BEDFORD
CHEESE
SHOP

A FIRST COURSE IN
CHEESE

CHARLOTTE KAMIN & NATHAN McELROY

Race Point
PUBLISHING

Quarto is the authority on a wide range of topics.

Quarto educates, entertains and enriches the lives of our readers—enthusiasts and lovers of hands-on living.

www.quartoknows.com

First published in the United States of America in 2015 by
Race Point Publishing, a member of
Quarto Publishing Group USA Inc.
142 West 36th Street, 4th Floor
New York, New York 10018
Telephone: (212) 779-4972
Fax: (212) 779-6058
quartoknows.com
Visit our blogs at quartoknows.com

10 9 8 7 6 5 4 3 2 1

ISBN: 978-1-63106-131-8

Library of Congress Cataloging-in-Publication Data is available

EDITOR: Susan Sulich
DESIGNER: Tim Palin Creative

Printed in China

CONTENTS

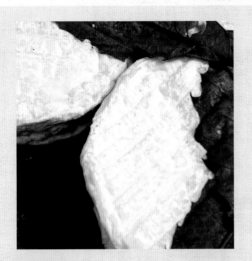

INTRODUCTION

Welcome to *A First Course in Cheese*. Here at Bedford Cheese Shop, we have built our business on the time-honored ways—similar to the small cheese shops found throughout Europe—in which we, as cheesemongers, present the craft of the cheese maker to you, the lactic-loving guest in our home. Cheesemongers are the gatekeepers of the traditions and ancestral ways of cheese-making, procuring and nurturing cheeses in order to educate the world about them. Our role is to support small dairy communities throughout the world, communities that are made up of farmers and cheese makers working in unison, supporting their villages, sustaining their way of life, connecting to the earth, and crafting something that evolves from a raw product into

a completely other experience. These are communities that depend on you, the consumer, who cares about what cheese you buy. Entire family lineages are rooted in the communal aspect that cheese represents. From the small village dairies throughout the Alps to the mom-and-pop producers in northern Vermont, we not only bring you their tastiest creations, but also the stories of these heroes.

Historically a way to sustain farmers during the winter months, cheese now has more varieties available than any other food group—literally thousands upon thousands of creations, all from a base of milk, salt, time, and love. Cheese is a sensory explosion—smell, touch, look, taste—and you will be submerged in lactic ecstasy when in the presence of real cheese. What do we mean by real cheese? When cheesemongers speak of cheese, we speak of those that are handmade following traditional artisanal methods. We are talking about craftsmanship that has evolved into a true, as well as an incredibly diverse and delicious, art form.

The goal of this book is to offer you a window into the daily endeavor of cheese-making. We want to give you a tool, a way to learn about this amazing world and also a way to enter into it, educating your palate and helping you to become an explorer and connoisseur of this incredible food. At the root, we want to give you a glimpse into the life that we have dedicated ourselves to protecting and sharing. Cheese is a journey from the earth to the plate, and we invite you to embark upon that journey with us.

WHAT IS A CHEESEMONGER?

We stand tethered to the counter as you enter the shop, brandishing knives, paying meticulous attention to every cheese, making sure it's cleaned, faced, wrapped, and placed just right for you to peruse. We are cheesemongers, that sect of the food world that may seem alien to the lay person, but is an essential aspect of the world of agriculture. The last person to handle a cheese before it ends up in your hands and in your home? Well, that's your cheesemonger. We are the voice of the cheese maker, the farmer, and the livestock. Making sure you are informed, fed, and happy is our job.

When people ask, "Why did you become a cheesemonger?" two words come to mind: love and respect. It is love for the history and practices of agriculture and for the ancient process of cheese-making; it is respect for the delicate dairy creations; and it is a combination of the two for the wonderful people who make up the cheese-producing industry. We have the honor of sharing the stories of the cheeses, their creators, and the communities that nurture them. We also get to educate you, the consumer, on the pleasure of these creations. Every day we come to work prepared to taste, smell, touch, and care for these little works of art so that they can make it to you as their most perfect selves.

You know you are a cheesemonger when the holiday crush pushes you to the brink of temporary insanity; when your knees, back, wrists, and neck are writhing in pain from hoisting eighty-pound (36 kg) wheels and breaking them down into hundreds of pieces; when a knife slips out of your hands and you automatically know how to dress a wound to perfection; and when you make the effort to get out to the countryside to see the proper treatment of the animals, meet the hardworking cheese makers, and take in the sweet smell of clean rural air.

Being a cheesemonger means coming home with cuts all over your hands; it means waking up in the middle of the night thinking about how all the highly perishable packages you sent out are faring; and it means wanting to see the cows in the field, frolicking in fresh spring grass with their young. Instead you have chosen to stand for hours, cutting and wrapping for a seemingly endless line of party throwers during the holiday season. The physical and mental toll it takes on us mongers to do the thing that we love to do is sizeable. But if you ask any true monger, he or she wouldn't have it any other way. This is what we do. This is what we love.

Cheesemongers play an important role in the delicate solar system that is the cheese family. If the farmer is the sun that gives life to the animals, sustaining and caring for them, and the cheese maker is the moon, pulling forth the cheese's inner potential and nurturing it toward greatness, then the monger is the gravitational pull that keeps the cheese grounded and moving forward.

We are a brotherhood, a sisterhood, a family that stretches around the globe, touching the present and the past. Sensory exploration and transcendence is what we are here for. Take our hand, talk to us, and let us lead you down the path of mind and palate expansion, into the promised land of real cheese.

—Charlotte Kamin and Nate McElroy

PART ONE
ON THE FARM—WHERE IT ALL BEGINS

MILK ANIMAL BREEDS

It all begins with the milk. If a cheese does not start with high-quality, fresh milk, there would be very little to speak about or be proud of in the cheese-making world. And without proper farming techniques and conscientious animal husbandry, it would not be possible for the creatures described in this section to produce the milk necessary to make the marvelous cheeses described in this book.

Over the centuries, different cultures have bred and raised animals that are suited to their specific environments. Livestock adaptation has either been an evolutionary development by the species in response to its climate or the result of cross breeding to produce an animal that has the characteristics necessary to survive and be of benefit to the people cultivating them (i.e., high milk or meat yield, able to withstand cold climates, etc.). With time comes the development of what are known as "landrace" animals. A landrace breed is one that has made its home in a specific environment for a long time, adapting to the climate and conditions of the land and being isolated from other breeds of their species.

There are a variety of animals and breeds of those animals whose milk is used in the cheese-making process. Here is a rundown of some of the more prominent beasts that are relied upon to provide the milk for our favorite cheeses.

COWS

The heavyweights in the dairy world, cattle produce more milk than any other species that contributes to the world of cheese, so it's no surprise that the majority of cheeses in the marketplace are made from cow's milk. While the common conception of a dairy cow is black and white and possibly named Bessie, there are a significant number of breeds that have specific attributes essential to producing the milk that cheese makers desire for crafting their various creations.

JERSEY

Originating on the island of Jersey in the English Channel off the northern shore of the French mainland, these cattle weigh in, on average, between 900 and 1,000 pounds (408 and 454 kg) and can vary in color from light gray to dark brown. These beasts have the highest output of milk per body weight of any breed, producing an average of thirteen times their body weight annually. In addition, Jersey cows have a higher fat content in their milk than any of their brethren, resulting in cheese that has a full flavor and rich mouthfeel. Their Bambi-like eyes and inquisitive-looking ears make them highly recognizable.

HOLSTEIN

When you think of cows, the image that most likely pops into your head is that of the Holstein breed, with black-and-white markings typical of a dairy cow. Originally bred in what is now the Netherlands, Holsteins have the greatest milk output of any breed overall, averaging almost 19,000 pounds (8,618 kg) of milk per year. The ability of this breed to produce such staggering amounts of milk has made them heavyweights in the dairy industry for centuries, leading to their vast exportation overseas, especially to America when the Dutch were settling here. Although the volume of milk produced by Holsteins is great, it has a relatively moderate fat content.

BROWN SWISS

These large, tough cattle originated in the mountains of Switzerland, where they had to adapt to harsh fluctuations in climate from season to season. Brown in color and weighing between 1,300 and 1,400 pounds (590 and 635 kg), on average—the bulls clock in closer to 2,000 pounds (907 kg)—these beasts yield close to 15,000 pounds (6,804 kg) of milk per year, making them the second-largest producer among dairy cattle. Coupled with a solid fat content in their milk (about 4 percent), these resilient and gentle beasts are a cheese maker's dream.

GUERNSEY

Another breed that takes its name from an island off the northern coast of France, Guernsey cows have a coloration of reddish-brown and white and a reputation for producing milk of outstanding quality. With a docile temperament (save for the bulls) and the production of milk with a spectacular golden hue, these cattle weigh, on average, 1,000 pounds (454 kg) and produce about 13,000 pounds (5,897 kg) of milk annually. Guernsey cows have the second-highest fat content in their milk of all dairy cattle. The combination of such richness and volume have made them a highly sought-after breed.

AYRSHIRE

Scottish in origin, these cows are the result of selective crossbreeding to produce an animal that would be of benefit to the butter and cheese producers in the region of the same name. Ayrshire cows range in weight from one thousand to twelve hundred pounds (454 to 544 kg) and are recognizable by their red-and-white markings. These animals produce over fourteen thousand pounds (6,350 kg) of milk per year, on average, that has a very balanced, moderate fat composition.

GOATS

Nimble goats have been relied upon for thousands of years for their meat and milk, and continue to provide sustenance and economic contributions to many cultures. As they are hardwired for foraging—nourishing themselves on shrubs, new growth, wild plants, and even thorn bushes—goats are often able to survive in places where other animals cannot, such as parts of the Middle East and Asia, making them a versatile animal to raise. Goat's milk is a good alternative for people who may have difficulty consuming cow's milk, as it has a lower amount of lactose, the carbohydrate many people have difficulty digesting. As they are fairly compact animals, goats have a milk output that is significantly less than cattle, averaging about 10 percent the total of the biggest bovine producers.

LAMANCHA

First bred in the United States in the state of Oregon, the LaMancha goat is a result of Spanish colonization of what is now California, with the missionaries bringing the spry beasts from their native land. Recognizable by their extremely short, almost nonexistent ears, these goats have an average weight of 130 pounds (59 kg), with an annual milk output of roughly 2,100 pounds (953 kg)—that's a whole lotta milk for such a tiny animal! Additionally, their milk has a high fat content, coming in behind only the Nubian breed (facing page) in average amount of fat.

NUBIAN

The Nubian (or Anglo-Nubian) are descendants of Middle Eastern goats, but were first bred in the United Kingdom. The inherent disposition of these sturdy and fairly large animals—the does averaging around 140 pounds (64 kg)—gives them the ability to withstand harsher climates, such as in the desert. Nubians have the highest fat content in their milk of the major dairy goat breeds, yet produce relatively low amounts, averaging about 1,800 pounds (816 kg) per annual lactation.

TOGGENBURG

Taking its name from the valley in the canton of St. Gallen in Switzerland where they were originally raised, Toggenburg goats are considered to be one of the oldest dairy breeds on record. With the does weighing an average of 120 pounds (54 kg), these solid-colored beauties range in hue from light brown to charcoal gray or even dark chocolate, and have ears that stand up and out from their heads. Toggenburgs produce a relatively high amount of milk, averaging a little over 2,100 pounds (953 kg) annually, but their liquid has a moderate fat content, which is low compared to other breeds.

SAANEN

Hailing and taking their name from the Saanen Valley in the Swiss canton of Bern, this breed of goat is known for its high milk output. A rather large breed, Saanen typically weigh around 140 pounds (64 kg), producing close to 2,600 pounds (1,179 kg) of milk, on average, per year, yet their milk has a fairly low fat content. Saanen are generally white or cream colored, and their high milk productivity, gentle temperament, and ease of management make them a popular breed among dairy farmers.

ALPINE

Sometimes referred to as French Alpine, these goats originated in the mountains of eastern France. Alpines come in a variety of colors—black, brown, white, and gray—and they have ears that stand fairly erect. Alpines average around 130 pounds (59 kg), producing approximately 2,200 pounds (998 kg) of milk annually, with a moderate fat content. Such milk production makes them a preferred breed in the goat dairy industry.

SHEEP

There are only a few breeds of sheep that produce the volume and quality of milk necessary to create cheese. East Friesian and Lacaune are the top dogs, so to speak, in the category of dairy sheep, and many cultures have their own landrace breeds that have been relied on for centuries to produce the liquid gold from these woolly beasts. Their average milk output is small and the fat content is high—it takes a large amount of sheep's milk to make a wheel of cheese, and this is usually reflected in the price point at the cheese counter.

EAST FRIESIAN

Originally from East Frisia in Germany, East Friesian sheep are recognizable by their wool-less faces, legs, and tail. Mature does average about 160 pounds (73 kg), producing approximately 1,300 pounds (590 kg) of milk in an annual lactation cycle, making them the heartiest producer of milk among dairy sheep breeds. They are especially known for their docile temperament and ease of demeanor when in a milking parlor.

LACAUNE

The Lacaune sheep has its origins in southern France, where its milk was made famous by the production of Roquefort (see page 190) and, in fact, is the only milk allowed to be used in making this cheese because it is a name-protected cheese (see page 38). Adapting to the rocky terrain of the region, these hearty sheep produce a good deal of milk—between 800 and 1,000 pounds (363 and 454 kg) per year—with a rich fat content. A mature Lacaune doe weighs around 150 pounds (68 kg) and can adapt to a variety of conditions, making this breed a versatile choice for dairy sheep farmers.

WATER BUFFALO

These gentle giants are the unsung heroes of the dairy world. Although rarely thought of as a domesticated, milk-producing animal, water buffalo have been relied upon by many cultures for centuries for their milk. These beasts can weigh anywhere between sixteen hundred and twenty-six hundred pounds (726 and 1179 kg), producing between four thousand and seven thousand pounds (1,814 and 3,175 kg) of milk, on average, annually. Their extremely rich milk has more protein than cow's milk, as well as more vitamins and minerals, while being lower in cholesterol. Their amiable disposition endears them to farmers, yet they have been known to have bouts of stage fright, making the milking process a delicate operation. There is nothing quite like tasting high-quality, full-flavored water buffalo milk in mozzarella di bufala.

SEASONS OF FEED AND FLAVOR

A simple and beautiful truth about the dairy industry is that it is a seasonal journey. The art of making cheese comes from knowing the nuances imparted to the milk with each changing season and how to create cheeses best suited to the flavor and quality of the milk produced throughout the year.

Like humans, our dairy-yielding brethren's bodies, moods, and hormones change throughout the year, following the cycle of the seasons. During the spring months, after having been cooped up in a barn for the long winter, they get to roam freely and indulge on the fresh grass and wildflowers in the pasture. The bulls and bucks begin to make eyes at the cute cows and does, and soon enough, there is love in the air and babies on the way. This time of year, the animals' diets are mostly fresh greens, which create an herbaceous, floral, rich-tasting milk that is a bit watery since it is being produced in great abundance. In the later summer months, after the animals have had a consistent diet of fresh greens, their milk is packed with a rich variety of nuanced flavors of all they have eaten and stored up throughout the season. During the long and cold months of winter, the animals get a special blend of hay and silage to supplement their dwindled outdoor diet. The animals' milk yield is very low in the fall and winter time, which increases the fat-to-liquid ratio, making for a rich and thick cream. This is the time of year when the milk is at its prime for buttery, decadent, gooey cheeses, such as Vacherin Mont-d'Or (see page 110) and Ardrahan (see page 87).

Each dairy animal also has its own mating process, gestation period, and time of year when its appetite is at its fullest; these things influence the flavors and ultimately the type of milk that is produced. During the first few months of spring, when the baby goats, known as kids, are arriving, their mothers' milk is bucky and floral, with citrusy notes. This is the time of year for the great fresh and rind-ripened cheeses, such as Mothais sur Feuille (see page 72) and Couronne de Touraine (see page 67). Toward the end of spring and beginning of summer, the kids are gobbling up grass and hay, while their mothers' milk production begins to lighten, creating a buckier, more barnyard-y flavor profile. Aged, natural-rind tommes made from this milk are great—think Tomme Chèvre Tunnel (see page 167) and Caprotto (see page 124).

Cheese makers understand the seasonal variations of their animals and milk, crafting a variety of cheeses that are best suited for the milk types and flavors produced during different times of year. The fun part is getting to taste the diverse cheeses or even the same cheese with the changing seasons.

FARMS AND FARMERS

There are two very different models—and polarized philosophies—of production in the dairy industry when it comes to the care of the animals and the farm: the large factory-run producers, known as Big Agriculture, and the smaller producers, who for us personally are part of the cheese-world family that we honor.

EVOLUTION OF BIG AGRICULTURE

Once upon a time, all food crafts were fabricated by hand, with an undeniable attention to detail, as it is hard not to pay attention to the little things when you are working with them directly. But for hard-working farmers, whose days began well before sunrise and often didn't end until after the moon's arrival, the introduction of time-saving innovations was a welcome reprise. With the industrial boom came the creation of large milking parlors with automated pumping mechanisms—basically a suction cup and tube to replace the hand and the pail. Along with farming and milking, the labor-intensive process of making cheese had begun to lose its appeal to the next generation, and most of the artisanal-made products found an accelerated process in a factory assembly line. Over time, more and more of the hand-crafted dairy delicacies morphed into industrial versions of themselves.

RESURGENCE OF SMALL FARM PRODUCTION

In recent years, there has been a return to the land, so to speak. A new generation has come to recognize the benefits and the beauty of the philosophies and ways of life associated with a small farm mentality, and more young people are setting their sights on returning to traditional practices and artistic possibilities in the agricultural world. Throughout the United States, we are seeing a resurgence of family-run farms—young couples and collectives learning and practicing the ways of the land and the trades of the past.

In small farm production, you will usually find the more rustic and traditional methods of animal husbandry (allowing animals to roam and graze where they please, caring for them with respect, etc.) and cheese-making being employed. The time-honored craft of milking by hand, being able to see and smell the freshness, and training the eye to catch any defects or imperfections are still valued. Even when small dairies are using milk from other sources, they still are taking the time to craft the cheese by hand. The heating of the milk, the cutting of the curd, the forming of the wheels—all of these laborious tasks are being done with a human touch instead of by machine. Obviously, the quantity yielded is drastically different; whereas "Big Ag" can literally crank out the product, small farms have a cap on how much they are capable of making, which translates into a bigger cost differential at the cheese counter.

The quality, however, is undeniable. We are not saying that all cheeses made in the larger processing farms are bad, but there is something special, nuanced, and seductive when eating a small-farm cheese and truly being able to taste the land, love, and attention paid to every step of the creation process. As cheesemongers, part of our mission is to educate you, the consumer, on the differences in the options out there to help you determine what kind of farming practices you want to support.

CO-OP VS. FARMSTEAD

When it comes to the world of food, there are a lot of catchphrases that are thrown about. You may hear terms such as "artisan" and "organic," "farmstead" and "local." Advertising honchos have zeroed in on what makes some foods desirable, and suddenly, these words have no meaning when they are spoken with the same conviction about a fast food chain's new offerings as about a family-run farm that goes above and beyond organic certification, but maybe does not have the resources to pay for organic certification documents. In the confusing contradictions of rhetoric and marketability, it's nice to take a step back every once and again to reconfirm that these words do have real meaning, with specific philosophies and practices behind them.

Two somewhat confusing terms used quite frequently in the cheese world are farmstead cheeses and co-op (or cooperative) cheeses. At the root of these two cheese-making models is where the milk actually comes from.

Farmstead cheese refers to a product that is made on the same farm where the milk is produced. This means that the herd of the cheese maker is the sole supplier of the milk. The advantages of farmstead is not only control of the quality of the milk—meaning the farmer can guarantee what the animals are eating, how often they are on pasture, and their general well-being—but also the ability to ensure freshness. Usually the milk only travels a few yards from the milking parlor to the cheese-making facilities. This timeframe guarantees that the milk is never sitting around unattended or getting jostled about in transit. Milk is a very delicate substance, and the protein strands can easily break down if roughed up. The downside to farmstead production is the undeniable amount of work that goes into raising and tending to animals. Cheese-making is an incredibly taxing and tiring endeavor on its own, and compounding the financial and physical burden with needing to be an animal farmer, too, can prove extremely challenging.

Co-op cheese-making can take a couple of forms. One is that the cheese maker works with a select group of nearby farmers who can guarantee the quality and freshness of their milk. In this way, the two entities work in tandem to make a complete product that showcases both the quality of the milk and the skills of the cheese maker. Trust and respect are nurtured, clear communication is maintained between all parties, and a set price for the labor of love is agreed upon and adhered to. Another form of co-op cheese-making is in sharing the use of the actual dairy. Cheese-making equipment is not cheap, so there are operations where different cheese makers take turns producing their cheeses within one facility. Then no one person has to shoulder the financial responsibilities of purchasing and maintaining the equipment. This model also creates an opportunity for collaboration and a place where shared ideas can be worked on and brought to fruition.

Both the farmstead and co-op practices rely on the principle of community, which is and has always been at the heart of cheese-making. With their feet firmly planted in the soil, these artists are able to see that their animals thrive, and create something outstandingly tasty and nutritious for everyone to enjoy.

PART TWO
CHEESE BASICS

MILK CHEMISTRY

Milk is a magical substance. The rich combination of calcium, protein, healthy fats, and enzymes make it a super food of sorts. This liquid that gives life and sustenance to future generations of animals is also used as a staple in our food world. Humans are the only creatures that take milk from other species and use it for the benefit of their own kind.

THE MAKEUP OF MILK

Although the nuances and structure of milk vary slightly depending on breed, feed, seasonality, and, of course, type of animal, all milk is basically made up of five components: water, lactose, milk fats, milk proteins, and salt. These ingredients create a chemical playground where the liquid form can be manipulated into a solid mass.

Milk is about 85 percent water, with lactose comprising about 5 percent. After cheese-making, the cheese retains only about 5 percent of both water and lactose. Bacteria consume the lactose during the cheese-making process, creating lactic acid in their wake. This process achieves the desired acidity level for cheese-making and can be regulated by the amount of bacteria that is added to the milk, as well as by washing the curds to remove bacteria. Milk fat, also known as butterfat, is less dense and thus rises to the top, creating the cream layer on top of whole-fat milk when it has been left to settle. Skimming milk is the act of removing this cream layer, which then makes milk that is lower in fat. When full-fat milk is used in making cheese, about 90 percent of the milk fat is retained and concentrated into the cheese. Milk proteins are comprised of two types: caseins and whey proteins, with casein accounting for about 80 percent of the proteins found in milk and whey proteins making up the other 20 percent. The caseins play an integral role in the cheese-making

process. These proteins bind together to create the solids, or curds, during the coagulation process. Liquid known as whey is released during the process. The chemical catalyst introduced with bacteria and rennet (an enzyme that aids coagulation) transforms the protein structures, which expel the liquids that are being held together in the chemical bond. Salt naturally occurs in low levels in milk.

Milk's structure is pretty fragile. Fat proteins are delicate beings that are not uniform in nature. The process of homogenizing milk pushes the liquid through narrow channels repeatedly, thus forcing the compounds to become a smaller and more consistent size. Most cheeses do not react well to homogenized milk; the variations and fragility of virgin milk are what are desired for a true artisinal product. The process of transferring milk from farmer to cheese maker can also cause deterioration in milk quality. The old technique of jostling about the milk pails or even pumping the liquid from holding vessel to milk tanker and then into a vat can compromise the integrity of the milk's structure. In recent years, gravitational milking channels have been implemented so that the milk flows freely from the milking parlor into the vats, eliminating the rough jostling and harsh movements that can affect the milk's structure.

Milk truly is a form of liquid gold and makes a substantial contribution to the agricultural marketplace. Liquid milk can be broken down, extracting whey to be dried and turned into whey protein for health shakes. Butterfat is skimmed off to be made into heavy cream. Butter is made from full-fat milk, and once the solids have coalesced, the milk that is leftover is what is sold as buttermilk. And of course, there are the two thousand–plus varieties of cheese that are crafted from this white wonder.

THE CHEESE-MAKING PROCESS

What makes cheese-making so fascinating is the complete transformation of one substance into another. Sure, you can dry out plums to get prunes, or evaporate seawater to harvest salt, but cheese is unique in that it is the only food substance that starts as a liquid form and comes out the other end as a solid mass that varies in density, texture, and flavor, with the help of a magical combination of chemistry—it is, in essence, a totally new creation.

Like all fermentation products, cheese-making has its roots in preservation. Milk is a highly perishable product, and farmers needed a way to extend its shelf life, so to speak, throughout the seasons. The history of cheese-making dates back at least five thousand years, when, rumor has it, a traveler was crossing the desert with goat's milk carried in the dried stomach of a goat. Over the journey, as a result of all the jostling, the milk coagulated. When the traveler attempted to quench his thirst, his lips encountered a curdy substance instead, not unlike a liquidy cottage cheese

The cheese-making process has evolved quite a bit from its beginnings, and has become an amalgam of chemistry and creativity that yields a wide variety of results.

Pressing the curd expels the whey and helps the mass to solidify.

The job of converting milk into cheese is not a difficult one. In fact, cheese-making is a simple process. Here are the steps to making cheese:

1. Place milk into a vat and heat it slightly. This step prepares the milk structure to begin the transformation into something solid. The bacteria in the milk feed on the lactose, turning it into a lactic acid. These bacteria may be present on their own, in the case of raw milk, or added to the milk before the heating process begins—this additional substance is called the "culture," or starter bacteria. Different starter cultures result in different flavor profiles in the end result. When a blue cheese is being crafted, for example, the blue spores might be added to the milk at this point to encourage the blue growth later on.

2. Once the milk is at the proper temperature, and the desired level of lactic acid has been achieved, rennet is added to begin the coagulation process. This process begins to remove the caseins from the milk, allowing the milk proteins to adhere to one another, creating a mass out of the liquid. Rennet contains the enzyme chymosin, which converts the casein into a substance closer to cheese curd. During this step, the liquid is left undisturbed for a while so that the full coagulation process can take place, eventually forming a large curd.

3. Once the curd has formed into a semi-soft to chewy texture, it is time to cut it. Within this large curd is an abundance of whey, the liquid by-product created when the milk proteins attach to one another. The process of "cutting the curd" allows the whey to drain. Depending on what cheese is being made, the larger block is cut down to different sized curds, allowing them to retain a certain amount of moisture. The actual cutting can be done in a few ways. Some cheese makers prefer to cut the curd by hand with a long-handled contraption that has thin cutting edges, resembling a rake with several small bow saw–like blades. It can also be cut by machine. For a drier end result, the curds are cut smaller, thus expelling more whey. For a softer and creamier cheese, the curds are left slightly larger, with more whey being retained. At this step, a lot of variations can take place, depending on the type of cheese being made. Once the curds have been cut, they can be salted to help dry them more and achieve the desired acidity level. The curds can also be washed at this stage, removing any remaining lactic acid—in order to stabilize the curds and also to achieve the desired flavor profile for the cheese.

4. Now comes the forming of the wheels. Once the curd reaches the size and texture the cheese maker desires for the cheese being produced, the curd is ladled, scooped, or piled into a cheese mold. Cheese molds are vessels that have tiny holes throughout their structure, to allow any remaining whey to drain while holding the curd in place. The curd is pressed down in some way—either by gravity, a press, or weights—helping to expel the whey while encouraging the mass to adhere to itself. This fresh cheese sits in the mold for varying amounts of time, depending on the specific cheese being made. Once the mass is removed from the mold, the exterior of the cheese may be salted, washed with a salt brine, or soaked in a salt bath to help the process of crusting the exterior of the cheese, which will become the rind. Some alpine-style cheeses, such as Challerhocker (see page 125), soak in their brine bath for several hours or overnight to help the structure form. Once the desired firmness has been achieved, the wheels are removed from the bath and placed into an aging environment that best suits the intended cheese's needs.

5. During the first few days and weeks of a cheese's life, it is tended to daily, being turned and rubbed, caressed and watched, making sure it is developing properly into the cheese it is intended to become.

TYPES OF RENNET

Remember the traveler carrying the milk in the dried goat stomach (see page 22)? Unbeknownst to him, the dried stomach in which he was transporting his milk contained living enzymes in the stomach lining, which were the catalyst for the coagulation process over the course of his journey. Nowadays, there a few types of rennet used in most cheese-making. The basic need is for the rennet to contain chymosin, which is the actual enzyme that curdles the milk. There are certain soft cheeses that are curdled with an acid such as lemon juice, omitting the need for rennet altogether—these include Cream Cheese (see page 53) and Indian paneer. The type of rennet used affects the flavor and texture of the cheese. Although there are more variations and subvarieties within the three types of rennet listed below, these are the basic types used in cheese-making.

TRADITIONAL ANIMAL RENNET

Traditional animal rennet is produced in the stomach of ruminant mammals. The term "ruminant" refers to animals (such as cows and sheep) that have more than one stomach, and as part of their digestive process, they swallow food and then bring it back up and continue chewing it. Rennet is a naturally occurring complex of enzymes in the stomachs of these types of animals, and it is a key element in how the offspring of the animals digest their mothers' milk. The enzymes help curdle the milk into a more solid form—as in cheese-making—once it has gone through the young ones' digestive systems. Most often, the rennet is procured as a by-product of the ecosystem of farm life. Most males at a dairy farm are sold off for their meat after a few have been chosen for future breeding purposes, but some of the young male animals are slaughtered for their stomachs, and the needed rennet. The stomachs are first dried to preserve their longevity. Pieces of the stomach are then cut off and reconstituted in a water or whey solution mixed with a bit of vinegar to help the acid levels. The liquid slurry is then added to the milk during the cheese-making process (see page 22). Traditionally, the stomachs used are from the same type of animals whose milk is being utilized (i.e., a sheep's stomach for sheep's milk, a goat's stomach for goat's milk, and a calf's stomach for cow's milk). It is important that the stomachs used are from animals who have only consumed their mother's milk, not ones that have already begun to eat grass or feed. The enzymes needed for the coagulation process are drastically reduced and sometimes completely eliminated in the stomachs of animals that have a diverse diet of more than just their mother's milk. Traditional animal rennet is thought to produce a more robust, desirable flavor profile.

MICROBIAL RENNET

Produced primarily in laboratories, these specialized bacteria enzymes are fermented and purified to control their conditions. The outcome is a consistent product that is easy to use and does not require the same process of reconstitution as traditional animal rennet. Although suitable for vegetarians, microbial rennet lacks the natural functionality of utilizing the unwanted male animals in the dairy communities. Cheeses made with microbial rennet tend to have a more bitter flavor profile, which is accentuated when the cheeses are aged.

VEGETABLE RENNET

There are several plants that contain a naturally occurring enzyme that can coagulate milk. Nettle and thistle are two plants that are used frequently in the cheese-making process. Thistle, most well known in the fabrication of Spanish and Portuguese-style torta cheeses, such as Torta la Serena (see page 109), introduces a vegetal, artichoke-like flavor note in the cheese. Although there is no large flavor effect in cheeses made with this rennet, this type of rennet is still not used often, for the fact that the cheeses tend to ripen better when traditional animal rennet is used. Cheeses made with vegetable rennet are suitable for vegetarians.

Rennet being added to cheese

MOLDS

Molds and bacteria may not sound very appetizing but they are a key component in creating cheese. Bacteria is purposely introduced into the cheese at either the milk stage or after it has been shaped. The molds that grow contribute to the flavor and help protect the cheese while it ages. Cheeses have to be carefully monitored, however, to make sure that the bacteria is helpful and not harmful. Below are some of the more common molds involved in the cheese-making process.

PENICILLIUM CANDIDUM

A trademark of bloomy-rind cheeses, this white, pillowy mold populates the surfaces of cheeses, such as Brie Fermier (see page 60), Camembert Fermier (see page 62), various triple crèmes, and numerous other cheeses that fall into the category of bloomy cheese. The mold is introduced either by adding it to the milk in the make process or spraying it on the surface of the cheese once it has been shaped. The cloud-like appearance of Penicillium candidum is cultivated on cheese through the management of the aging process in properly humidified and conditioned environments. Penicillium candidum enrobes and protects the cheese during its maturation, working to break down the fats and proteins present in the interior of the cheese to create a silky, gooey texture that has typical notes of earth, mushrooms, and asparagus.

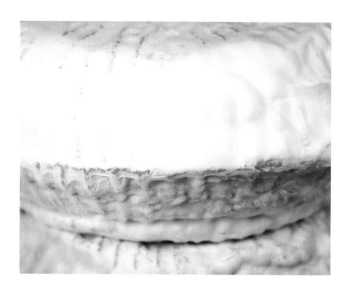

GEOTRICHUM CANDIDUM

Sometimes referred to as the "brainy" mold in the world of cheese, Geotrichum candidum (Geotrichum) is known for its worm-like appearance and ability to grow rapidly on the surface of cheese. Geotrichum lends definitive notes of yeasty sourdough bread and fermented citrus. Like Penicillium candidum, it may either be incorporated into the milk in the make process or sprayed on after the formation of the cheese. In many goat's milk cheeses, it is the only mold introduced, yet Geotrichum provides a very hospitable environment for other, stronger molds to grab onto—sometimes with a negative result. It is

not uncommon to see Geotrichum populated on washed-rind cheeses or growing in conjunction with Penicillium candidum. Too high a level of Geotrichum on a cheese can lead to other undesired effects, such as rind slippage, which is when the rind of the cheese is not solidly united with the paste, resulting in the exterior "slipping" off the cheese during handling.

PENICILLIUM ROQUEFORTI

The original source of the most common type of spores used to make blue cheese is something of a legend. Rumor has it that the naturally occurring molds were discovered on a certain type of rye bread that was accidently left out in a cave in the south of France. As the story goes, a young shepherd ditched his lunch of fresh sheep's milk cheese and bread in a cave while he went off to frolic with a local lass. When he returned several days later, the bread had become an incubator for the naturally occurring molds in the cave, and the same molds had coated the fresh cheese. The shepherd tasted the new creation and was pleased with the piquant depth. Regardless of whether the story is true or not, future generations did grind down mold-covered bread and use it as a starter for their blue cheeses. Penicillium roqueforti needs a lot of air and a good amount of moisture to blossom. In blue cheeses, the bacteria are usually added to the milk during the cheese-making process, and the completed wheel is pierced with hollow needles to create air channels for the Penicillium roqueforti to grow in. Nowadays, there are still naturally occurring versions of the bacteria, but the same structure has been replicated in laboratories, creating a uniformed strand. Depending on the type of milk the bacteria is added to, as well as the type of cheese being made, the flavor profile can run the gamut from tangy and peppery with notes of copper to sweet and citrusy with a tart lemony quality.

RHIZOMUCOR

Commonly referred to as "cat hair" among cheese people, Rhizomucor (Mucor) is a mold that is viewed as a problem if it appears in the ripening of soft, more fragile cheeses, yet it is viewed as a desirable mold to be cultivated on more aged, natural-rind wheels. Recognizable by the fact that it does indeed look like cat's fur standing on end, this highly aggressive mold can populate the surface of a cheese almost ten times faster than Penicillium candidum and spreads rapidly in a highly humid aging environment. Since the spores are easily transferred by ventilation, it can be a catastrophic, unwanted guest. It strikes fear in the heart of a cheese maker and affineur when

Mucor appears on their more delicate cheeses, as it imparts bitter notes in the flavor profile. But not all effects of Mucor are negative. As cheeses were developed in various caves around Europe, the flora of these environments, which includes Mucor, shaped some of the more famous wheels in their infancy into the stalwarts they are today. Early cheese makers discovered that the appearance of cat fur on wheels of Tomme de Savoie (see page 169), Saint Nectaire (see page 164), and Garrotxa (see page 156) protected and enhanced the desirable flavor profile of these wheels, imparting touches of pleasantly bitter woodland.

BREVIBACTERIUM

Most commonly referred to as B. linens, Brevibacterium is the rust- and orange-colored mold that is found on some of our favorite washed-rind cheeses. The famed "footy" aroma is not far from the truth, as these bacteria also live happily on human skin and may emit that scent from the presence of a certain sulphur. With the washing of the cheeses with salt brines, booze, or any desired liquid, the perfect environment is created to attract B. linens. Over a short amount of time of washing, the white cheese begins to crust over, developing a deep burnt-red coloring—that coloring is the colonization of Brevibacterium, and can range from a pale yellow to a dark brick. The bacteria encourage the cheese to ripen from the outside in, creating a creamy texture toward the rind with a dense, fudgy center. Ardrahan (see page 87), for example, can vary wildly texturally during its ripening process. Once the cheese has been ripened thoroughly, the paste should be consistent throughout. Brevibacterium also thrives on firmer washed-rind cheeses. Appenzeller (see page 86), for instance, attracts the same bacteria, but due to the less frequent washing and the elongated aging time, the colors are more muted, as is the funky aroma. Besides the coloring and aroma, the one significant characteristic of the bacteria is a slightly meaty, sometimes bacony, and wonderful flavor that develops when a cheese is aged.

CHRYSOSPORIUM SULPHUREUM

It's a mouthful, but, boy, it sure is pretty on the rinds of cheeses. Chrysosporium sulphureum is recognizable by its imparting of delicate, little yellow spots, or "flowers," on the exteriors of many natural-rind cheeses. These speckles of yellow bloom on earth tone–colored rinds of cheeses such as La Marotte (see page 157), Puits d'Astier (see page 162), and Corsu Vecchiu (see page 155), and create such visual character that they endear themselves to the hearts of cheesemongers and consumers. The bacteria are mainly the product of the aging environment, a testament to the positive seasoning of a "cave," and

hop from cheese to cheese in the proper conditions and ventilation. Known to impart a metallic battery-like taste when consumed, this seemingly off-putting element should lead the consumer to perhaps taste the rind but eat sparingly. Chrysosporium sulphureum delves deep into the sensory aspect of cheese—it is mainly a visual stimulant, and a beautiful one at that.

PENICILLIUM GLAUCUM

The lesser known of the two major blue molds found in cheese, Penicillium glaucum is described as a more mellow strain of blue mold in comparison to Penicillium roqueforti—a fruitier and less spicy yet still-pronounced strain that is introduced in the cheese-making process or injected by needles, in the technique known as needling, after the cheese has been shaped. This naturally occurring mold has been harnessed by cheese makers in order to help break down the proteins of the milk to create the desired texture, and to break down the fats in the milk to create the desired fruity and sharp nuances of a cheese. Finding the harmony of this mold with the milk being used and the cheese being shaped is the essence of artistry in cheese-making. By controlling

the aging environment and salt levels of a cheese, this blue mold may be cultivated slowly over time to bring out all the nuanced flavors that create a very special product. Some notable cheeses using Penicillium glaucum are Gorgonzola (see page 181) and Bleu d'Auvergne (see page 178).

SPORENDONEMA CASEI

Unique to the rinds of cheeses only, Sporendonema casei is a specialized bacteria that is slow to develop its bright orange patchwork. What begins as a white dusting slowly develops into the orange bloom spots on the rinds of cheeses, usually ones that already have other bacteria colonized on their rinds. Although little is known about how the bacteria affect the flavor profile of the cheeses, we get very excited when we see these little pockets developing on some of the natural-rind cheeses, as it is usually a good indicator that the cheese is developing nicely. Sporendonema casei should not be confused with Brevibacterium, which has a uniformity of coating on the rind that makes it easy to distinguish from Sporendonema casei.

AGING ENVIRONMENTS

After a cheese has been made and formed (or shaped), the next step is for it to be aged (with the exception of fresh cheeses (see pages 51–55), which, as their name implies, are not aged). The aging process can vary significantly from one type of cheese to another. Cheeses are fickle little beings that, like humans and animals, have an ideal environment where they will thrive and grow into their perfect selves. Each cheese needs a specific "incubator," if you will, to cultivate the flavors and textures desired for the marketplace.

"Cave" is a catchall term for a controllable aging environment that helps cheeses achieve their desired end results. These "caves" may be high-tech, white, sterile walk-in refrigeration units, or rustic mold- and bacteria-filled cellars that have been carved out of mountainsides. Regardless of structure, the key components of a successful aging environment for cheese are temperature control, ripening surface, humidity, and airflow.

RIPENING SURFACE

The ripening surface, or what the cheeses actually sit on while they mature, depends on the cheeses' particular needs. For some cheeses, such as the bloomy rinds (see pages 57–81), the preferred method is to place these unripened, "green" cheeses on stainless-steel airing racks, which allow airflow around them. As these rinds develop, they then "become one" with whatever

surface they are placed upon. The easily cleanable and aerated racks allow for effortless turning of the wheels as the rinds develop, as well as a quick clean between batches.

Other cheeses, such as the washed rinds (see pages 83–112), tend to thrive on wooden planks, most commonly pine and spruce. These planks have a porous nature that adapts quickly to the moisture levels of both the environment and the cheese. The wood also imparts a nuanced flavor from its natural material as well as has the capability to absorb the positive bacteria that help the cheese develop in a controlled environment.

Many DOP and name-protected cheeses (see page 38) are required to be aged on straw mats composed of dry grass or rye, or the like. This practice imparts a wholly unique flavor. The porous nature of the reeds and how they are woven together produce an environment that is positive for the rinds and thus the flavor profile of these cheeses as they develop.

Back in the day, farmers used natural materials that they had on hand as surfaces to keep the cheeses slightly elevated to allow airflow, which helped reduce the financial burden of the farmer having to procure new materials for the aging process. Nowadays, you will find variations on this theme with bar mat or plastic material that comes in a variety of tensile strengths and porousness to help with the aging process. In essence, it is all about creating the perfect airflow and environments to develop specific styles of cheeses.

BACTERIA

Each of these controlled environments also has a specific signature in the air that comes from years of use, and has seasoned the caves. The accumulation of bacteria in the atmosphere is the perfect nurturer to help future cheeses to mature with the different flora (plant matter) already present there. Different rinds require different enclosed environments to thrive. Bloomy cheeses (see pages 57–82) are very susceptible to cross contamination and need a relatively sterile environment to mature properly. Natural-rind cheeses (see pages 149–173) are a more sturdy lot and love a good mix of bacteria in the air to develop the proper rinds. A controlled area that has harbored many natural-rind cheeses to maturation has developed a force field, in a sense, of positive molds to protect the cheeses from harmful intruders, such as insects or negative bacteria that could harm the final product.

HUMIDITY AND TEMPERATURE

The key to cultivating the desired molds lies within the humidity levels of the aging environments. Many old-world "caves" have been constructed in an ideal location that has the proper airflow, temperature, and humidity levels. Most of the new aging facilities have to be fabricated with machinery to create the desired environment. The humidifier—the same one used by most parents to help with a child's cough—adds moisture to the environment in a regulated manner to create a temperature and humidity level conducive to positive mold cultivation. At the same time, too much moisture can be a breeding ground for all sorts of bacteria, including the negative ones, making the regulation and development of the humidity level integral to the artistry of cheese-making and affinage.

Airflow is just as critical to ripening as any of the other factors involved in the maturation of a cheese. Too much air movement can be harmful to the growth of certain bacteria and too little can create a stagnant environment in which no positive development is accomplished, and can even generate an area that harbors the growth of bad bacteria that thrive in cold, wet areas. (Cheese makers test and sample their cheeses during the aging process to make sure none of these bad bacteria invades their product.) The old-school "caves" were built to have the gentle breezes move through them to produce a cycle of air that would be beneficial to the seasoned environment. In modern aging facilities, especially in an urban environment, they rely on efficient ventilation systems to deliver air to the "cave." With this type of airflow comes the spread of beneficial molds—if it is a properly seasoned and maintained environment—to the ripening conditions of the cheeses aging there. This forced airflow requires regulation and tempering with dampers to prevent the air from blowing out too cold or in too aggressive a manner.

Dampers play an important role in that they not only regulate the velocity of airflow, but they also act as a filter for the aging environment, trapping unwanted materials before they can enter the aging environment and helping control the bacteria present, which is extremely important to the development of cheeses. Dampers can come in a variety of forms, everything from welded in and adjustable fan shrouds to garden mulch netting and even hair nets. Dampers produce a more stable environment for aging that takes into consideration the cheeses' need for humidity and temperature.

Creating a productive aging environment for cheese is impossible without all of these elements coming together. Establishing a harmonious home for a cheese to mature and develop into the piece that you bring into your home and enjoy is the goal of the cheese maker, the affineur, and the cheesemonger alike.

THE ROLE OF THE AFFINEUR

A time-honored trade throughout Europe is that of the affineur, a person who selects wheels of cheese from the producer and then ages them to their peak versions in his or her own specialized caves or aging facilities. Cheeses are sensitive, individual little beings, with each type needing different aging conditions to mature properly. The role of the affineur is to carefully calibrate that aging process to ensure that a cheese ages to perfection and achieves its ideal flavor and texture profile. While some affineurs specialize in a particular style of cheese, they understand the needs of all cheeses.

Aging facilities need to have optimal temperature, airflow, and humidity, and all of these aspects need to be controlled. When a "cave" or aging room is full, the cheeses themselves produce a lot of moisture and bacteria. When a facility is less full, the humidity and temperature is affected, and these elements need to be regulated by a watchful eye. It's a delicate process that requires constant monitoring to ensure just the right conditions for each cheese.

Bloomy cheeses (see pages 57–81) tend to need warmer, higher-moisture environments to help encourage the growth of the Penicillium candidum bacteria. Once this has been achieved, the cheeses then need to exist in an environment that is slightly cooler to slow down the ripening process. Bloomy cheeses are sensitive to other bacteria and have a tendency to pick up blue molds and a mold known as Mucor, or cat fur (see page 27). Due to this sensitivity, bloomy and Geotrichum cheeses need a relatively sterile environment to remain pure. Washed-rind cheeses (see pages 83–112) need a moister, slightly cooler environment than their bloomy brethren. Due to the high levels of salt that is used in most washes for cheeses, the rinds tend to dry out a bit faster, thus the need for a more humid room to prosper. Natural-rind cheeses (see pages 149–173) and blue cheeses (see pages 175–193) thrive in areas that are a cacophony of bacteria and fauna. The mixture of different spores in the air helps to season the cheeses properly.

Affineurs have specialized rooms that are designed and maintained for the different types of cheeses. Over time, these rooms harbor their own bacteria balance, creating a signature flavor that the cheeses take on as they age.

In some situations, affineurs simply select cheeses but do not age them further. Their keen eye for perfection and discernible taste help them choose their preferred wheels. Affineurs also work very closely with cheese makers, acting as a sounding board to help work through complications and innovations.

The affineur also plays a role in the economics of the cheese world. Farmers and cheese makers take on a large financial burden and a cash-flow concern with the cycle of investing in animals and cheese-making and then having to wait for a return on that investment for when the cheese is finally ready to sell. Finding a buyer for cheese also adds another layer of work for the cheese maker. Some cheeses also need several months—sometimes years—to age properly. It is a huge liability for cheese makers to basically sit on their money until it is time to sell their cheeses. Affineurs purchase the cheeses from the producers earlier in the process, so the producers, in turn, have liquid cash to pay bills, buy feed, and keep up with their everyday operating expenses.

Affinage, or aging, is a true art, and affineurs do hands-on training for several years before they are allowed to age cheeses on their own. In many instances, these affineurs have the craft rooted in their heritage, often being raised or apprenticed with cheese makers or other affineurs. In the United States, the role of the affineur is still very new and underrepresented, but as the artisanal cheese community grows, we expect the number of affineurs to similarly increase.

A fun cheese plating is to buy the same type of cheese from several different affineurs so that you can taste the differences and begin to learn the specific styles and signatures that each affineurstrives for. A Tomme de Savoie (see page 169), for example, is going to taste very different depending on who is aging the wheels.

PART THREE
CHOOSING CHEESES

VISITING A CHEESE COUNTER

So you arrive at the cheese shop and find yourself standing before cases filled with a vast array of cheeses of all shapes, sizes, and colors, many of which have names you are not sure how to pronounce. The cases you see are the result of hours spent every day by the cheesemongers caring and nurturing these wheels to perfection and then cutting and wrapping pieces for the customers' pleasure. Yes, we know that it can be intimidating.

We also know that you have a love or, at the very least, an interest in cheese. Whether you have very little knowledge about cheese and only a slight idea of what you like or have a fairly high level of cheese knowledge, the important thing to remember is that in the shop, we cheesemongers are there to help you articulate and understand what it is that you are actually looking for. You have come to the right place because cheesemongers are professionals—people who have dedicated years of their lives to learning and understanding the ways of the curd.

The first step is to engage with us. We are at your disposal. We don't expect you to know about the vast fromage laid out before you. Tell us what you want, what you desire, what you are looking for. Here are some questions you can think about that will make for a more productive exchange:

* Are you entertaining and want to have a cheeseboard for your guests? How many people are you having and is it for an appetizer or after a meal? How many cheeses would you like? What is your budget?

* Are there any flavors, styles, or names you want to avoid? Do you want hard or soft? Full-flavored or mellower?

* Are you cooking with the cheese? If so, what are you making? Here's a tip: we love food and want to know exactly what is going to be on your table. Whether your need is a slab of Gruyère (see page 128) for gougères, something meltable for mac 'n' cheese, or something to shave atop some vegetables you picked up at the farmer's market and are going to roast, if you talk to us about food, you're sure to see our eyes sparkle and hear rumbling pangs from our too-accommodating stomachs.

* What drinks are you planning to serve with the cheese? A sparkling white, or perhaps a dark port, or a summery mix of cocktails?

Giving us these parameters will help both of us. And don't worry if you happen into the store without any of these questions answered; we'll pull the answers out of you one way or another. We are here as sounding boards, as shepherds ready to guide you through the maze of cheese that we present before you. The most important two things to remember when approaching a cheese counter are to communicate with your monger and to taste everything.

WHAT'S IN A NAME: DOP/AOC NAME PROTECTION PROCESS

What is in the name of a cheese? If you look closely, you can learn several things about a cheese from what it is called. Its name may refer to location of production, the aging process or make style, or the type of animal from which the milk came. Some cheese names are quite creative, as there is a lot of freedom in naming many cheeses.

However, for certain cheeses, there is a regimented name designation protection process. By protecting a product under these designations, the farmer, the cheese maker, the cheesemonger, and the consumer are ensured that what is being produced and consumed is made in a traditional manner and meets certain high-quality standards of ingredients and production. These cheeses have a Protected Designation of Origin (PDO), meaning they must be made within a certain geographical area, using milk from a specific breed, and be made in a particular way or with a standardized process.

Protected Designation of Origin came about in the early decades of the twentieth century, when the development of mass-produced, industrialized dairy began to infringe upon the livelihood of the regional farmer, threatening traditional, artisanal cheese-making practices. At the Stresa Convention in 1951, European countries gathered to create the first international agreement on cheese names and their process of production. Italy, France, Switzerland, Denmark, Austria, Netherlands, Belgium, Sweden, and Norway participated in the convention. This is where cheeses such as Roquefort (see page 190), Gorgonzola (see page 181), and Parmigiano-Reggiano (see page 135) all gained their international protected status.

The naming regiment can vary from country to country, but they all have the same underlying premise: to make sure their national products are made in the proper manner and that the consumer is aware of the traditional methods employed to create a product of greater quality. In France, Appellation d'Origine Contrôlée (AOC) is used; in Italy, Denominazione di Origine Controllata (DOC); and in Spain, Denominación de Origen Protegida (DOP, or DO). To be called Comté (see page 125), for example, the cheese must be made in the Franche-Comté region of France, only from the raw milk of Montbéliarde or French Simmental cows that are pastured. Parmigiano-Reggiano (see page 135) may only be called such if it is produced in specific provinces in Italy from skimmed cow's milk. So when you see a cheese name followed by one of the various acronyms above, you are buying a product that is blessed by the country it came from, as well as the European Union, as one born from traditional methods of production and a guaranteed level of quality.

The name designation protection process benefits the region and people involved in the production. Farmers and cheese producers who adhere to the standards of quality and production methods indicated in the agreement receive recognition and a proper price for their product. Without these protections, many cheese makers would not be able to afford to make these high-quality artisanal cheeses, and for some cheeses, the art and tradition of making them might have been lost.

Cheeses protected by the PDO meet high-quality standards of ingredients and production, are made within a specific geographical area, use milk from a specific breed, and are made in a particular way or with a standardized process—thus maintaining the cultural heritage of cheese-making.

TERROIR/REGIONAL PAIRINGS

The word "terroir" is thrown around quite a bit these days. It is a term that refers to something very real and very special about the "taste of place," as it affects the flavors of the natural foods we enjoy. In some contexts, however, terroir is becoming another catchphrase to help sell food. As cheesemongers, we believe heavily in the truths that an animal grazing on the wildflowers of the Loire Valley will produce a milk and thus a cheese that tastes of the Loire Valley, and that herds of cattle that graze on the high alpine pastures during the summer will inevitably make a cheese that tastes and smells of the Alps and will be different from a cheese of the same variety produced in another locale. That is part of what is so great about the cheese world: you can travel the globe one bite at a time. True farmstead and artisanal cheeses are chock-full of the flavors of the season when they are made and the elements of the environment—soil content, temperature, moisture and humidity of the air, natural flora, etc.—where they are created. The time-tested saying "what grows together goes together" (or something to that effect) is clearly evident when the products of agriculture from the same region are paired up.

Terroir pairings are fun to try and exceedingly pleasing to the palate. To get you started, here are some of our favorite pairings.

GARROTXA (SEE PAGE 156) AND CHORIZO A heavenly combination from Spain, the tart acidity and touch of earthiness from Garroxta meshes together with the sweet, smoky heat from Spain's classic cured sausage, chorizo.

JASPER HILL FARM HARBISON (SEE PAGE 70) AND HILL FARMSTEAD EDWARD The gooey, lactic, treat Harbison has all the grassy, sweet notes of the lush land of northern Vermont. The mouth-coating goodness pairs extremely well with Edward, a pale ale from Hill Farmstead Brewery, which is crafted down the road from where the cheese is born. The hoppy notes of the beer break through the indulgent flavor of the cheese and bring out a hint of caramel.

COURONNE DE TOURAINE (SEE PAGE 67) AND SANCERRE Goat's cheese and white wine are a traditional and divine match. This flinty cheese with a slight barnyard flavor balances the floral, honeysuckle notes found in the wine. Texturally, the chalky, slightly supple paste plays off the light-bodied nature of the wine

MONTGOMERY'S CHEDDAR (SEE PAGE 159) AND ENGLISH ALES Cheddar cheese was born to be paired with beer. The buttery, grassy tang of the cheese is a natural partner to the wild fermentation and slightly sour fruit notes and refreshing qualities of farmhouse ales, such as Somerset Saison.

ANDANTE DAIRY CONTRALTO (SEE PAGE 86) AND NORTHERN CALIFORNIA PINOT NOIR This slightly full-flavored, washed-rind goat's milk cheese loves a good, round-bodied light Pinot Noir from the Sonoma Valley. Touches of red fruit and a pleasant mineral flavor of the wine combine with the sweet, creamy goat's milk.

VERMONT SHEPHERD "VERANO" (SEE PAGE 172) AND LOCALLY GROWN AND PICKLED VEGETABLES This flinty, slightly woolly, full-flavored sheep's milk cheese is complemented by the vinegary tang and subtle sweetness of pickled vegetables, such as string beans and peppers.

FETA (SEE PAGE 113) AND MARINATED GIGANTE BEANS An appetizing nibble for the gods or even us mortals, the slightly salty feta pairs wonderfully with the extremely supple, creamy, and tomato-marinated white beans.

BRIE FERMIER (SEE PAGE 60) AND ELDERFLOWER COMPOTE Sweet and savory are a match made in heaven, and this gooey, earthy, green garlicky Brie goes great with the sweet, chunky, and aromatic elderflower jam.

CAMEMBERT FERMIER (SEE PAGE 62) AND CALVADOS The fudgy Camembert with its mushroom overtones is lightened with a sip of this apple brandy. The earthiness breaks through to a fruity swish in the mouth, and the two flavors disappear rather quickly, which is ideal because you will want to keep imbibing in this pairing.

CHALLERHOCKER (SEE PAGE 125) AND DARK CHOCOLATE You wouldn't think it, but this nutty, creamy Swiss cheese is a perfect vessel for a piece of dark Swiss chocolate. Think of the best s'mores you have ever had—salty and sweet and melt-in-your-mouth good.

BLAUSCHIMMEL/CHIRIBOGA BLUE (SEE PAGE 177) AND GERMAN DESSERT WINE Some blue cheeses love a sweet wine, and the marshmallow, buttery treat Blauschimmel cries out to be paired with a gewürztraminer or another slightly floral white wine with a touch of viscosity.

TOMME D'ESTAING (SEE PAGE 169) AND GAMAY FROM CÔTES D'AUVERGNE This fuzzy and gamy natural-rind sheep's milk wheel is a good match for the lighter-bodied yet fruity and mineral-tinged reds from the Auvergne, such as gamay. Slightly nutty with hints of mushroom, the cheese is balanced by the mellow acidity and subtle dustiness of the gamay.

BRA TENERO (SEE PAGE 153) AND A BOTTLE OF BARBERA D'ASTI The extremely balanced and drinkable red wines of the Piedmont region of Italy are the perfect match for the straightforward table cheeses of the region. Sitting around a table with a chunk of Bra Tenero and a nice bottle of Barbera with family and friends should be on your Sunday schedule sooner rather than later.

ROS (SEE PAGE 164) AND SIDRA NATURAL Pairing the aged sheep's milk cheese Ros with its dry texture and flavor profile of toasted hazelnuts and wool, alongside a glass (or bottle) of naturally fermented Spanish cider (sidra) makes for a highly enjoyable afternoon snack. The acidic bite of the beverage matches up nicely with the fatty complexity of the cheese.

TOOLS OF THE TRADE

Cheeses are like safes that beg to be cracked open. Here are some of the tools we employ on a daily basis to make sure each wheel is split in a way that maintains the integrity of the cheese and reduces any loss of product.

PARM KEYS

Designed to separate a wheel of Parmigiano-Reggiano (see page 135) so that the structure of the curds stay intact and the cheese is gently pulled apart, parm keys are a very specific set of tools to be used only for this task. There are four essential tools in this category: the scoring knife to penetrate the tough rind and create avenues for the other tools; the two almond-shaped knives that are inserted into the score and used to pry the cheese apart; and the spatula that plunges deep into the heart of the cheese to create separation of the two halves of the wheel.

GUILLOTINE

This is our preferred name for a large, double-handled knife. It allows for complete control, balancing the heft of the cut from hand to hand as the blade is typically "walked" through the cheese—by "walked" we mean that the blade is rocked back and forth while applying a proper amount of pressure to make progress in cutting. We use this knife on large cooked and pressed wheels such as Gruyère (see page 128) and Comté (see page 125) to break them down into manageable sizes to sell on the counter. An added bonus: handling such a large piece of sharpened steel really makes you feel like a boss.

ASSORTMENT OF KNIVES

Knives are an integral part of the job, but without proper care and attention, they can become a serious hazard. Knives come in all shapes and sizes, and knowing which one is right for cutting a specific cheese is part intuition, part common sense. Thinner filet blades are better for soft cheeses, as the drag of the knife face isn't as dramatic as the one from a larger chef's knife. On the other hand, you wouldn't want to use a filet blade to get through a wheel of Appenzeller (see page 86), unless you have a lot of time and really strong forearms. Knives allow for communication with the cheese you are handling. You feel the strength of the rind and paste as it gives way to the blade; you can also feel if the cheese is going to splinter, crumble, or come out perfectly. Using knives appropriately makes for a connection to the product that every good cheesemonger develops and prizes.

WIRES

Sometimes, your only choice for cutting is a wire. These simple instruments are comprised of a steel wire of a specified length and two handles to create tension on the wire, allowing it to pass through wheels of cheese. A preferred method by many in the industry to cut cheese, wires, for the most part, make clean cuts, and are helpful in splitting larger wheels (particularly if you can't handle a guillotine) and cutting softer cheeses. Many people are trained on wires, which require practice and finesse to create the correct wire tension for the cut. With proper technique, they are an efficient tool in the cheese-cutting game.

HARPS

Harps are simply wires that have controlled tension by the design of the handle. They are good for splitting softer cheeses. A lot of blue cheeses are best cut using this tool, as it penetrates the cheese in a controlled and steady manner without a significant amount of drag on the cheese, lessening the chance of a cheese crumbling, resulting in loss of product.

CHEESE-CUTTING BOARD

These slabs of either steel or hard plastic are another version of employing a wire to cut cheese. Like the harp, there is a controlled tension on the wire thanks to a spring mechanism that rests on the underbelly of the board. Boards are good for making precise, clean cuts and are an easy tool to handle for any level of cheesemonger or even a serious connoisseur.

BREAKING DOWN BIG WHEELS

Ensuring the integrity and quality of cheese is one of our greatest passions. Making sure we receive the cheese in optimum condition and maintaining that healthiness is something we take pride in. So when you see that chunk of Parmigiano-Reggiano (see page 135) or that slab of Comté (see page 125) sitting on the counter, you best believe that we didn't receive it in that adorable, ready-to-buy size. One of the lucky mongers behind the counter got to break down a mammoth wheel of cheese that was likely over fifty pounds (23 kg)— probably closer to eighty pounds (36 kg). Breaking down wheels is not a willy-nilly process. There are certain techniques and procedures that ensure the integrity of the cheese, and cheeses are split using the preferred tools of the monger (see page 42).

One of the most important things to remember when breaking down a large wheel of cheese is to try to leave as much of the wheel intact as possible and to create a section of the wheel that is a manageable size for selling on the counter. Each wheel of Parmigiano-Reggiano (see page 135), Comté (see page 125), Gruyère (see page 128), clothbound Montgomery's Cheddar (see page 159), etc., is initially split in half, with one half faced (which means

cleaned of any rind or debris from the paste, and then covered in paper (waxed paper) and then wrapped tightly in plastic to avoid exposure to air and tagged with the split date. The remaining half is then split to create two quarters of a wheel. One of these quarters undergoes the same process as that first half (faced, wrapped, and labeled). Ta-da: you now have a quarter to start breaking down for your customers, which, more times than not, gets broken down into an eighth or even a twelfth, and so on.

Meticulously breaking down cheeses into smaller parts allows a proper paste-to-rind ratio, ensuring that the piece of cheese you are buying represents the evolution of the cheese and the full spectrum of flavors in each wheel.

We take pride in being able to understand and communicate with the wheels of cheeses with the tools we use, walking a guillotine through the dense paste of a wheel of Comté (see page 125) or using a fine wire to cleanly separate two halves of a massive piece of Gruyère (see page 128).

By receiving these cheeses in their true, whole state, rather than precut and shrink-wrapped in smaller pieces considered suitable for sale, we are able to maintain the cheeses in an environment that allows for their maturation to continue until they are ready for consumption. This results in cheeses that are expressive and, more often than not, in prime condition when they hit the counter and end up in your home.

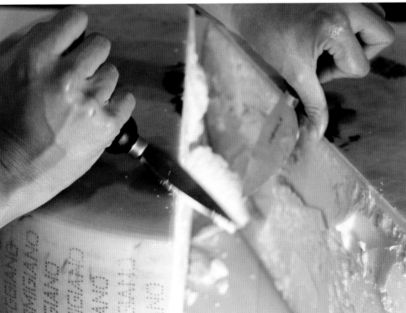

STORING CHEESE

Cheese is a living breathing thing. When we get these fragile little forms on our counter, we spend hours, days, and even weeks tending to them and ensuring that they are existing in the best environment possible for them to ripen into their peak forms, or that they are being sustained in their perfect state. Once a wheel of cheese is cut, it immediately begins to die. This is a fact that cannot be helped; it is part of the reality of dealing with a perishable product. Cheese, in essence, is controlled rot, a fragile fermentation. There is a fine line between milk being developed into a product of exceptional quality or decaying into a spoiled, inedible hunk of something no one wants.

There are several different beliefs when it comes to the proper care and storage of cut cheese. As the consumer, you are choosing to invest in a perishable delicacy that you would like to enjoy in its best possible state. As cheesemongers, we highly recommend getting smaller amounts that you know you can consume within a week or so.

Cheese is not a porous material, so any surface mold that grows can be scraped or cut off without jeopardizing the quality of the interior. Certain cheeses, specifically bloomy cheeses (see pages 57–81), may omit an ammonia scent when they are in decline, indicating that the cheese is past its prime; however, this ammonia scent can be confusing because some aged cheeses, particularly alpine styles such as Gruyère (see page 128), will omit the same scent, which is a natural part of their aging process and should not be cause for alarm.

There are many options in the marketplace for cheese storage, including specialized papers and bags designed to elongate the life of a wedge or sealed plastic container–like contraptions that assert that their "cave-like" environments will make cheese last weeks longer than normal.

When you purchase a piece of cheese from a reputable cheese shop, they will properly wrap it in a slightly breathable paper with a barrier, such as wax paper, to protect the exposed sides of the cheese. The best thing to do is to put the already wrapped piece of cheese into a glass or plastic container with a lid and store it in your refrigerator, or you can place the wrapped cheese directly into the vegetable bin of your refrigerator. When purchasing a piece of cheese that is already wrapped in plastic wrap, the options are to eat it quickly to prevent excess molding from the moisture buildup, or to transfer the cheese to a piece of parchment paper and store it in the cheese or vegetable drawer of your refrigerator.

In the end, your best option is to purchase smaller pieces more often to ensure the best quality.

It is of the utmost importance that you never freeze your cheese. Once cheese drops to a temperature of freezing, the bacteria dies and the entirety of the cheese becomes compromised.

PART FOUR
ENCYCLOPEDIA OF CHEESES

FRESH

Fresh cheeses are the group of young and usually quite soft and velvety cheeses that are made when the curds and whey are left to mostly mingle together in an indulgent creamy mass that solidifies only slightly as some of the whey is drained out. The term "fresh" refers both to the cheeses' light and mellow tastes and the fact that the cheeses are not aged—as in sometimes only for a few hours and up to a few days. Characteristically, this group is on the mellower, milkier side of the cheese world. While most cheeses have both rennet and an enzyme added to the milk to begin the cheese-making process, many fresh cheeses have a high acid-based component added, such as lemon juice, to help curdle the milk. Fresh cheeses are pleasantly mild and tend to pair well with fresh fruits and berries, and are an incredibly versatile ingredient to incorporate into breakfasts and desserts—think of a bowl of Fromage Blanc with ripe blackberries folded into the cheese and a drizzle of wildflower honey adorning the top, or Ricotta (see page 54) and lemon curd mixed together and then baked in a small ramekin for an incredible pudding-like treat.

HOMEMADE BUTTER RECIPE

1 cup (240 ml) heavy cream, chilled

1 pint (475 ml) container or mason jar, with lid

Salt to taste, optional

1. Place chilled cream in a container or mason jar and shake it until the cream develops into the consistency of whipped cream.

2. Continue to shake vigorously until the cream separates into butter and buttermilk.

3. Rinse with cold water and squeeze out remaining buttermilk.

4. Mix in salt, if desired.

5. Store in the refrigerator for up to 3 weeks.

BUTTER

MILK TYPE: Cow, goat, sheep, water buffalo, yak, etc.

In simple terms, butter is the product of separating the majority of fats and proteins in milk from the other components of the liquid. By agitating the milk cream, the fats that reside in it join together to form the rich paste we know as butter. The remaining fluid is known as buttermilk. You can tell the quality of the milk and the feed of the animals by the color of the butter—the more golden yellow it is, the more minerals and nutrients the animal has been consuming, a sign of being out on pasture and eating fresh green growth.

One of the great things about butter, besides its sweet, creamy, and smooth character, is that it can easily be made at home. The next time you need to put your kids to work, have them shake some cream, following the recipe on the left.

CHÈVRE *(SHEV)*

MILK TYPE: Goat

Chèvre can be a confusing word in the context of cheese. Chèvre literally translates from the French word for "goat," but chèvre is also a cheese, and not just any French goat's cheese; it is a very specific creamy yet crumbly, citrusy yet lactic super-fresh cheese that is kind of like the perfect blend of Fromage Blanc, Cream Cheese (see below), and farmer's cheese. The process of making chèvre is similar to other fresh cheeses in that the milk is fermented with the help of an enzyme and then heated for a bit to enliven the chemical reaction between the milk proteins and the chosen enzyme—and then it is pretty much ready to be consumed. Goat's cheese is usually lower in fat and has no real amounts of lactose, so it's easier on the system to digest. Goats yield milk from mid-March through October, and the flavors of the milk, and thus the cheese, vary wildly during this time. Toward the beginning of the season, there are a lot of bestial, bucky overtones of the milk, with the floral, grassy after notes coming as a more delicate wave. The flavor balance begins to shift throughout the season, becoming more forwardly grassy and floral by the end of the milking cycle. Fresh chèvre is great rolled in crushed nuts, crumbled on a big green spring salad, or simply smeared on a bagel with some smoked salmon.

CREAM CHEESE

MILK TYPE: Cow (traditionally)

Cream cheese has a long history. First accounts of this super fresh, super fatty, rich, and tangy creation go back as far as the late 1500s in England. Cream cheese is actually very easy to make; it is only a two-step process, and pesky equipment such as a cheese vat or cutting instruments are not necessary. Different countries have different standards of what they require in a cheese to be considered "cream cheese," but the consensus is that there needs to be a high level of fat—higher than what occurs in milk—thus the addition of cream. To make cream cheese, full-fat milk (meaning no skim or low-fat versions) has a lactic acid bacteria added to it to help lower the acidity level of the milk. This creation is then heated up to a very specific temperature—72°F (22°C)—so that the molecules in the milk relax and stick together, thus thickening. Once the desired consistency is achieved, the whole shebang needs to be heated up a bit more to kill off any remaining lactic-acid bacteria so that the product becomes stabilized. If the bacteria were allowed to continue to grow, the

acidity levels would drop so low that the milk molecules would collapse and turn back into liquid. Most mass-produced cream cheeses have some sort of stabilizer added so there is not as much pressure on reaching exact heat levels or having the need for quick consumption. Because this is a fresh dairy product, it is best to eat it within a few days of acquiring. Go beyond smearing it on a bagel and try it stuffed into squash flowers.

HOMEMADE RICOTTA-STYLE CHEESE RECIPE

½ gallon (1.9 l) whole milk

1 cup (240 ml) heavy cream

1 teaspoooon citric acid, dissolved in
    ½ cup (120 ml) cool water

1 teaspoon salt

1. Pour milk and cream into large pot.

2. Slowly heat the milk and cream on low, stirring frequently until it reaches 180°F (82°C). Remove from heat.

3. Add citric acid, then stir gently for 20 seconds to distribute evenly—you will see the curds begin to form.

4. Add salt and gently stir for 10 additional seconds.

5. Let the curds rest for 10–15 minutes.

6. Gently scoop curds into draining baskets (these are available online where cheese-making supplies are sold), or with a finely slotted spoon, scoop into a bowl with a netting of cheese cloth suspended over the rim.

7. Refrigerate and let drain for at least 15 minutes and up to several hours.

8. After draining, store in an airtight container in the refrigerator for up to 3 weeks.

RICOTTA

MILK TYPE: Cow, sheep, or sometimes goat

Ricotta cheese is one of the most ubiquitous fresh cheeses out there. From its humble beginnings as a way for cheese makers to get the very last bit of salvageable proteins from the leftovers of a hearty day of cheese-making, it has now morphed into a centerpiece in the culinary world. Literally translated as "recooked" from the Italian, ricotta first came about when a cheese maker decided to cook the leftover whey from a day of production, and the few remaining bits of milk protein clumped together, providing the cheese maker something to feast on for the evening. What most people encounter as ricotta is not actually ricotta (a product made from the reheating of the whey), but instead is a whole-fat milk that has been heated then had citric acid (or lemon juice or white vinegar) added to it to encourage curdling. The recipe on the left is a version of ricotta-style cheese that is extremely easy to make at home and is an impressive starter to any meal with a drizzle of good olive oil and a sprinkle of salt.

SEIRASS *(SEAR-AS)*

MILK TYPE: Sheep and cow

ORIGIN: Piedmont, Italy

What looks like a bird's nest cocoon is actually an incredibly dynamic cheese that is filled with all the grassy nuances of its hay exterior, and the saline tang of a sheep's milk Ricotta (see above). This mountainous production gets its name from the local word for "ricotta," and is made with the leftover whey from the firmer toma, the common cow's milk wheels made primarily for the farmers to sell at market. The whey of the cooked-curd cheese produces a firmer second curd, which gives these wheels their dry, brittle texture. After receiving a hefty sprinkling of salt, the small-cut curds of mixed milk are then rolled in salt as well. Once a thin crust has formed after a few hours, the glob of dairy is enshrouded in fresh grass, the same fresh grass that the beasts that provide the milk graze upon. Unlike a lot of the more common salted ricottas, Seirass is an excellent centerpiece and not just as an ingredient to cook with. The slight saltiness reveals a lactic depth of woolly sweetness and hearty cream.

Enjoy with a bright white, such as a crisp Pinot Grigio, or a summer cocktail, such as a sloe gin fizz.

3-CORNER FIELD FARM
BREBIS BLANCHE *(BRAY-BEE-BLAHN-CHE)*

MILK TYPE: Sheep

ORIGIN: New York, United States

Located near the border of Vermont and New York in the Battenkill Valley, 3-Corner Field Farm creates these little dumplings of decadent sheep's milk that have a fatty, earthy aroma with a dense and sometimes crumbly texture. They're great when very young, but when left to age and tighten up over a few days, they can take on a more pronounced woolly and gamy flavor profile, representative of the purity of the sheep's milk used. 3-Corner Field Farm raises predominantly East Friesian sheep (considered to have the greatest milk output of the sheep world) that graze on their pastures during the warmer months, where they enjoy the naturally cultivated flora of the land. During the frigid winters, the sheep are kept indoors and eat a feed that is primarily cultivated from the farm. So while Brebis Blanche is produced year-round, the cheese has two distinct flavor profiles depending on the season.

YOGURT

MILK TYPE: Cow, goat, sheep, water buffalo, yak, etc.

A rich and tangy treat, yogurt is an incredibly healthy dairy delight with an appeal that crosses several continents and people. It's made by warming up milk and adding bacteria known as yogurt cultures, and then allowing the milk to slightly cool for a few hours so that the milk cultures, after which the milk thickens into the silken texture that is so seductive. The culturing process turns the proteins into live enzymes known as probiotics, which help to regulate the digestive system. Extremely versatile, yogurt is great when topped with fresh fruit for breakfast, incorporated into a savory salad dressing, or added to help cool a spicy stew. Make some at home using the easy recipe on the right and have fun experimenting with the world of cultured milk.

HOMEMADE YOGURT RECIPE

1 quart (946 ml) whole milk

1 package yogurt starter culture (this can be found online where cheese-making supplies are sold) or 1 tablespoon yogurt with live active cultures

1. Heat milk on the stove or in a microwave on high until it reaches 180°F (82°C).

2. Let cool to 110°F (43°C).

3. Add starter culture or yogurt with live active cultures and stir to combine.

4. Pour into glass jars, with lids and incubate at 110°F (43°C) for 8–12 hours, undisturbed, using a controlled water bath, heating pad, etc.

5. Store in the refrigerator for up to 3 weeks.

BLOOMY

The pillowy white mold you see on the outside of Bries and triple crèmes—that puff that looks so soft and cloud-like—is what is known as the bloomy rind. Bloomy-rinded cheeses are born from two types of bacteria. Penicillium candidum gives cheeses a characteristic chalky color and soft-looking appearance. Bries, Camemberts, and triple crèmes all have the cakey, meringue-white appearance from this mold. Geotrichum candidum gives cheeses a more wrinkly, brainy texture and appearance, and is most commonly found on slightly aged goat cheeses, such as Couronne de Touraine (see page 67) and Crottin de Chavignol (see page 68) from the Loire Valley, and Capriole Farms Wabash Cannonball (see page 64) from Indiana.

During the cheese-making process, the milk is inoculated with the bacteria, which develops into the white rind as the cheese is aged, anywhere from a few days to a few weeks. In some production facilities, the bacteria is introduced in a spray form once the cheese has set and begun to age. This process tends to create a bit of a thick, chalky rind that can peel apart from the paste, resulting in a poor eating experience.

Also known as soft-ripened cheeses, bloomy-rind cheeses age from the outside of the cheese toward the center, creating a lovely cream line near the rind and a gooey, sometimes dense or velvety interior. Depending on the bacteria used, as well as the starting culture, bloomy-rind cheeses can run the gamut in flavor profiles from mushroomy and earthy to sweet and creamy. (Bloomy rinds should never emit an ammonia scent or be orange or brown in color.) When lush and ripe, the cheeses in this much-loved category are especially delightful when paired with a sparkling wine.

ALEMAR CHEESE COMPANY BLUE EARTH

MILK TYPE: Cow

ORIGIN: Minnesota, United States

When Keith Adams of the Alemar Cheese Company in Mankato, Minnesota, began his cheese-making career in 2009, he worked tirelessly to create a French-inspired soft-ripened cheese. The end result was Alemar's Bent River Camembert, which won the hearts of cheesemongers and consumers across the United States. A few years later, he set out to make a large-format bloomy-ripened cheese that would be a different expression of the organic cow's milk used in his Camembert. This was the birth of Blue Earth. When we first receive this American Brie at about six weeks of maturation, it feels like a baby's diaper at capacity. Clocking in at about two pounds (907 g) each, these lush and lactic wheels have an amazing, runny cream line and a dense buttery core that provide excellent variations of texture. Subtle aromas of mushroom and asparagus complement the rich, fatty paste. The next time you're in the mood for a Brie, this one is truly worth seeking out.

Enjoy with a bottle of Zweigelt, as well as slathered across homemade brandied fruitcake.

ALEMAR CHEESE COMPANY

Mankato, Minnesota, United States

When life gives you lemons, you either gotta make lemonade or...well, what's the alternative? When Keith Adams of Alemar Cheese Company of Mankato, Minnesota, found himself at a crossroad in life, he decided to dedicate his time and talent to creating American cheese influenced by French-style bloomy rinds. By converting an old commissary kitchen into a cheese-making and aging facility and outfitting an old pickup truck with a vessel to transport the high-quality milk from the neighboring farm to his dairy, Mr. Adams has worked outside the box to build Alemar into one of the most exciting cheese producers in the United States. Alemar Cheese Company is continually pushing to elevate the caliber of the cheese they produce, and their forward-thinking is an inspiration to the cheese community. In addition to Blue Earth, look for their Bent River Camembert and the little stinker Good Thunder, which is washed in a local brown ale.

ANDANTE DAIRY DUET

MILK TYPE: Goat or goat and cow

ORIGIN: California, United States

These little briquettes of creamy, sweet pure goat's milk or a blend of goat and cow's milk come from the magical genius that is Soyoung Scanlan, proprietor of Andante Dairy in Petaluma, California (see page 60). With the dairy situated on a rolling hillside, the goats that provide Soyung's milk graze on Northern California's finest greens before being lovingly milked by her neighbor. Once the milk has been delivered via a long pipe that runs straight from the barn to her kingdom, Soyoung gets to work figuring out what kind of cheese the milk wants to become.

For Duet, she was inspired by the herbaceousness of the goat's milk and decided to "infuse" the milk with fresh herbs—the same fresh herbs that the goats graze on. She warms the milk with a bouquet of lavender, or thyme, or whatever they're munching on at the moment, before adding the cultures. Once the milk has been through the magic machine (you know all about this by now; it's when the cheese gets made, see page 22), she hand-ladles the curd into the little brick molds and lets them ripen in a warm, humid, still room. They develop a slight cream line just under the rind, while maintaining a delicate, velvety center, all with just a faint nuance of the fresh herbs.

ANDANTE DAIRY

Petaluma, California, United States

Soyoung Scanlan is a chemist and classically trained pianist. After an extensive education in both of these fields, she fell in love with milk and its complex chemical makeup. After moving to California, Soyoung decided to indulge her lactic curiosity and began making cheese. Her small dairy is situated on top of a rolling green hill in Petaluma, California. From the window in her cheese-making room you can see directly into her neighbor's barn, which houses all the goats that produce her grade-A milk. Soyoung's cheese-making philosophy is rooted in her trust that the milk will tell her what cheese it wants to become. All of her cheeses are handmade, hand-ladeled, and truly unique expressions of her craftsmanship. The floral, sweet, and balanced milk yielded from the Northern California landscape is distinctive and expressive in each of her creations.

ANDANTE DAIRY METRONOME *(MET-ROW-GNOME)*

MILK TYPE: Goat and cow

ORIGIN: California, United States

Soyoung Scanlan of Andante Dairy in Petaluma, California, loves shapes, crafting little dairy wonders into the shapes of hearts, miniature drums, bricks, and especially elongated pyramids, which mirror the tempo-keeping machines that all musicians know so well. This mixed-milk blend begins with the same ingredients as most of Soyoung's other creations: milk, enzymes, rennet, heat, curd cutting, love, etc. After being hand-ladled into the molds, she let's them ripen in her warm, moist, and quiet aging room so that they develop a fine bloom. The end result is an altogether dense yet light dairy contradiction that is both sweet and milky, with slight hints of buttercups and all the freshness of morning dew.

BRIE FERMIER *(BREE FAIR-ME-EH)*

MILK TYPE: Cow

ORIGIN: Île-de-France, France

Since we are unable to import true raw milk Brie from France, we're always on the hunt for the closest thing we can get to those wheels we savor while in that country. With its beautifully delicate and developed rind and lush paste, Brie Fermier holds all of the aromas that are found in a true Brie: mushroom, asparagus, and broccoli. This cheese is a rich, lactic paste that becomes fudgy and earthy as it ages. Fermier refers to the fact that the milk that goes into this Brie is from the same farm where the cheese is made and, as a result, is the freshest it can possibly be, making this a high-quality cheese.

Enjoy with a glass or two of Calvados.

BRILLAT SAVARIN (BREE-AHT SAV-UH-RAN)

MILK TYPE: Cow

ORIGIN: Normandy, France

What can be said about this wheel of salty, buttery goodness that hasn't already been said? Named after the famous French politician and gastronome Jean Anthelme Brillat-Savarin, this cheese is a triple crème, meaning that it contains a minimum of 75 percent butterfat. Wow, that's a whole lotta fat! Perhaps the greatest gateway cheese of them all, Brillat Savarin has a plump, powdery rind that shows slight brown wrinkles as it ages and loses moisture. The interior, when young, is akin to a softened brick of butter, with a small amount of gooeyness near the rind. Age makes the paste tighter and fudgier, with subtle hints of dank earth. It's one helluva seductive cheese.

Enjoy with sparkling wine and fresh fruit.

CAMEMBERT FERMIER *(KAM-IN-BEAR FAIR-ME-AIR)*

MILK TYPE: Cow

ORIGIN: Île-de-France, France

Camembert originated in Normandy, France, where both apple orchards and happy cows have been staples of the agricultural system there since the beginning of time. Camembert came about as an adaptation of Brie, the pillowy white-rind cow's milk delight that was an institution in every French home. Marie Harel, the famed female French farmer who invented Camembert, was looking for a tasty cheese to craft with the rich and decadent milk from her herd of cows. Produced in smaller-sized wheels than Brie, Camembert ripens much faster, developing a lovely mushroomy, earthy, slightly buttery taste encased in a wave of gooey love. During the agricultural industrialization era, wooden boxes were crafted to house Camembert, allowing it to be shipped farther for sale. Nowadays, there are several different producers of Camembert, but Fermier represents that the milk used to craft the cheese comes from the same farm where it is made. The flavor of a true farmhouse Camembert is much fuller, rounder, and richer than those that are made from commercially produced milk.

To enjoy this decadent treat, toss the whole Camembert—wooden box and all—into the broiler for about 10 minutes, until the top chars, and the cheese itself becomes bubbly and scrumptious. Note: Be sure to remove the top of the box before placing in the broiler.

CANA DE OVEJA *(CON-AH DAY OH VAY-HA)*

Milk Type: Sheep

Origin: Murcia, Spain

When you think of Spanish sheep's milk cheese, what's the first thing that comes to mind? Yeah, that wonderful cheese known as Manchego (see page 158). But Spain is so much more than that famous wheel, as evidenced with these bloomy sticks that are created in the southern part of the country near the Mediterranean Sea. These pleasurable logs weigh about one and a half to two pounds (680–907 g) when we receive them. When sliced open, Cana de Oveja presents a gooey cream line with a cakey paste that unleashes simple hints of orchard wood and toasted nuts. This can be a difficult cheese to find at times due to its popularity and its modest price point.

Enjoy with a bottle of funky, unfiltered Spanish cider.

CAPRIOLE FARMS OLD KENTUCKY TOMME *(TOHM)*

MILK TYPE: Goat

ORIGIN: Indiana, United States

This dense goat's milk cheese from Capriole Farms (see page 65) in Greenville, Indiana, has the slightly firm texture of a young American Jack cheese with all of the nuances and depth of a cellar-aged goat cheese. Made from the milk of the herd that grazes in the beautiful pastures bordering Kentucky and Indiana, this cheese develops notes of moss and clay as it ripens in the caves. The flavor is extremely mellow and unassuming for a goat, and borders on the sweet and lactic nature most often found in the milk of a younger cow.

This cheese melts extremely well, lending itself to be the star ingredient in the best cheese quesadilla you will ever have.

CAPRIOLE FARMS PIPER'S PYRAMIDE

MILK TYPE: Goat

ORIGIN: Indiana, United States

The ancient Egyptians may have built the pyramids, but the cheese maker has perfected them, especially Judy Schad and her crew at Capriole Farms (see page 65) in Greenville, Indiana, where Piper's Pyramide is produced. This super dense, stunning pyramid of superbly cultivated goat's milk with its dusting of paprika is aptly named after the cheese-maker's red-headed grandchild. This cheese takes on a fantastic layer of brainy Geotrichum candidum as it ages, and the subtle smokiness of the paprika is a perfect complement to the sweet, grassy goat's milk.

Enjoy with a bright, crisp rosé.

CAPRIOLE FARMS SOFIA

MILK TYPE: Goat

ORIGIN: Indiana, United States

Another true American classic, these little barquettes of goat's milk bliss are covered—as well as veined with—vegetable ash. Named after a phenomenal cheese maker who assisted at Capriole Farms (see page 65) in Greenville, Indiana, for a short time, this creation is dense and velvety, with an unassuming sweetness that can only be attributed to the foliage that the goats graze upon daily. As the cheese develops, it takes on the typical brainy layer of Geotrichum candidum and breaks down into a seductive cream line that can become quite runny when the time is right. The paste never loses its cakey texture, revealing pleasant earthy notes from the ash that meshes with the sweet lemon-peel notes of the goat's milk. Sofia finds a new legion of followers at our counters every day.

Enjoy with a glass of Muscadet followed by a bowl of mussels.

CAPRIOLE FARMS WABASH CANNONBALL

MILK TYPE: Goat

ORIGIN: Indiana, United States

Produced since 1992, these little nuggets of pure goat's milk possess very thin and delicate rinds that develop over their dense, sweet centers after just a few days in the warm cellars of Capriole Farms in Greenville, Indiana (see facing page). A light dusting of vegetable ash is sprinkled on prior to the aging process, encouraging a mellow, almost floral flavor to develop. As these little dumplings age, they grow a bit denser but retain their mellow flavor profile of fresh flowers and sweet corn. Their petite shape makes them almost too cute to pass up when shopping for cheese.

Enjoy with most white wines or a lightly hopped lager.

CAPRIOLE FARMS

Greenville, Indiana, United States

In the mid-1970s, a young couple, Judy and Larry Schad, purchased an eighty-acre farm in the heart of the land that borders Kentucky and Indiana. Part of the original plan behind purchasing their own farm was to raise animals and live off the land. Their first goat proved to be a challenge, displaying all the bullheadedness goats are known for, and they quickly gave him up. When they saw a cute, little charmer at a county fair in Indiana, they decided to give it another try. Soon enough, Judy fell in love with goats, but unfortunately, her sons did not fall in love with their milk. Judy decided to put the milk from the goats to another use, learning how to make cheese and creating fresh versions in her kitchen. In 1985, she and her husband took the plunge and invested in professional cheese-making equipment, and there has been no looking back. Thought to be the Grandmother of American Goat Cheese, Judy continues to inspire and educate.

CASATICA DI BUFALA *(CAH-SA TEE-KA DE BOO-FALA)*

MILK TYPE: Water buffalo

ORIGIN: Lombardy, Italy

This fatty, dense brick comprised of rich water buffalo's milk (which averages twice the fat content of cow's milk) is a no-brainer if you are looking for a soft bloomy-rinded cheese that will not offend even the most timid cheese consumer. Made by two brothers in northern Italy, Casatica di Bufala is enrobed in a gentle layer of Penicillium candidum and possesses a dense, chewy, ivory-white paste that holds hints of toasted hazelnut—which at times can be difficult to sense due to the highly seductive texture and luscious, sweet fat that melts over the tongue.

Enjoy with a glass of Nebbiolo and even try melting it on your next pizza.

CAZELLE DE SAINT AFFRIQUE *(CA-ZALE DUH SAINT AFF-REAK)*

MILK TYPE: Sheep

ORIGIN: Midi-Pyrénées

Inspired by and crafted like its brethren Crottin de Chavignol (see page 68), this sheep's milk wonder is handmade in the foothills of the Pyrenees in France. Instead of using the relatively low-in-fat goat's milk, the fattier sheep's milk creates an extremely luscious, somewhat woolly, yet all-around gentle cheese that is so unique, only one producer has brought it to the United States. The floral nuttiness of the sheep's milk is enhanced with a little age—about six weeks—when the delicate rind develops to encase the rich, creamy center.

Enjoy baked briefly in an oven and then nestled atop a steamy pile of rice pilaf for an impromptu risotto-esque experience (without all of the exhausting stirring).

CHÈVRE D'OR (SHEV DOOR)

MILK TYPE: Goat

ORIGIN: Loire Valley, France

These little discs of Loire Valley goat's milk enrobed in
Geotrichum candidum are quintessential to any decent cheese
counter. Best in the spring and early summer, when the goats have
had their kids and the milk is lushly flowing, each piece of Chèvre
d'Or weighs in at about five ounces (142 g) and is fairly plump and
supple when young, with a dense, cakey interior laden with notes
of lemon peel and fresh grass. As it ages, this cheese takes on a
more intense, minerally flavor profile and a fudgy yet somewhat
stone-like texture. At any age, this is a goat cheese that beautifies
any cheese plate and leads the way to any cheese lover's heart.

Enjoy with a crisp Sancerre and stone fruit.

CLOCHETTE (CLOW-SHETTE)

MILK TYPE: Goat

ORIGIN: Poitou-Charentes, France

Rumor has it that this unique Loire Valley goat cheese got its bell shape when a cheese maker used the cups of one
of his wife's brassieres as molds after running out of traditional draining molds. Whether this is true or not, the
distinctive shape of this cheese, along with the distinctive way it ripens, is a real treat for any true goat cheese lover.
The dense and velvety center combined with the quick gradation to the lighter, softer cream line presents a pleasant
balance of textures. The robust and gamy goat flavor is pronounced under the Meyer lemon notes. After these little
bells have aged for two weeks, they develop a wrinkly, white rind that grows even more wrinkly and tangier with
age. This cheese is a real showstopper as the centerpiece of a cheese plate and a lovely end to a springtime dinner of
vegetables and roasted rabbit.

Enjoy with red grapes, sweet breads, and honey.

COULOMMIERS (COAL-LOOM-EE-AIR)

MILK TYPE: Cow

ORIGIN: Île-de-France, France

Coulommiers is basically the slightly chubbier, shorter, less popular cousin of Brie. France has the whole gooey
cow's milk indulgence on lockdown, and here is another example of why. Whereas a Brie can run the gamut in
flavors from mushroomy and wild to buttery and tame, Coulommiers is lactic and sweet with hints of burnt caramel
and brown sugar. Although this cheese has been made longer than Brie, it is still relatively unknown in the U.S.
market. Coulommiers is a great treat for anyone who loves a soft, spreadable cow's milk cheese and wants to try
something that is less commercial.

COURONNE DE TOURAINE *(CUH-ROAN DUH TOUR-AN)*

MILK TYPE: Goat

ORIGIN: Loire Valley, France

A member of the Loire Valley goat-cheese family, the Couronne (or "crown" in English) are halo-shaped, ash-covered pieces that come our way thanks to the affineur Rodolphe Le Meunier (see page 68). Enrobed in a brainy layer of Geotrichum candidum with some powdery white blooms that spot on the rind, this goat cheese has a cakey, brilliant white paste that, when perfectly ripe, possesses a moist cream line, adding to the already decadent and lush mouthfeel. The slight bitterness of the rind combines with the citrusy core of the cheese to produce a sweet and savory flavor profile. With age comes bitterness (ain't that the truth), and though this cheese will still be of high interest to those who like more intense notes of barnyard, we find this cheese to be at its best when pliable and with a higher moisture content.

Enjoy with a Sancerre.

RODOLPHE LE MEUNIER

Rodolphe Le Meunier was born and raised in the cheese world. His father was a maître fromager, and the younger Le Meunier learned the art of affinage from watching this wizard. Nestled in the idyllic Loire Valley in France, Rodolphe has taken over his father's cheese-making facility and updated it with a state-of-the-art aging house with four different caves—all humidity-, climate-, and temperature-controlled to best suit the variety of cheeses he selects to age. Known for his magic touch, Rodolphe works closely with producers to ensure the best quality for collaboration. Within the aging facility, he has created an education center so he, too, can continue the Le Meunier legacy of teaching the next generation the craft of cheese aging.

COWGIRL CREAMERY MT. TAM

MILK TYPE: Cow

ORIGIN: California, United States

A true American original, these little drums hale from the beautiful rolling hills of Northern California. Cowgirl Creamery in Point Reyes Station, California, has been a staple in the U.S. cheese revolution since its inception, and this buttery, dense, organic cow's milk cheese shows you why. The light, delicate rind encases a supple yet firm decadence that is so sweet and milky, it's as if full-fat milk magically solidified. Working with the Strauss Family Farm, the ladies at Cowgirl can ensure that their milk comes from happy grass-fed cows that graze upon some of the loveliest emerald green pastures around. Almost all of the other ripened cheeses that Cowgirl crafts are a variation of their staple, Mt. Tam, which is named after nearby Mount Tamalpais, the glorious mountain that runs along the spine of Marin County.

CROTTIN DE CHAVIGNOL (CROW-TAN DUH SHA-VEE-NOLL)

MILK TYPE: Goat

ORIGIN: Loire Valley, France

Perhaps the most famous goat cheese of the Loire Valley, Crottin (or "animal dropping" in English) is a small cylindrical cheese that is made anywhere from western France to the northern coast of California, with subtle variations of flavor and rind development based on the cheese-maker's desire and the microbiology of the milk and ripening facilities. This French example of the style arrives to us green, allowing us to ripen it in-house. As the cheese blooms, the flavor of the goat's milk transitions from fresh grass and citrus into a bucky, musty, animalistic character. Depending on your flavor preference, ask your cheesemonger to let you examine the state of the Crottin you wish to purchase. This cheese is a great bang for your buck and helps create diversity in any cheese spread.

GOAT LADY DAIRY SANDY CREEK

MILK TYPE: Goat

ORIGIN: North Carolina, United States

Goat Lady Dairy in Climax, North Carolina, is making some of our favorite domestic goat cheeses at the moment. Enrobed with a brilliant, ashy, powdery rind, Sandy Creek is a luscious, full-flavored cheese that averages six ounces (170 g) a dumpling. With a line of vegetable ash through the middle, this cheese has a goopy, runny character beneath the rind, with a citric paste that is cakey when young and dense like a stick of butter when quite ripe. The compact size and shape of Sandy Creek lends itself to being a perfect cheese to share with a small group of loved ones.

Enjoy with fresh peaches.

GOAT LADY DAIRY SNOW CAMP

MILK TYPE: Cow and goat

ORIGIN: North Carolina, United States

Snow Camp, produced by the Goat Lady Dairy in Climax, North Carolina, is made with a blend of tart, acidic goat and cow's milk and developed into a pudgy cylinder that is at once sweet and salty. For anyone who has an aversion to goat's milk cheese, this could be the one that breaks through. Snow Camp is a great cheese to share with two to three people, no matter what level of cheese connoisseur you are with. The pleasantly bitter rind adds a touch of earthiness to the creamy paste. A great cheese for enjoying at brunch or after-dinner, if you see one of these little guys on the cheese counter, don't pass it up.

Enjoy with Champagne or a tart cider, as well as spread over hazelnut crackers or paired with sultanas.

JASPER HILL FARM HARBISON

MILK TYPE: Cow

ORIGIN: Vermont, United States

The folks at Jasper Hill Farm in Greensboro Bend, Vermont (see page 130), have revolutionized the way American cheese makers engage in their craft. Jasper Hill not only acts as an aging facility for a selection of local farmers— similar to the role of the affineur in Europe—but they also craft a few cheeses. Harbison is their spruce bark–wrapped cow's milk goodie that is so coveted, it can oftentimes become a challenge to find. Similar to its cousin, Vacherin Mont D'or (see page 110), Harbison is meant to be x-ed along the rind and peeled open to reveal the oozing puddle of earthy, buttery treasure that is the heart of this cheese. Developed in a warm and humid cave, these little guys are a showstopper any time they are presented.

Enjoy with a loaf of crusty bread, dipping it into the decadent, gooey center of the cheese.

LINGOT DU QUERCY *(LIN-GO DO CURR-SEE)*

MILK TYPE: Goat

ORIGIN: Quercy, France

The world of French goat cheese is made up of a wonderful assortment of shapes and sizes, including this small brick. Lingot, the English "ingot," is a precious oblong-shaped cheese made in the south of France, among the plateaus that provide the wild sustenance for the goats to graze upon. A full-flavored representation of the milk from the region, Lingot du Quercy has a distinct cross section of textures: a seeping cream line surrounds a dense interior of sweet, yeasty, and somewhat gamy goat's milk, while the rind imparts a simple bitterness that adds to the complexity of the cheese on the palate.

Enjoy with a Crémant du Jura and fresh strawberries.

MANY FOLD FARM CONDOR'S RUIN

MILK TYPE: Sheep

ORIGIN: Georgia, United States

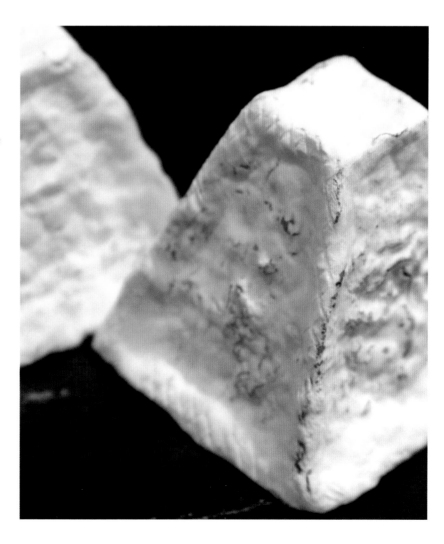

Based on the Loire Valley–classic Valençay (see page 80), these ash-covered pyramids of farmstead sheep's milk cheese from the fine folks at Many Fold Farm in Chattahoochee Hills, Georgia, arrive to our shop as fresh as possible so that we are able to participate in their ripening process. They have a pleasant, dank aroma, and when they are at their peak, the pyramids have a pillowy layer of bloom on the exterior and a smooth cream line, with a dense and pleasantly chalky paste that boasts notes of sweet grass and a bold yet not overpowering nuttiness. It's rare to find such high-quality sheep's milk cheese in the form that Condor's Ruin is made, so if you're able to score one of these beauties, you won't be disappointed. Just make sure it still has some moisture and suppleness to it.

Enjoy with a dry American cider.

MANY FOLD FARM GARRETTS FERRY

MILK TYPE: Sheep

ORIGIN: Georgia, United States

Many Fold Farm in Chattahoochee Hills, Georgia, produces these top hats of pasteurized sheep's milk from February to October, when the ewes' milk is at peak form. Garretts Ferry is essentially a large-format Crottin-style cheese that we receive green (unripened but inoculated) and develop in a humidity-controlled environment. The cheese takes on a healthy layer of Penicillium candidum over the pristine white exterior, giving the cheese a pillowy, cloud-like appearance, while the interior of Garretts Ferry develops a gentle cream line that wraps around the cakey, somewhat crumbly paste. Notes of burnt caramel, toasted nuts, and herbs permeate this cheese. This is a bright and refreshing cheese to enjoy during the warmer summer months.

Enjoy with a crisp pilsner and some fresh peaches.

MOTHAIS SUR FEUILLE *(MOE-THIGH SIR FWEE)*

MILK TYPE: Goat

ORIGIN: Poitou-Charentes, France

This small round comes from a region known for its goat's milk cheeses, and this particular cheese sets itself apart by being wrapped in a distinctive chestnut leaf as well as having a unique aging process. Placed in an extremely humid aging room with no ventilation, this cheese quickly takes on the flavors of a cellar and the leaf it is wrapped in. Softer when younger and becoming denser as it ages, this cheese has an earthy, woodsy quality that blends nicely with the tangy animal flavors of the goat's milk. It develops spots of blue-gray mold on the rind as it ages, which can be easily scraped off but actually add beautiful floral notes and depth to the bucky paste. Mothais is a cheese to try at varying ages to see exactly where your flavor preference lies with it.

NETTLE MEADOW FARM KUNIK *(KEW-NICK)*

MILK TYPE: Goat and Jersey cow cream

ORIGIN: New York, United States

Located about four-and-a half-hours north of our New York City shop, Nettle Meadow Farm in Warrensburg, New York, produces this decadent triple crème–style cheese (meaning it contains at least 75 percent milk fat) and is one of our most popular locally sourced cheeses. Luscious and voluptuous, this rich, spreadable Brie-style wonder has all the flavor, tanginess, and citrus notes of a fresh chèvre, with the buttery, earthy, mushroomy Jersey cow cream. Quite plump when ripe, this cheese makes a pleasant addition to any cheese plate.

Enjoy with fresh fruit and sparkling wine, or as part of a decadent breakfast spread with rye toast and jam.

PAINTED GOAT FARM CINDERELLA

MILK TYPE: Goat

ORIGIN: New York, United States

With about eighty goats on one hundred acres in upstate New York, Ilyssa Berg and Javier Flores do just about everything on Painted Goat Farm to create these beautiful ash-coated logs. From raising the goats and milking them to shaping the cheese, this couple is creating one of our favorite cheeses to age in our caves. Similar in style to Sainte-Maure (see page 76), Cinderella arrives covered in ash and takes on a fine layer of Geotrichum candidum, facilitating the breakdown of the interior of the cheese to a smooth cream line and a rich, creamy texture. Aside from how great this cheese tastes, it brings

us much pleasure to be supporting small farms in what we in New York City affectionately call our backyard.

Enjoy with acidic whites, ciders, and yeasty farmhouse beers, as well as fresh berries.

PAVÉ DE JADIS (PA-VUH DE JAH-DEEZ)

MILK TYPE: Goat

ORIGIN: Loire Valley, France

This ash-covered goat's milk brick is an excellent example of the high-quality cheeses that come from the Loire Valley. With a moist, fudge-like consistency, this cheese is tangy, citrusy, and creamy with a slight mineral finish. When we receive this cheese, there is no noticeable rind development, only the layer of vegetable ash that enrobes it. After a few weeks of maturation, the rind begins to bloom, ripening slowly from the outside in. This creates a wonderful cross section of textures and a fuller, more luscious flavor profile that abounds with wild yeast notes (but nothing so much as to overpower the palate). But what really sets this cheese apart from the other Loire Valley goat cheeses is its larger size and its shape, which allows for the development of the flavor and rind without compromising the moistness and texture.

Enjoy crumbled over a beet salad or matched up with a traditional lager.

PIERRE ROBERT (PEE-AIR ROW-BEAR)

MILK TYPE: Cow

ORIGIN: Île-de-France, France

A rich cheese that has extra cow's cream added to it, these plump discs are an exercise in decadence. Made by two former producers of Brillat-Savarin (see page 61), they decided to take this triple-crème cheese that they were making and loved, and age it in a cave. The result is Pierre Robert—a buttery, salty, earthy, and decadent cheese that spreads like a dream. Each wheel weighs about one pound (454 g) and is wrapped in a puffy Penicillium candidum bloom with a paste that is akin to softened butter. Often referred to as the ice cream of the cheese world, it is a great introduction to the world of cheese and a guaranteed winner on a cheese plate.

Enjoy with a sparkling wine. As it ages, its salinity pairs well with fruitier reds or even crisp lagers.

POULIGNY SAINT PIERRE (POO-LEAN-E SAN PEE-AIR)

MILK TYPE: Goat

ORIGIN: Berry, France

Hailing from the heart of France, Pouligny Saint Pierre is a treat for the mouth and the eyes. Shaped as a regal pyramid and name protected (see page 38), these bloomy-rind masterpieces of rich, minerally goat's milk are a testament to the fertile soil and the quality of water from their region of production, attributing to the rich pastures the goats graze upon. Each piece of cheese weighs around a half-pound (227 g) and is beautifully covered with a pillowy layer of white Geotrichum candidum that blossoms small flowers of blue and green mold as it ages. The flavor profile is similar to goat cheeses from the Loire Valley, though Pouligny Saint Pierre tends to have a bit more earthiness to it when it is perfectly ripe. This cheese has a subtle cream line when ripening, giving it a nice variance of texture. With age, the pyramid shape tends to sag a bit, the paste tightening into a denser, more uniform texture—yet the flavor profile is uncompromised. Pouligny Saint Pierre is a great cheese to share with two to three people.

Enjoy with fresh berries and a sparkling wine.

QUATRE FEUILLE *(K-WHAA-TRA FAH-WEE)*

MILK TYPE: Goat

ORIGIN: Loire Valley, France

Most French cheeses made from the milk of younger goats are known for their dense, velvety, slightly bucky taste. This dense yet gooey variation brings together the longstanding traditions of France's creamy cheese lineage with the high-quality dairy from their goats. Hailing from the goat capital of France, the milk is collected from a selection of surrounding farmers, cultured, curdled, cut, and then hand-ladled into a unique four-leaf-clover mold—hence the cheese's name.

ROBIOLA TRE LATTE *(ROW-BE-OH-LA TRAY LATTE)*

MILK TYPE: Cow, sheep, and goat

ORIGIN: Piedmont, Italy

Hailing from the mountainous region of northern Italy, these mixed-milk little patties are a source of regional pride. Most commonly produced as pure goat's milk delights, the addition of cow and sheep's milk elevates the goo to a fatty euphoria that tastes like a barn with the door open in springtime. Filled with hints of dry grass and fresh clovers, the center is dense and velvety, while the rind houses a thin layer of cream that is an oozy, slightly pithy, bestial treat. Because these little guys are ripened in very humid caves, almost all moisture is retained, and the end result is a sublime introduction to an Italian tradition. To really enliven a get-together, wrap one of these bad boys in a thin layer of pastry dough, bake for 15–20 minutes, and serve as a golden brown, creamy treat.

SAGE FARM BELVIDERE *(BELL-VAH-DEAR)*

MILK TYPE: Goat and Jersey cow cream

ORIGIN: Vermont, United States

When Molly Pindell first set out to make cheese, she felt that she needed to master making the Loire Valley classic Valençay (see page 80). Working to hone her craft at goat dairies in the United States, she and her husband purchased Sage Farm in Stowe, Vermont, in 2007. They began raising their own goats and converted existing farm structures into a milking parlor, cheese room, and aging facility. Belvidere is a disc of farmstead goat's milk cheese that is fortified with Jersey cow cream from nearby Butterworks Farm. Roughly the size of a beverage coaster, we receive the discs when they are very green—about three days old—and allow the rind to develop Geotrichum candidum in a high-moisture environment. When ripe, this cheese possesses aromas of sweet grass, wildflowers, and wet earth. The paste is slightly tart from the goat's milk, and the cream creates a rich mouthfeel and smooth finish. The fortifying fat from the cream allows Belvidere to maintain interior moisture and ripen for a longer period of time. With significant age, the flavor profile turns to flinty stone and hazelnut with blossoms of green and blue mold on the rind.

SAGE FARM STERLING

MILK TYPE: Goat

ORIGIN: Vermont, United States

Another cheese from the tranquil lands of Stowe, Vermont, Sterling is named after the peak of a nearby mountain, and is a great take on French-style goat cheese. Covered with a layer of vegetable ash, these little pyramids arrive to us unripened, full of moisture, and delicately packed. As the cheese ages and the rind develops, a perfect graying cream line enrobes a delicately flakey, brilliant white paste of tangy goat's milk that holds notes of fresh grass and subtle citrus. The youthful aromas of bright yeast and hay deepen with age, morphing into a more dank and musty, almost cellar-like scent, while the flavors of the paste take on a soily, animalistic quality.

SAINTE-MAURE *(SANT-MAAH)*

MILK TYPE: Goat

ORIGIN: Méan, Belgium

Hand-ladled by Daniel Cloots at La Fromagerie du Gros Chêne in the Belgian Ardennes, we receive these beautiful logs of goat's milk cheese unripened, which allow them to develop over time with the proper temperature and humidity until a healthy layer of Geotrichum candidum enrobes the paste. Traditionally a French cheese, these logs of Sainte-Maure are larger than their French counterparts and do not contain the characteristic straw through the middle (which is used to aerate and help ripen the center of the cheese along the same timeline as the rind). The result is a dense yet sometimes delicate cheese that when young, holds beautiful notes of lemon peel and grass, and when left to age, takes on a mineral and gamy quality, with a pronounced sharpness and a chewier texture.

Enjoy with a saison or light white wine.

SAINTE-MAURE DE TOURAINE *(SAN MORE DUH TOUR-RAIN)*

MILK TYPE: Goat

ORIGIN: Loire Valley, France

A lovely little log of pure goat's milk bliss, Sainte-Maure de Touraine is a name-protected and recipe-regulated cheese (see page 38) that has been distinguishing itself from the commercially made Sainte-Maure since the 1990s. Covered with a delicate rind of blue-gray mold, the paste that develops is dense and slightly crumbly, with a gooey creaminess toward the wrinkled rind. The lemony front breaks through to a wave of floral gaminess, that ends with a round hay-like flavor. The salt level is very balanced and delicate, but tends to be more pronounced as this cheese ages. A straw of dry hay is inserted into the cheese when young and fresh to help facilitate the aging process. With the slight aeration to the paste, the center develops a creamy denseness.

Enjoy with a Wit beer or a light, fruity white wine.

SCIMUDIN *(SHEE-MOO-DEEN)*

MILK TYPE: Cow

ORIGIN: Lombardy, Italy

The Italian response to French Brie, this almost triple crème–style (meaning more cream has been added) cow's milk cheese is unique to the Italian cheese lexicon. Not as buttery as a Robiola Tre Latte (see page 75), and without the beefy, nutty funk of a Taleggio (see page 108), Scimudin is extremely lactic and creamy, with very delicate hints of mushroom and earth. If you have tired of the options in the Brie family, this is a cheese to seek out. Look for wheels with pronounced runniness, as this is when the full flavor of Scimudin presents itself. Approachable without being banal, Scimudin always flies out of our case.

Enjoy with a bottle of Barolo.

SECHON DE PAYS *(SAY-SHAWN DUH PAYS)*

MILK TYPE: Goat

ORIGIN: Rhône-Alpes, France

Don't let these small, delicate discs deceive you. This petite goat cheese packs a wallop of intense flavor of moist fur and stony minerality in each bite. Slightly more aged than other small-format goat cheeses, Sechon de Pays is on the firmer side, and is often covered in blue-gray-green molds, which are all positive signs of cheese maturation. With a super tangy, nutty, slightly sour flavor, this cheese is as complex as it is delicious, and can be enjoyed when it is very young as well as when it is extremely aged.

Enjoy with a minerally Chablis.

SELLES-SUR-CHER *(CELL SURE CHER)*

MILK TYPE: Goat

ORIGIN: Loire Valley, France

These little discs of pure goat's milk from the heart of goat country in France are bucky and sharp, with an alluring salt front balanced with a robust finish. After the milk has been cultured and the rennet added, it is left for several hours to coagulate. Once the curds are cut, the soupy mixture is ladled into molds with small holes that the excess whey drains out of for the twenty-four hours they are left out to dry. Once drained, the cheese is dusted with vegetable ash, traditionally used to protect the cheese from unwanted elements (insects being a main culprit). The result is a sensually creamy paste with a dense, velvety allure when aged. Selles-Sur-Cher is a great served on its own as a dessert cheese after a light meal of grilled trout and spring veggies.

Enjoy with green grapes, a drizzle of wildflower honey, and raisin bread, as well as a fruit-forward Chablis.

ST. HANNOIS *(SANT-HAN-WAH)*

MILK TYPE: Goat

ORIGIN: Loire Valley, France

Looking like a small goat's milk marshmallow pillow, this Crottin-style cheese arrives with a furry exterior due to the molds cultivated during aging. Usually white, blue, and green-gray on the outside, this slightly aged goat cheese has a dense center that is tangy, somewhat bestial, and fungal. Pliable when young and chalky with a bit of age, the minerally and dense St. Hannois is one of the more unique cheeses to discover. And its small size makes it the perfect cheese for one.

Enjoy with a yeasty farmhouse cider.

SWEET GRASS DAIRY GREEN HILL

MILK TYPE: Cow

ORIGIN: Georgia, United States

By implementing the system of rotational grazing, the folks at Sweet Grass Dairy in Thomasville, Georgia, ensure that their cows are moved to new pastures every twelve hours so they can feed on the best grass and roam about the land. You can literally taste the happiness of these cows in all of SGD's cheeses, but this supple, decadent, Camembert-style cheese is the one that tugs at our hearts (and stomachs) the most. A thin, pillowy rind of Penicillium candidum embraces a rich, straw-colored, slightly tacky, and gooey paste that releases notes of buttercups, yeasty hay, and sweet butter. Look for Green Hill when it is young and supple—give it a squeeze and feel the plumpness of the high-quality milk.

Enjoy with a sparkling wine of your choice, some fresh fruit, and crusty bread.

TICKLEMORE

MILK TYPE: Goat

ORIGIN: Devon, England

Formerly produced by Robin Congdon of Ticklemore Dairy, the production of this cheese has moved to Sharpham Farm, where it is now made by Debbie Mumford and Mark Sharman. Pressed into colanders, giving the cheese its distinct "flying saucer" shape, Ticklemore is a mild, semi-firm goat cheese with a thin layer of gooey crème beneath the rind and a dense center. Light, floral, and grassy with hints of chive and lemon, Ticklemore tastes like a delicate, goaty springtime kiss. Neal's Yard Dairy exports this cheese to us across the pond, and though it is slightly more expensive than other soft-ripened goat's milk cheeses, the craftsmanship, quality of milk, and care during the aging process shine through with each bite.

Enjoy with a Sancerre or a light, dry cider.

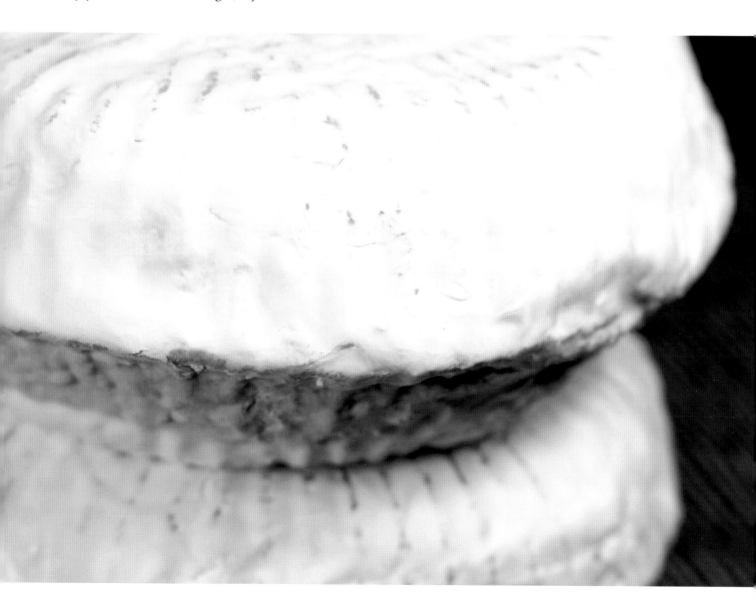

TOMME PÉRIGORDINE *(TOHM PEAR-OH-GO-DEAN)*

MILK TYPE: Goat

ORIGIN: Aquitaine, France

A real treat of a goat's milk cheese from southwest France, this cheese resembles a decadent vanilla-frosted cake, with its cream-colored, wrinkled rind and dense, alabaster-white paste. The flavors are floral with hints of fresh hay and clean barn, with the aroma of baby goats and wild clovers. Not as aggressive as some of the Loire Valley goats that can take on a very petting zoo-like quality, Tomme Périgordine maintains a lovely balance with a great salt level and slight citrus flavor. The center of this four-pound (1.8 kg) tomme is dense with a pleasing melt-on-your-tongue quality. The paste lightens gradually toward the rind, eventually forming a thin cream line beneath the slightly more bucky-tasting rind. Tomme Périgordine is a great companion to green salads filled with seeds and legumes.

Enjoy with a sparkling white or a rosé and spring fruits. Also try pairing with thinly sliced strawberries macerated in a drizzle of lemon juice and garnished with finely chopped mint.

TOMME VAUDOISE *(TOHM-VA-DWAHZE)*

MILK TYPE: Cow

ORIGIN: Canton of Vaud, Switzerland

A small hockey puck of goo brought to us by Maître Fromager Rolf Beeler, Tomme Vaudoise is an example of the marvelous bloomy-rind cheeses produced in Switzerland. With a smooth rind and an almost-liquid center, this cheese showcases the high-quality milk found in Switzerland. Weighing about four ounces (114 g) each, these little discs have a rich and creamy character with hints of earth and grass when young, becoming earthier and assertive as they age. Tomme Vaudoise can pack quite a strong flavor wallop with some additional maturation time.

VALENÇAY *(VALE-NN-SAY)*

MILK TYPE: Goat

ORIGIN: Loire Valley, France

This classic French goat cheese from the Loire Valley encapsulates the long-standing cheese-making history of this region. Once upon a time, this area was the center of goat farming. The rolling pastures of wildflowers, lilacs, mustard, and onions made for an exceptional diet for these free-grazing beasts. Delicate and balanced, the goat's milk in this cheese manifests itself as bright and luscious, as opposed to animally and robust. The dense and velvety center lightens toward the rind, where a thin cream line of more goaty goo forms. Legend has it that these ash-covered, truncated pyramids were once made in the form of a pointed pyramid. After Napoleon's defeat in Egypt, on his way back home, traveling through the south of France, he encountered this cheese during a meal, and in a fit of rage, chopped off the pointy top—shaping the cheese ever since. This springtime treat appears in April in its freshest form, lemony and bright. Toward the end of the season—late summer—it develops a grassier and more goaty quality.

Enjoy with a Menu Pineau white, a Loire Valley grape that makes a stupendous wine.

Facing page: Clockwise from top right—Cinderella, Sterling, Garretts Ferry, Condor's Ruin

WASHED RIND/BRINED

When someone is in the mood for some real stink—for cheese that usually keeps the spouse or kids at bay—they are looking for this group of (usually) orange-colored-encrusted, funky rounds of dairy. Washed rind, also known as smear-ripened, cheeses become very aromatic by being washed with a specific solution—whether it be brine, wine, beer, eau de vie, or some other type of liquid—to encourage the growth of bacteria (Brevibacterium, specifically) on the rind of the cheese. The aromas run the gamut of sweet decay, moist feet, and barnyard manure to roasted nuts, wet leaves, and naturally occurring notes of ammonia. The cheeses may vary in texture from oozing rounds of goo produced in Burgundy to fudgy, rotund wheels created in the Swiss Alps. Cheeses are washed in the process of their maturation to encourage the development of their rinds, to protect them from drying out, and to enhance the flavor profile of the paste. This section looks at those cheeses that tend to take on the more pronounced elements of the washing process. This collection of cheeses is a good match for sweet wines and hard liquors, such as scotch, whiskey, and gin.

A CASINCA *(A CA-SINKA)*

MILK TYPE: Goat

ORIGIN: Corsica, France

This rare and exquisite treat from the island of Corsica is born from the milk of Mediterranean goats that feast primarily on the land's *maquis*—the dense forestation of various shrubs, herbs, and trees. The goats' natural diet is expressed in the dense and doughy paste that is encased by the typical orange-colored rind that can bloom with speckles of white and blue mold. Using traditional animal rennet, A Casinca is aggressive without being overpowering, pungent and bestial without knocking you completely off your feet. Its small size—about five ounces (142 g)—makes it a perfect cheese to share among a small group of adventurous cheese lovers. Because this cheese is such a showstopper, it is best featured as the centerpiece of any cheese plate.

Enjoy with a wild fermented wine, such as a Coturri Zinfandel, that can match the cheese's feral notes and herbaceous nose without overpowering the delicate nuances of it.

ABBAYE DE TAMIÉ *(AH-BEE DUH TAH-ME)*

MILK TYPE: Cow

ORIGIN: Rhône-Alpes, France

True abbey-made cheeses are a rarity in today's world. Once upon a time, the monks who lived in the abbeys throughout France and Belgium were known for their food craft. From beer to jam, these men focused their love and energy on the cultivation of food traditions. The cheeses of the abbeys were most often washed-rind cheeses, usually washed with the beers being made simultaneously. The Abbaye de Tamié was established in 1131, and the monks have been making its namesake cheese almost since the abbey's inception. This cheese is known for its pungent aroma—reminiscent of woolly socks and wet cardboard—but its flavor is so nuanced and mellow at its prime that the smell can be deceiving. Once the milk has been heated to the desired temperature, the producers use enzymes that have been made at the abbey to begin the coagulation process. After the curd is formed and cut down to pea size, the leftover whey is processed into methane to heat the abbey's hot water system. The cheese is then set to bathe in a salt brine to help encourage the crust and what will become the rind. It is then moved to the relatively balmy—almost 60°F (16°C)—and humid cellars and tended to daily as it ripens. Finally, it is washed by hand and nurtured until it is perfectly supple and ready for consumption.

ALEMAR CHEESE COMPANY GOOD THUNDER

MILK TYPE: Cow

ORIGIN: Minnesota, United States

Alemar Cheese Company (see page 59) creates these little squares of rich Minnesota cow's milk and bathes them in healthy doses of Surly Bender beer, a locally brewed brown ale, during their maturation process. Weighing in at about one-third pound (151 g) each, this cheese can range from thick, funky bricks of sweet cream to a more unctuous, nutty, and runny pile of goo. The milk is sourced from a farm a few hours' drive away and transported by Keith Adams and the gang back to their dairy, where the bricks are hand-formed and gently washed during their maturation process. The rind's aromas of barnyard, wet wood, and slightly piney hops give way to a buttery paste with hints of soil. Good Thunder is a relatively new cheese on the market and one that should be picked up if you see it on a cheese counter.

Enjoy with just about any cured meat and a pint of malty, bitter brown beer.

ANDANTE DAIRY CONTRALTO
(CON-TRAHL-TOE)

MILK TYPE: Goat

ORIGIN: California, United States

One of Andante Dairy's (see page 60) only washed-rind cheeses, Contralto is a floral goat's milk puddle of goo that is disarmingly mellow and sweet for being both a washed rind and a goat cheese. While most washed-rind cheeses can take on a "footy" or manure-esque scent, this bacteria-smeared dream is much closer to the scents of wet grass and peanut shells.

Cheese maker Soyoung Scanlan uses the technique of ripening the cheese in a relatively dry environment so that the rind develops slowly and smoothly. The center of the cheese is fudgy and dense, becoming more gooey and rich as it ages for the few weeks it is held and washed in its slightly humid home. The creaminess at the rind takes on a sharp bite with time, while remaining balanced and buttery.

APPENZELLER (AP-EN-ZELL-ER)

MILK TYPE: Cow

ORIGIN: Canton of Appenzell Innerrhoden, Switzerland

This firm, Swiss wheel has all the sweet and oniony notes of an alpine cheese, but with the hearty zip of a washed-rind wonder. All Appenzeller producers craft their own special washes, sometimes incorporating wine or wild herbs from their land; thus, each producer's wheels have his or her own signature flavor profile. The production of Appenzeller is protected by a consortium that supports the producers and guarantees a certain pricing for their products (see page 38). This allows the cheese makers to focus on their craft and not have to worry so much about the marketplace. Wheels range in flavor from a delicate sweetness, like a milky taffy candy, to a more robust, salt-riddled bite that rivals the savoriness of some of the best country ham, depending on how long the wheels are aged and who is producing them. Appenzeller melts extremely well and is the best secret ingredient in any gratin dish, as well as being appreciated on its own.

Enjoy with a yeasty cider or an herbaceous gin martini.

ARDRAHAN (R-DRA-HAN)

MILK TYPE: Cow

ORIGIN: County Cork, Ireland

First made in 1983 by cheese maker Mary Burns, Ardrahan is one of those cheeses that is great at any stage of the aging process. The milk from her herd of Friesian cows is pasteurized and then coagulated with vegetable rennet to produce a cheese that when young, is soft and bulging with a luscious cream and a cakey, chalky heart. Ardrahan's pungency is backed by notes of sweet soil and a hearty meatiness, bordering on smokiness, when on the palate. With age, the chewy texture of the cheese takes on a pronounced minerality.

Enjoy with three fingers of Knappogue Castle Whiskey.

BANON (BAN-ON)

MILK TYPE: Goat

ORIGIN: Provence, France

Encased in chestnut leaves that are gathered by the cheese makers in the autumn months, Banon, which has a history dating back to the Roman times, is wholly unique and inventive to this day. Nestled just north of Aix-en-Provence, the town of Banon is the only area that can produce this name-protected cheese (see page 38). These little, pure goat's milk discs are wrapped in the chestnut leaves after two weeks of aging, and then dipped in a brine of eau de vie. Sometimes the leaves are dipped in an additional vinegar solution or a liquor to impart a more pungent aroma as they age. After a few more weeks, Banon develops little pockets of blue-gray mold on the rind. When young, the cheese is a bit brighter and citrusy on the palate, with a crumbly yet moist texture. The leaves help maintain the moisture in the cheese, as well as imparting a vegetable note. As the cheese ages, the discs become gooey, strong, and goaty, with a rather robust assertion of booze and fur. A great finish to a hearty meal, Banon is best consumed with fresh crusty bread and a good snifter of something special.

Enjoy with brandies, cognacs, and dry sherries.

BERGFICHTE *(BURG-FICK-TUH)*

MILK TYPE: Cow

ORIGIN: Canton of St. Gallen, Switzerland

Made by the legendary Swiss cheese maker Willi Schmid, this fir bark–wrapped stinker is a dream come true for people who love a little something funky on their palette. Although the recipe for this "lumber jack" cheese has been around for centuries, Willi, along with Ernst Dirriwachter, were the first to produce it for the American market. You can now find the pasteurized version, called Forsterkase and produced by Ernst, while Willi chooses to use raw milk in his creation. The scent of Bergfichte has a manure-esque tinge, and can be a bit aggressive for the faint of heart, but the taste is so balanced and textured that one bite really is a flavor joyride. The fir tree bark, which is hand-sheared by Willi himself, not only adds a gorgeous aesthetic note to the overall presentation of this beauty, but it also imparts a sappy, woodsy tang to the otherwise buttery stink of this exceptional washed-rind cheese over the course of the aging process.

Enjoy with a balanced Grüner or yeasty white ale.

BRESCIANELLA STAGIONATA *(BRESH-EE-NELL-AH STAH-GEE-OH NAH-TA)*

MILK TYPE: Cow

ORIGIN: Lombardy, Italy

This super gooey stinker is reminiscent of both Taleggio (see page 108) and Robiola Tre Latte (see page 75). A sweet and floral cheese, the healthy washing with a salt brine adds a deep funk that has hints of yeast and barn. When aged, the paste becomes extremely runny and can take on an extreme funkiness to rival any gym locker. Although this cheese can appear aggressive to the nose, the taste is so complex and fruity that it defies the senses. A great cheese to smear on a crusty country bread or pair with thin ribbons of prosciutto, the balance and complexity of it make Brescianella Stagionata a showstopper.

Enjoy with any wild cider or sour beer.

CABRICHARME *(CAB-RE-SHARM)*

MILK TYPE: Goat

ORIGIN: Méan, Belgium

Made from the raw spring and summer milk of Belgian goats, Cabricharme, or "charming goat," is a lactic, oozy blast of barnyard funk made by La Fermier de Méan (see page 90). Following their policy of non-homogenization, the dairy produces wheels that vary from flavors of sweet grass and citrus in the early months of lactation to a more porky and feral taste during the warmer months. Brined in baths that have been used numerous times over, the rind attracts positive bacteria, thanks to the heritage wild microbes inhabiting the brining solution. These wheels are best served when they are runny and plump, but as they firm-up over time, a fudgy texture and more bestial flavor notes will permeate the senses.

Enjoy with a glass of Moinette Blond or other bottle-conditioned, lighter, yeasty ales.

LA FERMIER DE MÉAN

Maffe, Belgium

Nestled in the town of Maffe in the Belgian Ardennes, La Fermier de Méan is a cooperative that has been in existence since the mid-1980s, selling the organic products of the region and aiming to promote a way of life for the farmer and the consumer based in local, sustainable agriculture. In the early 1990s, the cooperative began producing cheese sourced solely from the surrounding farms and made exclusively with raw milk. Within a rustic building, inconspicuously situated off a small road that traverses the rolling hills, La Fermier de Méan makes roughly a dozen different types of cheeses in very small amounts daily. With a few different aging rooms and a brine solution that is said to date back decades, they are creating delicacies from the Belgian landscape that are loved around the world. In addition to Cabricharme (see page 89) and Charmoix (see page 93), look for their Tomme de Chèvre, a sour, natural-rind goat's milk wheel.

CAMEMBERT AVEC CALVADOS *(CAM-UM-BEAR AH-VECK CAL-VAHD-OOS)*

MILK TYPE: Cow

ORIGIN: Normandy, France

The Normandy region of France is known for its long agricultural history. Two of the best known products from this area are apples and cow's milk. This sweet, slightly earthy, wholly indulgent cheese is the perfect marriage of what Normandy is famous for. The rich, full-fat cow's milk comes from the beautiful bovines grazing along the fertile pastures, eating the fallen apples as they go. The long-standing orchards here yield an abundance of juicy and sweet fruit. The mushroomy, earthy, creamy Camembert is washed with Calvados (apple brandy), introducing a sweet, layered, vegetable aroma. The gooey paste oozes out a fungal joyride that is accented with the boozy sweetness of the wash. A great treat is to bake the Camembert, wooden box and all, for about fifteen minutes in the broiler, until the top is charred and blistered. When sliced open with a serrated knife, the cheese's bubbling center is a puddle of lactic bliss, waiting to be plunged into with crunchy bread and sliced apples. Note: Be sure to remove the wooden lid before putting cheese into the broiler.

Enjoy with a chilled cider or a warm Calvados.

BAKED CAMEMBERT

Camembert is a great centerpiece for any small get-together. Served at room temperature, these beefy little guys become supple and creamy, elevating to a warmed butter quality. A great way to present one of these is to cloak it in pastry dough and bake in a hot oven at 400°F (200°C) for about 15 minutes. The pastry crust browns and becomes toasty, as the cheese heats through, creating a molten core of lactic wonder. Smear a small amount of spicy French Dijon mustard on the top a few minutes before you remove it from the oven, and the mustard turns into a dark glaze of tang and spice. Your guests will delight at this quick and simple appetizer. Serve alongside a crisp dry white, such as a Pinot Grigio, and some sliced dark rye bread.

CAPRIOLE FARMS MONT ST. FRANCIS

MILK TYPE: Goat

ORIGIN: Indiana, United States

From the famed farm that revolutionized goat's milk cheese comes Mont St. Francis, the only washed-rind cheese made by Capriole Farms (see page 65). Its dense and fudgy paste is ivory white, while the rind is shocking orange, reminiscent of a ripe pumpkin. These small wheels average about one pound (454 g) each and ripen quickly as they are washed for about a month. Inspired by the abbey-style washed rinds of France and Belgium, Mont St. Francis has a salt-forward encounter, with a funk-filled end, packing notes of damp hay and seared steak. The scent is a bit more aggressive than you would think, considering the relatively mellow flavors. The aroma is manure-esque with notes of a full

compost bin, and the fudgy paste has a more meaty musk. The goaty kick is elevated with age, and the uncanny herbaceousness of the milk is balanced with the salty brine.

Enjoy with Kentucky bourbon and a big plate of fried chicken.

CAROMONT FARM RED ROW

MILK TYPE: Cow

ORIGIN: Virginia, United States

Located in the town of Esmont in Virginia's Piedmont region, Caromont Farm produces Red Row, a raw Jersey cow's milk cheese bathed in a local cider from a nearby orchard. Aged a minimum of sixty days and weighing about three pounds (1.4 kg) each, these wheels have been a hit with cheesemongers and customers since they rolled through our doors. The sweet, funky exterior gives way to a rich, buttery paste that presents notes of fresh grass and hints of wildflowers and clover. The aroma of an apple orchard is present, as the active yeasts on the rind are naturally occurring and carry the hint of apple from the local orchard. This cheese is aromatic without being too confrontational.

Enjoy with some cooked sausage and a bottle of small production, off-dry (not overly sweet or overly dry) cider.

CARDO

MILK TYPE: Goat

ORIGIN: Somerset, England

Mary Holbrook fashions the rare treat known as Cardo from the raw milk of her mixed-breed goat herd. Using cardoon stamens in lieu of traditional rennet, these wheels are influenced by Spanish and Portuguese cheese-making traditions, yet hold a unique flavor profile that is expressive of the land where they are produced. Cardo is a gamy, full-flavored cheese that has a funky barnyard sweetness. Its soft paste is pleasant on the tongue, with the touch of herbal bitterness from the cardoon. When aged, it takes on an intense but pleasant dankness, with musty notes of wet hay.

Enjoy with bright, dry ciders or light white wines.

CATO CORNER FARM DESPEARADO

MILK TYPE: Cow

ORIGIN: Connecticut, United States

Similar to its brother Hooligan (see below), Despearado is a raw Jersey cow's milk wheel that receives a healthy washing of fermented pear mash and Pear William eau de vie from Connecticut's Westford Hill Distillers. The rind is a rich burnt umber color and has a distinct fruitiness on the nose. The aroma is far less stinky than most washed rinds because of the pear booze, which reveals the uncanny smell of an orchard after a rainstorm. The sweetness permeates the paste, allowing the funkiness to become balanced with an earthiness that rivals a sweet-and-tart candy. When ripe, Despearado has a contrast of textures, ranging from gooey just beneath the rind to a dense, cakelike core. The richness of the milk balances out any astringency from the Pear William washings.

Enjoy with some sliced pears and a cider.

CATO CORNER FARM HOOLIGAN

MILK TYPE: Cow

ORIGIN: Connecticut, United States

The fine folks at Cato Corner Farm have been perfecting the artisanal cheese craft since 1997. This operation, shepherded by a mother-and-son team, turns out a bouquet of raw cow's milk creations. Hooligan is their "signature" washed-rind cheese, which they then use as a jumping-off point to produce their other washed-rind cheeses. These plump little stinkers have less of an aggressive, "footy" scent, and lean more toward a toasted nut shell, wet soil aroma. They are washed with a salt brine twice weekly during the two months they're aged to help encourage a lovely orange-tinged rind. The paste is supple, sometimes with tiny eyes, or holes, forming toward the center and a lush cream line toward the rind. The texture is slightly firm, but melts incredibly well, screaming out to be pressed between two slabs of a buttery white bread for an incredible grilled cheese.

Enjoy with stouts and ryes.

CHARMOIX *(SHARM-WAH)*

MILK TYPE: Cow

ORIGIN: Méan, Belgium

Produced by La Fermier de Méan (see page 90), a cooperative in the Belgian Ardennes, Charmoix is a lush raw cow's milk cheese with notes of sweet sausage and soil. The milk for these wheels is sourced from neighboring farms that the folks at the cooperative never homogenize, which allows the liquid to express itself fully, resulting in slight variations from batch to batch. The rich, lactic paste is enrobed with a lovely bacteria-laden rind, giving the cheese a wonderful spectrum of flavor and texture. Charmoix is a gateway cheese for anyone who is timid of flavorful washed-rind cheeses but desperately wants to dip a toe in the pool.

Enjoy with Trappist ales.

CONSIDER BARDWELL FARM DORSET (DOOR-SET)

MILK TYPE: Cow

ORIGIN: Vermont, United States

The fine folks at Consider Bardwell Farm have been making this washed-rind, raw Jersey cow's milk cheese since 2004. The richness of the milk is heightened with a continuous healthy scrub of salt brine as the cheese ages out on wooden planks in the dairy's aging barn. The milk comes from their neighbors down the way, Jersey Girls Dairy, who believe in the same ethos of sustainable farming and open grazing for their cows that Consider Bardwell believes in for their goats. Although this is a washed-rind cheese, the aroma is more savory and mellow than some of its bathed brethren. The flavors develop from rather tame bacon to a slightly soured, nuanced grassiness. The undertones of green almonds and blanched hazelnuts develop alongside the sweet yeastiness. This is an incredible cheese as a stand-alone on a cheese plate or melted on toasted sourdough bread with a vine-ripened tomato for a sensational grilled-cheese delight.

Enjoy with a spicy Gose-style beer or a glass of Pig's Nose whiskey.

COWGIRL CREAMERY RED HAWK

MILK TYPE: Cow

ORIGIN: California, United States

From the ladies at Cowgirl Creamery come these little stinkers that weigh in at about a half-pound (227 g) each when perfectly ripe. They use the same base as their triple crème cheese, Mt. Tam (see page 68), but Red Hawk receives a washing of salt brine to encourage the wild yeasts to develop into a glowing red rind. The cheeses are aged in West Marin, where the salty sea air meets with the flora of the surrounding area, creating a bacteria culture specific to the region. Red Hawk is a Northern California original and tastes of the land that these cows graze upon. A slight stink of the rind dissipates when it is allowed to breathe a bit, turning the funk into a more saline, oceanic scent. The center is dense and sweet, while toward the rind, a rich, salty, beefy quality develops.

Enjoy with Anchor Steam beer or the light white wines that are produced throughout the Sonoma Valley.

DURRUS *(DER-US)*

MILK TYPE: Cow

ORIGIN: County Cork, Ireland

On the Sheep's Head Peninsula of Ireland's southwest coast, Jeffa Gill has made Durrus since 1979. The cheese is traditionally made with the unpasteurized milk of a Fresian herd nearby; however, we only receive a pasteurized version in the United States. These lucky cows get to roam the rolling green hills in some of the most picturesque and calming environments on earth. Durrus arrives at our shop in a supple, youthful state where the lush, sea breeze–kissed grass of County Cork is expressed through the milk. Meaty notes of dank basement and peanuts are present throughout and intensify as the cheese tightens up with age.

Enjoy with a hoppy ale.

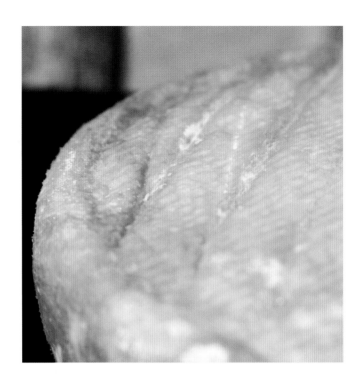

DURRUS FARMHOUSE CHEESE

Durrus, County Cork, Ireland

One of the leading pioneers of farmhouse cheese production in Ireland, Jeffa Gill has been creating at her dairy in the County Cork village of Durrus for five decades. Beginning with kitchen experimentation and developing into a fully operating dairy, the cheese here is a model of the high-quality dairy that can be found throughout Ireland, and a prime example of the country's agricultural revitalization. All the cheeses begin their lives in a copper vat, which facilitates even heating throughout the process. The wheels are then formed, drained, brined, and taken to the aging room within the production facility to mature until they are ready for market. Occasionally, you may find Dunmanus, another one of their cheeses, on a cheese counter. Produced in a similar way to Durrus, this cheese has more moisture extracted and is aged for a longer period to produce a product of earthy character and chewy texture. The focus and care by Jeffa and her crew are evident with every wheel of cheese we receive from them.

EPOISSES *(EE-PA-WAHS)*

MILK TYPE: Cow

ORIGIN: Burgundy, France

If there is one cheese that exemplifies a stinky French washed-rind cheese, Epoisses would be it. Made in the Burgundy region of France by the famed Berthaut producers, these wooden box–bound beauties receive a healthy washing of Marc du Bourgogne brandy as they ripen. The brandy, produced from the leftover grapes after winemaking, is tangy and tannic and helps to form the pale orange rind that can develop into a deep-burnt-brown color. The flavors run from big and beefy, with an almost smoky note—similar to a cured speck—to a mellower butteriness that can be compared to bacon fat or charred kidney beans. At its ripest, the stinky rind is elevated by a salty kick from the paste. In a region known for its big wines, this cheese, with its liquid center, is another contributor to the region's culinary fame. The curd-and-whey mixture is hand-ladled into the molds before being sent off to a cave for aging. This technique allows the cheese to ripen into a soupy wonder that is best served with a spoon, a fresh baguette, and a room full of people who know how to indulge in the finer things in life.

Enjoy with a snifter of Sauternes, and prepare yourself for a gastronomic experience of a lifetime.

GRÈS DES VOSGES *(GRAY DUH VOH-JUH)*

MILK TYPE: Cow

ORIGIN: Alsace, France

An attractive little oval of a cheese, Grès des Vosges is typically sold in four-and-a-half-ounce (127 g) pieces. It is produced in Alsace, a region known for another stinker, Munster. With a small fern leaf adorning the top of the cheese, Grès des Vosges has a damp, yeasty exterior that gives way to a dense, buttery core, and is an elegant addition to a cheese plate. It is sweet and salty with a luxurious texture that smears well on crusty bread. Grès des Vosges is an excellent step up for anyone who enjoys something a little stinky, such as a Reblochon (see page 105) or Taleggio (see page 108), and is ready to try something a bit more randy and funky.

Enjoy slathered over a slice of miche, while eating saucisson sec and quaffing an Achel Trappist beer.

GUBBEEN *(GOO-BEAN)*

MILK TYPE: Cow

ORIGIN: County Cork, Ireland

Keeping up the tradition of farmhouse production, Tom and Giana Ferguson create Gubbeen from the milk of their mixed herd that roams the 250 acres (101 ha) of their coastal farm. The Fergusons use only non-genetically modified (non-GMO) feed for their animals and have developed and cultured their own flora for the ripening of Gubbeen, preventing them from having to import bacteria cultures from abroad and creating a cheese that is expressive of the natural molds inherent on their property and in the ripening room. The cheese varies in texture when it arrives to our shop, but it always has a bright flavor from the richness of the milk. Deep notes of peanuts, pleasant porkiness, and fresh decay are enveloped in each bite, with the flavor of soil becoming bolder as the texture tightens over time. If you're in the mood for a hearty meal, pick up some potatoes, a good amount of bacon, onions, and Gubbeen, and make tartiflette. See recipe on page 101.

JASPER HILL FARM WINNIMERE *(WIN-EE-MEER)*

MILK TYPE: Cow

ORIGIN: Vermont, United States

Inspired by the famed creation Vacherin Mont-d'Or (see page 110), this Vermont original from Jasper Hill Farm (see page 130) is wrapped in spruce bark and is intended to be enjoyed in the same savage manor as Vacherin Mont-d'Or of x-ing the rind with a knife and then pulling back the corners to reveal a pool of pure stinky bliss. Made exclusively in winter, when the herd of Ayrshire cows are hay-fed and producing super-fat, rich milk, these raw-milk wheels are a fleeting glory in the American cheese world. The encompassing bark, which is harvested on the dairy's property, imparts a sappy, slightly tannic bite, while the cheese itself develops a deep, meaty, almost ham-like note that balances incredibly well with the woodsy aroma. These wheels are great as a centerpiece for any meal.

Enjoy with a big Burgundy wine and some nice cured ham.

L'AMI DU CHAMBERTIN *(LAH-MI DO SHAM-BER-TAN)*

MILK TYPE: Cow

ORIGIN: Burgundy, France

Another stinker from Burgundy, L'Ami du Chambertin is produced in the village of Gevrey-Chambertin and comes encased in an attractive little lidded wooden box. Like Epoisses (see page 97) and Trou du Cru (see page 109), it is washed with a marc (or liquor) of the region to give it a pungent, wet exterior that gains a studding of salt crystals as it matures. When opened, the cheese becomes quite runny with a dense dollop of lactic cake in the center. The sweetness of the milk is cut by the earthy, dried-straw flavors of its exterior. L'Ami du Chambertin is traditionally made with raw cow's milk, but only the pasteurized versions are presently allowed into the United States. This is a great cheese to cut the top off of and dip crusty bread directly into it.

Enjoy with a glass of Eagle Rare bourbon whiskey alongside a slab of game pâté.

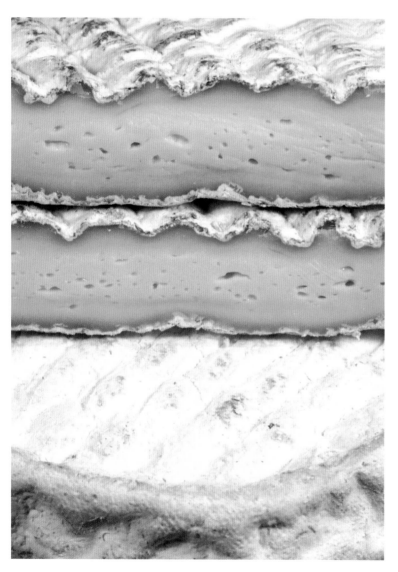

LE DREAN *(LE DREE-AN)*

MILK TYPE: Cow

ORIGIN: Auvergne, France

A supple cow's milk cheese from Auvergne, Le Drean receives sporadic washings in a salt brine during its few months of aging in caves. Inspired by Saint Nectaire (see page 164), Le Drean is also known as Saintalin, and is a true farmstead, or fermier, cheese, meaning the milk comes from the same farm where the cheese is made. The deep red rind develops its coloring from the washing, but the second aging step—maturing in humidity-controlled cellars—allows bright flowers of yellow and white mold to develop on the washed rind, displaying a hodgepodge of earth tones. The scent is muskier and earthier than most washed rinds, and veers away from the overtly "stinky" to more earthy and dirt-driven aromas. The paste is gooey without being runny, and develops a lot of little eyes as it ages. The flavor is both buttery and slightly bacony, with notes of peanuts and earth.

Enjoy with big round reds, such as Burgundys and Barolos, and present alongside glazed ham and rye bread.

LIMBURGER *(LIMB-BURR-GURR)*

MILK TYPE: Cow

ORIGIN: Duchy of Limburg

First created in the region of Duchy of Limburg in the nineteenth century, the land soon broke into different territories with arms in Belgium, Germany, and the Netherlands. Limburger is an aggressively stinky, washed-rind cow's milk cheese that has inspired cheese production within these three countries, as well as in the United States, for years. Most people's association with Limburger is its "footy" scent and big, buttery, beefy flavor. When younger—under two months of age—these little bricks of cheese—about a pound (454 g) per loaf—have a crumbly, slightly dry texture. After a few more weeks and months of washing, they begin to get gooey and creamy at the rind, and start to take on the signature smell of manure and funk. At their ripest, around three to four months of age, the center is a gooey mess and the smell is reminiscent of full diapers and crowded barns in the summertime. An old-school way to enjoy Limburger is smeared between two slices of brown bread with a thick cut of raw onion.

Enjoy with a lots of lager and a bold-flavored snack.

LIVAROT *(LIVE-OR-OH)*

MILK TYPE: Cow

ORIGIN: Normandy, France

With a rich history of dairy production, Normandy is a land of buttery, indulgent cow's milk cheese. Livarot is a stinky little sucker that has been a name-protected production (see page 38) since 1975. Slightly earthy with notes of peanut butter and caramel, these washed-rind wheels are a supple, gooey mess of a soil-scented lactic dream. Bound with either bark, hay, or paper, these wheels bulge out under their own weight when perfectly ripe. Although these wheels are bathed with a salt brine as they age, annatto is often introduced to the slurry (washing solution) to help darken the golden rust-colored hue of the rinds to an almost burnt red. This process also contributes a musky aroma.

Enjoy with a glass of Calvados, alongside a meal of roasted squab and a wild rice pilaf.

TARTIFLETTE RECIPE

4 tablespoons unsalted butter, divided

½ pound (225 g) slab of bacon, cut into lardons (small cubes)

1 medium red onion, chopped

½ cup (120 ml) dry white wine

2½ pounds (1.1 kg) Yukon Gold potatoes, thinly sliced

Salt and pepper, to taste

1 pound (450 g) Gubbeen cheese (see page 98), sliced matchstick thin

1. Preheat oven to 350˚F (175˚C). Grease an 8 x 8-in (20 x 20 cm) baking pan with 2 tablespoons butter.

2. Heat remaining butter in a cast iron pan until melted.

3. Add bacon and cook until fat has been rendered.

4. Remove bacon and sauté onions in drippings until translucent.

5. Add wine and cook until liquid has reduced by half.

6. Add potatoes, salt, and pepper and cook until tender.

7. Place half the potato and onion mixture into the baking dish and cover with half the bacon lardons and half the cheese.

8. Add the remaining half of potato and onions on top, layering the remaining lardons and cheese on top of this.

9. Bake for 20–25 minutes, or until the top is golden brown and bubbling.

MEADOW CREEK DAIRY GRAYSON

MILK TYPE: Cow

ORIGIN: Virginia, United States

Made from the milk of the farm's herd of eighty Jersey cows, Grayson is a funk-driven, washed-rind cheese that is shaped like a square paving stone and is bright orange, similar to the color of a Cheetos-stained fingertip. The aroma is musky and funky, with an uncanny bacony quality. The rich yellow-hued paste is filled with little eyes, making the texture almost elastic-like in its pliability. There are hints of roast beef and charred onions, with a salty finish that has notes of boiled peanuts. The Feete family who produces these slabs practices sustainable agriculture, providing herbicide- and pesticide-free pastures for their herd to graze upon. Grayson is only produced from April to October when these cows are grazing the green. A few hours after the cows are milked, cheese production takes place. This commitment to using the freshest, richest milk comes across in the cheese. An incredible creation from amazing farming practices, Grayson is an American original that will please anyone who loves a little funk.

Enjoy with a malt-driven brown ale and some grilled ribs.

MUNSTER GÉROMÉ (MUN-STIR GARE-OM)

MILK TYPE: Cow

ORIGIN: Vosges, France

Not to be confused with the orange spice-encrusted deli slices, this French classic has been a name-protected product (see page 38) since the 1970s, but dates back to the Middle Ages when the monks in the abbeys that speckle this region made this cheese. One of the stinkier cheeses found in the marketplace, Munster Géromé is an indulgently gooey creation of pure cow's milk that is cradled by a thin, sticky orange rind. Because of the AOC regulations, the production of this devilishly delightful dairy treat has strict guidelines about how it is created and where it is produced. Chalky and dense when young, these wheels are produced in two sizes—one a larger size, about three pounds (1.4 kg), that gets cut up and a smaller version made to be offered in its entirety—and get a hearty washing of salt brine as they mature, turning the larger version into a robust puddle of barnyard ooze. The best representations of this cheese come about in summer and autumn, when the herds are grazing on the higher pastures of the hillsides.

Enjoy with stouts and dark beers, as well as the starchy pairings of roasted potatoes and crusty breads.

NABABBO (NAH-BAH-BO)

MILK TYPE: Goat

ORIGIN: Val Taleggio, Italy

Another cousin of Taleggio (see page 108), this goat's milk brick is produced in northern Italy. The milk is left out to culture in open vats in a mountainous cave before being turned into cheese. This process allows the milk to take on more of the musty aroma, as well as the healthy microbes, that live in this lair. The wheels are washed a few times a week during their aging life, to help develop the pale peach rind. The yogurty center has the undeniable hint of goat, but with a floral sweetness that is riddled with wisps of buttercups and wild lilacs. The texture is pliable and moist without becoming too gooey or runny. The yeasty quality of Taleggio also appears in these wheels, but with more of a barnyard-like funk than an overt yeastiness. This is a great cheese for anyone who loves goat's milk cheeses but wants an unusual and new flavor.

Enjoy with a lighter red, such as a young Nebbiolo, or a floral wheat beer.

PONT L'ÉVÊQUE (PONT LEE-VECK)

MILK TYPE: Cow

ORIGIN: Normandy, France

Hailing from the lush land known for apple orchards and rolling acres of farmland, Pont l'Évêque is oftentimes a misunderstood cheese here in the United States. The production of this washed-rind stinker dates back to the twelfth century, and is rumored to have been birthed by a pack of Cistercian monks. Cheese-making, as well as fermentation in general, was a popular trade among the monks throughout France, and their gift to today's cheese world is prevalent. Pont l'Évêque is most often found in grocery stores well past its prime, so the intended dirt stink of the rind takes on an aggressive, somewhat ammoniated aroma. When handled respectfully, the flavors of fresh manure and dank cellar develop into a lush wave of warm milk that is sweet and seductive. This is a great cheese to try when the rind is still peach-colored with a tinge of orange glow. The creamy paste will begin to ooze out almost immediately upon cutting, and you will want to scoop it all up with a crusty baguette.

Enjoy with a yeasty hard cider or a balanced IPA.

QUADRELLO DI BUFALA *(QUAD-DRILL-OH DEE BOO-FAH-LA)*

MILK TYPE: Water buffalo

ORIGIN: Lombardy, Italy

The two brothers who make this Taleggio-inspired buffalo's milk cheese have revolutionized the way people think about the ultra-fatty, protein-rich milk often used primarily for making mozzarella. This washed-rind, chubby square takes on the depth and funk of the cellars it is aged in. After the making and initial wash, the cheese continues to receive a healthy rub down of brine, until the yogurty paste becomes fudgy and pliable. The rind holds notes of musk and wet paper, but the flavor is a mellow ride of freshly churned butter with a slight tang of heavy cream. When they first leave the caves, these squares are plump and peach-colored, but they continue to evolve well after leaving their aging environments. The rind develops patches of healthy molds—some yellow, some orange—all adding a complex richness to the buffalo's milk.

Enjoy with a light nebbiolo or even an herbaceous gin, such as Junipero.

QUESO DE CABRA DON MARIANO *(K-SO DUH KAH-BRA DON MARY-ON-O)*

MILK TYPE: Goat

ORIGIN: Extremadura, Spain

One of the favorites among our cheesemongers, this raw goat's milk cheese made with thistle rennet comes to us in dense, fudgy two-pound (907 g) wheels. This cheese arrives at our shop with a bright orange rind, and the ivory-white paste tends to be studded with small eyes from the fermentation process, presenting a sweet, feral flavor profile that resonates well with people who prefer strong cheeses. We like to serve it with sliced serrano ham, but if you want to get really crazy, melt it over potatoes and add a dash of pimentón picante.

Enjoy with a glass of white wine from Rías Baixas.

RACLETTE WITH WHITE WINE

MILK TYPE: Cow

ORIGIN: Canton of Obwalden, Switzerland

Raclette cheese can come in a variety of shapes and sizes—just take this square, washed-rind slab of raw cow's milk, for instance. Caroline Hostettler selects these "wheels" produced by Seiler Käserei in the city of Sarnen for export to the United States. They have a peach-colored rind that presents aromas of pleasant rot, wet earth, and a pronounced sweetness from the white wine used in the washing. The paste is a pale straw color, with a slight studding of eyes and a balanced, earthy flavor profile—the influence of the wine on the cheese is unmistakable. Like all raclettes, it is a highly meltable affair, and the sweetness of the wash explodes aromatically once things start warming up.

Enjoy with a glass of any white wine and slathered over smoked ham, potatoes, and cornichons.

REBLOCHON FERMIER (RE-BLEW-SEAN FAIR-ME-AIR)

MILK TYPE: Cow

ORIGIN: Rhône-Alpes, France

Fermier refers to the fact that the milk for the cheese comes from the same farm as where the cheese is made. This means that the cheese maker is in full control of the quality of the milk, guarantees freshness, and allows for careful oversight of the entire cheese-making process. Reblochon is a traditional French cow's milk cheese that gets a healthy washing of brine comprised of leftover whey from a different day of cheese-making and a basic saltwater brine. There are several reblochon producers, but very few true fermier producers. The difference in flavor is night and day. While the larger producers develop rather one-note, sometimes rubbery wheels, the fermier versions are rich, with notes of soil and an unmistakable nuttiness that comes across as toasted cashews and ripe honeydew melon. History tells us that reblochon cheese was actually a by-product of tax evasion. Once upon a time, dairymen were taxed on the amount of milk their herds yielded, so conniving farmers would only partially milk their beasts so they would be taxed less. Once the tax man journeyed on to his next destination, the cheese maker would finish the milking, producing richer, fatter milk, which would be used for these lush little wheels that were sold on a sort of black market. The aroma is nuanced and mellower compared to other washed rinds and takes on more of a sweet, musky note, rather than a "footy," beefy scent.

Enjoy with a floral white, such as a Sancerre or a Grüner.

REBLOCHON KUNTENER (REB-BLEW-SEAN COOT-NER)

MILK TYPE: Cow

ORIGIN: Canton of Jura, Switzerland

A true Swiss reblochon, these funky patties are an incredible treat for anyone who appreciates a little something stinky. Balanced in both its meatiness and tang, the healthy washing of whey they get during their maturation creates a hefty waft of manure and dirty diapers, as well as helps quicken the ripening process. Although the scent might lead you to believe this cheese has a really aggressive taste, the opening notes are of rare roast beef and toasted almonds. As these wheels open up in their ripening process, they become gooey and supple, but without turning into the runny mess sometimes found with ripe washed rinds. The ultra-rich raw milk that is used in the making of these wheels develops a luscious creaminess that is as close to the taste of freshly cultured heavy cream as can be found in a washed-rind cheese. This cheese is a personal favorite of ours.

Enjoy with a slightly smoky whiskey, such as High West Campfire, or a hearty stout beer, such as Left Hand Milk Stout Nitro.

SOUMAINTRAIN *(SEW-MAH-TRAN)*

MILK TYPE: Cow

ORIGIN: Burgundy, France

Similar in appearance and creation to its cousin Epoisses (see page 97), Soumaintrain is named after the village in which it was originally produced, near the Yonne River in eastern France. Unlike Epoisses, it is larger in form—twelve to fourteen ounces (340 to 297 g)—causing the interior of the cheese to develop a denser consistency when young rather than the general runniness of Epoisses. While both of these cheeses are washed in the same Marc du Bourgogne brandy, Soumaintain exhibits blooms of Geotrichum candidum on the rind when young, evolving into a glistening exterior when aged. The result of aging is a runnier, more animalistic flavor profile with notes of deep soil and seared sausage. Grab some crusty bread and fresh pears, and hop on board the Soumaintrain.

Enjoy with a bottle of Burgundy.

SPRING BROOK FARM READING RACLETTE

MILK TYPE: Cow

ORIGIN: Vermont, United States

Another great French-inspired creation from Spring Brook Farm (see page 138), this raclette is a melting dream. After the cheese is formed, a healthy washing of salt brine creates the rose-hued rind that is slightly tacky to the touch. There is a robust aroma of wet straw and burnt sugar, with an undercurrent of cherry pipe tobacco. The flavor is rather mild and buttery, and a great blank canvas to be used in numerous recipes, or as an addition to any meal that needs a gooey cheese component. Amazing melted over thinly sliced roast beef on a crusty baguette for an open-faced sandwich of your dreams, or grated over roasted brussel sprouts and then broiled to get brown and bubbly, there really is no wrong way to enjoy this cheese. As a stand-alone on a cheese plate, Reading Raclette goes very well with savory chutneys, which bring out the meaty notes in the high-quality milk.

Enjoy with a sparkling rosé to highlight the cheese's sweet hints of fresh berries and milk chocolate.

ST. JAMES

MILK TYPE: Sheep

ORIGIN: Cumbria, England

An exceptional rarity from the English countryside, this washed-rind sheep's milk slab is a heavenly creation by a heavenly man. Having the privilege of growing up with a flock of sheep, Martin Gott learned cheese-making the old school way—by getting his hands into the curd. After traveling around and apprenticing with some of the best British cheese makers, he and his partner decided to buy their own flock of sheep and start making this Tallegio-inspired production. Named for the first cheese maker Martin worked with, St. James is a beast of a cheese. Emitting scents of freshly cut grass and shorn wet wool, this cheese also possesses an unmistakable funk to the rind. The paste is gooey and decadent, sometimes with a cakey center. The rich sheep's milk is elevated with the daily salt-brine washing, creating a glazed-ham effect on the finish. A floral delight that is truly a masterpiece from this young cheese maker, St. James is not to be missed on the rare occasions it can be found. Present a wedge alongside a spread of grilled lamb chops and smoked sausages.

Enjoy with a bottle of chilled Sancerre.

STRACCHINO DI VEDESETA
(STRAW-KEEN-OH DUH VA-DES-TAH)

MILK TYPE: Sheep

ORIGIN: Lombardy, Italy

Thought to be the precursor of Taleggio (below), this funky, washed-rind cow's milk cheese from northern Italy has all the visual characteristics of its offspring, but a much more floral, caramelly, rich taste. These square slabs are washed daily with a salt brine during the first few days of their aging lives, but the bathing becomes less frequent as they firm up and develop their rosy orange-tinged rinds. There are scents of warm, buttered Parker House rolls and cherry taffy on the rind, and the paste holds a decadent sweetness that is both bready and meaty. The floral notes merge on honeysuckle and lilac for a slight perfumey hit.

TALEGGIO (TALL-AGE-EE-OH)

MILK TYPE: Cow

ORIGIN: Lombardy, Italy

Made in the northern region of Italy, Taleggio cheese has been produced since the Romans were in charge. Once made exclusively in the Val Taleggio caves, this ubiquitous stinker is now made throughout the Piedmont region. The cow's milk produced during the autumn months is only used when the yield is lesser and richer. After the alchemy of enzyme and rennet, turning the liquid into a solid, these square cheeses are aged on wooden planks to help maintain moisture and to impose a sappy, robust taste that is heightened with the funky scents of wet soil and yeast. The relatively sweet paste takes on hints of rising white bread and green hay—fruity yet savory. They are washed with salty seawater during their maturation to help stave off any unwanted bacteria, as well as to help regulate the moisture to encourage the cheese to become gooey and creamy as it ages. There are several different Taleggio producers, but because this is a name-protected cheese (see page 38), all versions must maintain a fat level of 48 percent and a minimum of forty days of aging on wood planks.

Enjoy with floral white wines or a lightly oaked Chardonnay.

TORTA ESPRIMIJO (TORE-TAH ESS-PRAH-ME-HO)

MILK TYPE: Sheep

ORIGIN: Extremadura, Spain

Another excellent example of the full-flavored queso that comes from Extremadura, Torta Esprimijo is made solely from the raw milk of the Merino sheep in the area, with vegetable rennet used in the production. Like all raw-milk cheeses sent to the United States, it is aged a minimum of sixty days before arrival. With this youthful state, the paste is gooey and lactic, with a pleasant sheen from the rich, fatty milk of the sheep. It is soft, smooth, and creamy with a bouquet of farm aromas and wet wool. Like most torta-style cheeses, Esprimijo is traditionally served with the top cut off to allow direct access to its seductive paste, which should be spooned onto Iberian ham or roasted vegetables.

TORTA LA SERENA (TORE-TAH LA CER-AI-NAH)

MILK TYPE: Sheep

ORIGIN: Extremadura, Spain

A pudgy and pungent round of raw Merino sheep's milk, Torta La Serena is a Protected Designation of Origin (see page 38) cheese from a region near the border of Portugal. Made in roughly one-and-a-half- to two-pound (680 to 907 g) wheels and coagulated with vegetable rennet—cardoon thistle, specifically—this cheese is said to have been in existence since the Middle Ages. It holds deep notes of mutton and wet fur, with a pleasant, piquant sweetness from the rich fat of the milk and vegetable rennet used in the production process. We prefer these wheels when they are ripe and oozing away from the rind, but there's nothing wrong with one that's a little more aged, as the texture tightens and the gaminess becomes more pronounced.

Enjoy with a dusty red wine at its later stages, but when young, it is great served with a wild Spanish cider.

TROU DU CRU (TRUE DO CREW)

MILK TYPE: Cow

ORIGIN: Burgundy, France

From the mind of cheese maker Robert Berthaut comes these little dumplings from Burgundy, which are essentially pocket-sized versions of Epoisses (see page 97). Washed in Marc du Bourgogne brandy—a local spirit made with the remnants from winemaking—Trou du Cru is an extremely aromatic and damp cheese that holds notes of straw, manure, and decay. Weighing only a couple of ounces (57 g), this cheese shows a cross section of maturation when cut into—a chalky, cakey center with a surrounding gooey cream line. As part of a cheese plate, it provides the fantastic option of presenting a rich and funky cheese without having to buy a large piece or break the bank.

Enjoy with something bubbly, such as a Crémant de Loire, as the texture of the wine will cut into the boisterous nature of the cheese.

THINK BIG

You'll see throughout these pages that there are certain cheeses that are well suited to be consumed in their entirety. Depending on the size of your gathering, on occasion you might want to purchase an entire wheel of cheese so that there will be enough for everyone to snack on, and the integrity of the cheese will be very high. We like to cut the top off a Torta Esprimijo (see page 109) and let people get direct access to the feral, sweet paste, as if it were a bowl of guacamole. Playing around with cheese is a lot of fun when you're with a group. A great way to show off your culinary prowess in front of peers is to throw a whole Vacherin Mont d'Or (right) into the oven, and then watch the resulting bubbling, runny cheese disappear in front of your very eyes.

TWIG FARM WASHED RIND WHEEL

MILK TYPE: Goat

ORIGIN: Vermont, United States

Made by one of the loveliest couples in the cheese world, Twig Farm's proprietors, Michael Lee and Emily Sunderman, handcraft true American originals. Their Washed Rind Wheel is their only washed-rind cheese and is an incredible example of what the combination of great milk, a little washing, and some time can do for a cheese. The milk for these plump little tommes comes from the herd that gets to graze in the woodlands around Twig Farm. Michael Lee milks his fifty goats daily to get the freshest milk for his creations. He washes these wheels by hand with a mixture of leftover whey from a different day of cheese-making and the spent pulp of apple cider. The exterior aroma is one of sweet, salty decay, and when sliced open, notes of hay and rich cream bounce from the fudgy, sometimes elastic paste. The wheels may vary in size, but weigh, on average, around one and a half (680 g) pounds each. Try pairing with sliced stone fruit in the depth of a sweltering summer.

VACHERIN MONT-D'OR

(VAASHH-ERR-IN MOUNT DOOR)

MILK TYPE: Cow

ORIGIN: Canton of Vaud, Switzerland

One of the most sought-after cheeses, this highly seasonal, indulgent mess of a cheese is only made the few short months when fall meets winter. Encased in a wooden box made from fir trees, this luscious and buttery beauty has all the depth of flavor of a vat of warm, raw milk that has been fermented in the dank cellars underneath a hay-filled barn. The origins of this cheese are a bit disputed, as it is produced in the hilly region that both France and Switzerland border. The French produce both raw and pasteurized versions, while the Swiss prefer to focus more on the pasteurized product. This is a name-controlled cheese (see page 38) in France, so every step of the production process must adhere to the specified guidelines. When perfectly ripe, this cheese is a goopy puddle of perfection. Basically the consistency of fondue, these wheels are meant to have the rind x-ed with a knife and peeled back, revealing a liquid center that is bestial and seductive, buttery and fluid. The rind emits the aroma of wet leaves and wood, with a hint of leather and sap. An incredible treat, this cheese is best enjoyed at room temperature with a spoon and a loaf of good crusty bread.

VULTO CREAMERY MIRANDA

MILK TYPE: Cow

ORIGIN: New York, United States

Named after the beloved wife of cheese maker Jos Vulto, Miranda is a gorgeous representation of a domestic, washed-rind cow's milk cheese. The whole-fat, raw milk used in these little drums is collected daily from a neighboring farm. After the curds have been formed, cut, and ladled into molds, the cheese is briefly salted to help develop the crust. These little guys receive a continuous washing of a special brine of absinthe from a distillery down the road. The herby booze imparts a sweetness to the cheese, which develops into a buttery goo

as it ages. There are two sizes of Miranda: The three-inch-tall by two-inch-wide (7.5 x 5 cm) buttons develop a rich, decadent center with a plush texture that is not too gooey. The larger wheels are about an inch tall by four inches (2.5 x 10 cm) wide, and develop a denser, buttery texture. The aroma is on the sweeter side and has none of the funky scent sometimes associated with washed rinds.

Enjoy with an herb-driven cocktail or a mineral-forward white, such as a Moscato.

VULTO CREAMERY OULEOUT *(OOH-LEE-OH)*

MILK TYPE: Cow

ORIGIN: New York, United States

This raw-milk specialty hails from the wooded countryside of the Catskills, about three hours north of New York City. The aggressive stink of this brine-washed rind is deceptive compared to its earthy and slightly sour paste, which eventually develops a richness that borders on softened, cultured butter. The recipe for this cheese has been perfected over years of play from cheese maker Jos Vulto. It started out as a rather salty, funky, curdy creation and has gradually transformed into the luscious, velvety beauty it is today. Loosely inspired by such classics as Taleggio (see page 108) and Ardrahan (see page 87), this  moister, slightly stinkier cousin has all the robust nature of a young cheese. The balance of the funky-musk and sweet-cream taste elevates this American original to new heights in the domestic cheese world. The milk comes from a neighboring farm and is collected daily for the cheese's production. The wheels are aged about sixty days before arriving onto the cheese counter. This is a great introductory cheese for anyone who likes a little stink and is ready to try something new.

WOODCOCK FARM CHEESE COMPANY TIMBERDOODLE

MILK TYPE: Cow

ORIGIN: Vermont, United States

In addition to the farmstead sheep's milk cheeses produced by Woodcock Farm Cheese Company, they also source Jersey cow's milk from a local dairy that prides itself on proper animal husbandry. Timberdoodle always makes us think of skateboards when it comes into the shop, because it looks exactly like one. Made with pasteurized milk and animal rennet, this cheese—produced in the style of Taleggio (see page 108) —is gently treated with a brine wash over its three months of maturation. The rust-colored rind encases a paste that is semi-soft and a rich butter yellow in color. Notes of peanuts, sweet sausage, and barnyard give way to a very lush mouthfeel, with pleasant chew, as the fat opens up with the warmth of the mouth. Timberdoodle is a great melter and will kick a homemade pizza up another level, but it's just as excellent served by itself on a cheese plate.

BRINED CHEESES

Developed by the Greeks as a way to lengthen the shelf life of cheeses, brined cheeses are a family of cheeses that are soaked in a salt bath once the cheese has been formed. This step is actually taken with most firmer cheeses once the wheels are aged to help build the crust that will develop into the rind. In the brined-cheese category, the wheels are left in the brine longer so that no rinds develop. After the initial cheese-making process, the desired amount of whey is pressed out of the bricks of curd. Once this process is completed, the bricks are then left to soak in a salt brine that begins to "crust" the outside. These cheeses tend to be salty and a bit brittle and are great for crumbling. Depending on the milk that is used, brined cheeses develop a high acidic tang that is usually balanced nicely with the saline levels. Dense and firm, these are excellent cheeses to use in cooking, as they will hold their shape, and not goo out or run. Think of cubing up some French feta with leeks and mushrooms, encasing it in pastry dough, and baking it for a savory, wrapped pie of perfection. There is a whole spectrum of flavors in just the feta family alone, from tannic and tangy to musky and yeasty, truly there is a brined cheese for every occasion.

FETA *(FET-AH)*

MILK TYPE: Sheep, goat, and sometimes cow

Origin: Greece

There are several varieties of feta in the marketplace. Although it is a name-protected product of Greece (see page 38), feta is produced around the world, from a raw goat's milk version in Petaluma, California, to a mixed-milk production in Bavaria. Greek feta must be made from only sheep's milk, or with the addition of a small amount of goat's milk. All feta is soaked in a salt brine. This step helps to solidify the cheese, and also gives it a salty, tangy bite. The French sheep's milk feta is luscious and velvety, with a mellow flavor. The Israeli feta is brittler, saltier, and has more of an animally bite. Most fetas are a mixture of sheep, goat, and cow's milk. Although the textures vary with the milk type, and country of origin, they all have a somewhat grainy quality that can run from crumbly and sandy, to more moist with just a slight chewiness. There is a "creamy" version of feta found in several countries, wherein there is a higher fat content left in the milk before the make process, thus creating an almost solidified cream-like texture. Feta is most commonly used in salads, such as Greek salad, but is great to crumble over mezzi dips like hummus or white bean spread, or sprinkled over chilis and stews for a great addition of flavor and texture.

HALLOUMI *(HA-LOO-ME)*

MILK TYPE: Cow, sometimes goat and sheep

Origin: Cyprus

Salty and chewy, Halloumi is a semi-firm, sturdy brined cheese that is set using traditional rennet but has no starter culture added—that is, there is no acid-creating bacteria introduced in the make process, resulting in a cheese that is firm with a high pH. This creates a high melting point for the cheese. It is a popular ingredient in many Mediterranean and Middle Eastern cuisines and the sturdiness of the cheese gives it a portability that makes it a favorite among many nomadic tribes throughout those regions.

Believed to have been in existence for over a thousand years, Halloumi has been affectionately dubbed "the cheese that grills." Fry it up until a golden crust is achieved, and then dress it with olive oil and mint and serve with some flatbread.

WASHED CURD

"Washing the curd" is a process that results in cheeses that have a sweet, mellow flavor and smooth consistency. With this cheese-making method, the curd—once it has been cut and the whey has drained—is then washed with hot water (or beer or lambic) changing the pH and mineral content of the curd, and setting off a reaction in the bacteria that is present. This process produces cheeses that are supple and buttery when young, and sweet and studded with amino acid crystals when aged. Perfected by the Dutch centuries ago for the making of Gouda, the washed-curd process is now used to create many different cheeses. Washed-curd cheeses are great paired with whiskey or a full-flavored beer.

BRYARDE *(BREE-ARD)*

MILK TYPE: Cow

ORIGIN: West Flanders, Belgium

Situated in the town of Veurne near the Belgian seashore, Beauvoordse Walhoeve is a family-run dairy that produces numerous traditional farmhouse cheeses, including this one that we are completely gaga over. This large brick of raw milk from Holstein cows is enrobed in deep-maroon-colored wax. The curds of this cheese are washed in Brugse Zot, a Belgian pale ale with a wild yeastiness and bright acidity from the hops. These elements from the beer combined with the rich milk and cultures used in the cheese produce a wild and sour spectrum of flavors on the palate that is held together by a semi-firm, fudgy paste. Bryarde is a versatile, user-friendly cheese—its price point is reasonable, it melts extremely well, and it is a great addition to a ham sandwich.

Enjoy with a yeasty pale ale.

COOLEA (COO-LAY)

MILK TYPE: Cow

ORIGIN: County Cork, Ireland

From the rolling, stony hillsides of West Cork, Ireland, comes this Dutch-inspired treat. Handmade by Dick Willems and his son, Dicky, Coolea is a standout Gouda recipe, with all of the richness and caramelly depth of a Boerenkaas ("farmer cheese") Gouda, but with the flinty notes of the damp, rocky lands that the cows graze upon. The base of this perfection is the whole-fat milk that is treated like the liquid gold that it is—there is nothing added and there is nothing taken away. The handful of neighboring farms that the Willemses get their milk from are all a short distance away. Every evening, the milk is collected from the dairies and then left out at the cheese-making house to begin the slow fermentation. After the initial cheese-making process (rennet, enzyme, heat, and time), the resulting curd mass is cut down to release the whey, and then the curds are washed through with water while being heated a second time. This process ensures the ideal texture: a dense, firm, and sometimes grainy paste that Goudas are known for. Because the cheeses age for up to a year, they are coated with a form of breathable Plasticine that allows the cheeses to age slowly without losing too much moisture.

KRIEK (CREEK)

MILK TYPE: Cow

ORIGIN: West Flanders, Belgium

The family-run dairy Beauvoordse Walhoeve produces numerous traditional farmhouse cheeses, many of which include fresh herbs and spices. But the cheese that is a stand out among their creations is this little wheel—about one and a half pounds (680 g)—of red wax–encased raw cow's milk that is simply called Kriek, named after a type of lambic (a beer that is produced by spontaneous fermentation through the exposure of grain to wild bacteria and yeasts) of the same name. The beer kriek is shaped by taking lambic and re-fermenting it with cherries, resulting in a tart and wildly yeasty beverage. The cheese maker at Beauvoordse Walhoeve washes the curds with kriek and molds these little rounds that age about three months. The result is a sour, yeasty, and lactic creation, with a smooth mouthfeel and a chewy paste.

Enjoy with a kriek or a gueuze, as well as some shrimp croquettes.

MARIEKE GOUDA *(MAH-REE-KAY GOO-DAH)*

MILK TYPE: Cow

ORIGIN: Wisconsin, United States

In 2002, Marieke Penterman relocated from her native Holland to the dairy-rich land of Wisconsin. Having grown up on a dairy farm, Marieke chose to cure her longing for the cheeses of her native land by making them herself. After learning the cheese-making craft both stateside and abroad, she has now blessed us with her farmhouse cheese known as Marieke Gouda. The raw cow's milk from the Wisconsin farm is shaped with ingredients from Holland and formed into dense wheels that are left to age on pine planks also from Holland. The wood wicks away moisture and provides subtle tannins to the sweet milk developing within the wheels. Marieke Gouda comes in a variety of flavors and ages, but we prefer the more mature versions, with their rich burnt-caramel note and lovely salt-studded paste. This Gouda is a surefire hit among cheese fans.

Enjoy with a can of Bitter American pale ale and seasonal fresh fruit.

QUADRUPEL *(QUAD-ROO-PELL)*

MILK TYPE: Cow

ORIGIN: West Flanders, Belgium

Produced in a region of Belgium between the North Sea and the French border, Quadrupel is a rich Flemish cow's milk cheese by producer De Moerenaar that is made by washing the curds in a quadrupel ale—a beer with a strong, dark character. During World War I, this area of Flanders was flooded with seawater to prevent the advance of the German army. This maneuver not only impacted military history but also the future of agriculture in the area, as the grass (thus the milk) took on a higher level of salinity, resulting in the cheese maker having to use less salt during the make process. Encased in a tan-colored wax rind, Quadrupel is a semi-firm, lactic cheese with a fresh yet somewhat tart milk flavor that has a pleasant added sweetness from the beer's malt composition.

Enjoy with a bottle of La Trappe Quadrupel and some pickled herring.

STOMPETOREN GRAND CRU *(STOMP-UH-TORE-EN GRAND CREW)*

MILK TYPE: Cow

ORIGIN: North Holland, Netherlands

Aged Gouda is one of the most popular styles of cheese on the market. Its pronounced sweetness, crystal crunch from the amino acid breakdown, and rich mouthfeel make it a winner among the cheese-consuming populace. There are many well-made Goudas out there, but the one we prefer is produced by Cono and aged by a man in the

small town of Stompetoren. Aged around eighteen months, our friend Peter collects these roughly thirty-pound (14 kg) wheels of cow's milk that are enrobed in wax and green paper and mails them to us across the Atlantic to be received in our loving arms. Stompetoren Grand Cru has a rich orange–colored paste, thanks to the annatto added during the make process, and smells of burnt caramel and toast. The flavor is pleasantly sweet and very straightforward as the cheese melts on your tongue. Stompetoren is a wise choice for any fan of Gouda, let alone cheese in general.

Enjoy with a glass of robust porter.

WILDE WEIDE *(VILL-DUH VAI-DUH)*

MILK TYPE: Cow

ORIGIN: Holland, Netherlands

The amazing husband-and-wife team Jan and Roos van Schie fabricate this cow's milk dream on their small island in the middle of a lake in South Holland. A mixed herd of Montbéliard and Friesians graze freely on the lush idyllic pastures that are filled with a botanical bounty of wildflowers and grass. The small herd only produces a limited amount of milk, so just a few wheels are made a day. They are then aged on the island for several months before they arrive to shore. Unlike the majority of Goudas that are extremely caramelly and candy-like in flavor, Wilde Weide is tangier and more tropical, with a citrusy hit that waves into a savory finish. As with most Goudas, Wilde Weide is a great addition to any

picnic, chunking off pieces to bite into rather than slicing a slab. Because of its briny after note, this cheese is great paired with buttery green olives or cubed up into an herb-filled grain salad.

Enjoy with copious amounts of pilsner.

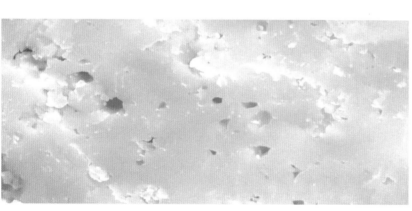

COOKED/PRESSED

Another method for making cheese with a smooth and dense consistency is by cooking the curds and/or pressing them. Cooked cheeses are developed by reheating the curds at a slightly higher temperature to extract more whey and affect the chemical structure of the curds so that the cultures develop the flavor profile and texture desired by the cheese maker. Pressed cheeses are made by pressing out excess moisture, either after the curds are cut or after reheating. The result is a fudgy, somewhat elastic cheese with good melting properties. This section will look at a variety of cheeses that are cooked and then pressed—a process that is associated with the production of alpine-style cheeses. The flavor profiles of these cheeses range from sweet, lactic, and floral to nutty, dank, and earthy. They love to mingle with funky, yeast-driven wines and robust beers.

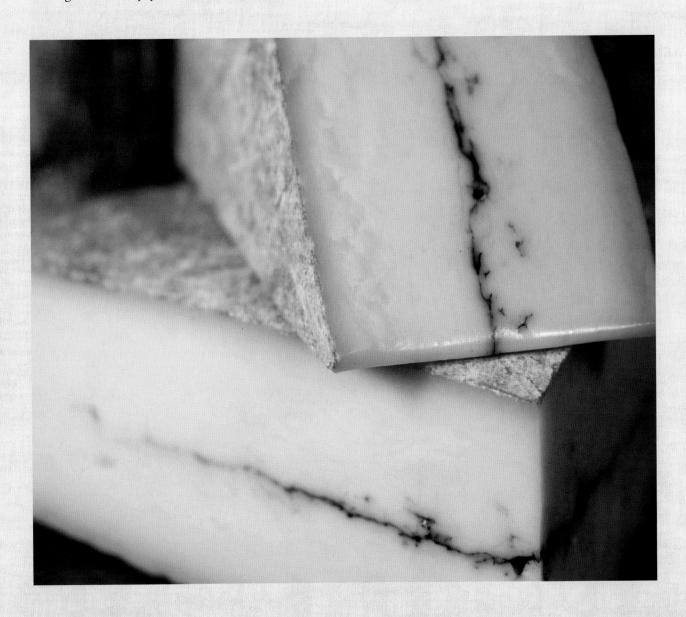

ADELEGGER *(ADD-AH-LEG-ER)*

MILK TYPE: Cow

ORIGIN: Bavaria, Germany

The milk for this German alpine cheese comes from seven organic farmers that all reside within the Allgäu region. The entire dairy is operated as a "green" facility, using steam to both clean and heat the dairy. For over fifteen years, the relationship between master cheese maker Evelyn Wild and her team of farmers has resulted in unique cheeses that balance the sweet richness familiar to the alpine-cheese family with the texture and depth of this exceptional milk. Adelegger is a seventeen-month-old, lightly washed cow's milk creation that cradles the nutty roastiness of the hillside with a wave of tropical fruit and tart cherries in the finish. The fudgy paste holds the coveted "crunchy bits," also known as a cluster of amino acids that form when rich milk is aged for over a year. The addictive flavor pop makes these wheels as seductive and alluring as a savory sweet. Adelegger is a real treat for anyone who likes the nutty, caramelly notes of a Swiss cheese but is looking for something with more of a tangy bite.

Enjoy with a hoppy IPA or a slightly smoky scotch, as well as with dense dark bread and dried figs.

BEAUFORT *(BOW-FOUR)*

MILK TYPE: Cow

ORIGIN: Savoie, France

The king of the French Alps, Beaufort is a majestic beauty of a cheese that truly encapsulates the historic traditions of mountain cheese-making. This cheese has had AOC status (see page 38) since 1968, which means that everything associated with how this cheese is made has been regulated for nearly fifty years. The Abondance and Tarentaise cows that lend their milk for these behemoth wheels—about eighty pounds (36 kg) each—graze along the alpine pastures. After the milk has been coagulated and cut, large beechwood hoops are used to collect the curd. It is then left to set overnight, thus giving the distinctive concave sides of the cheese. The wheels are then moved to spruce planks, where they receive a daily massage of salt to help form their thick crusts. After a few days of being flipped on the wood, the wheels receive a washing of brine, which introduces the pale yellow hue to the rind. Beaufort is left to age anywhere from six months to a few years. The flavors are rich with the grassy diet of the cows, as well as a nutty roastiness from the wooden aging environment, followed by a slight funk from the dank, cool mountain cellars where they mature. A great treat is a slab of Beaufort with some smoked salmon and fresh chives.

Enjoy with a light white wine, such as a Chablis or a not-too-oaky Chardonnay.

CALCAGNO *(KAL-CON-YO)*

MILK TYPE: Sheep

ORIGIN: Sardinia, Italy

Here's a little secret: When the drain of the day-to-day routine really starts to take hold, and the grind of the job edges on the precipice of despair, the mind likes to wander to Sardinia, with its ocean-kissed breezes and aquamarine waters. It's at these times when this raw milk pecorino comes in handy—one bite and the cares of the day drift away as you picture yourself on the beaches of Sardinia. These large wheels—roughly forty pounds (18 kg)—are aged for about a year and are made from the milk of sheep that graze upon the island's craggy terrain, munching on its natural foliage. When the wheels have set, they are then sent to the aging facilities of Casa Madaio in the town of Castelcivita in the southwest of Italy. Calcagno has a sweet, herbaceous flavor profile with a dense, salt-studded paste. You can practically taste the sun-drenched hillsides with each bite.

Enjoy with a dusty bottle of red wine and shaved over roasted cauliflower and anchovies.

CANESTRATO *(CAN-S-TRAH-TOE)*

MILK TYPE: Sheep

ORIGIN: Basilicata, Italy

There are many varieties of Canestrato found throughout Italy, but we find there is no better representation of the cheese than the ones selected and aged by the Madaio family. Taking its name from the reed basket it was traditionally formed in, this raw sheep's milk cheese is made in southern Italy and wears a beautiful relief on the rind from the forms the wheels are drained in. Aged for a minimum of twelve months and upward of two years, the paste is dense and minerally, with a bright sharpness presenting notes of straw and hazelnuts. The rind is often used for flavoring stock, as it possesses rich oils that are released when heated.

Enjoy with a spicy red, a strong dark ale, or even a sweet white at dessert.

CAPROTTO *(KAH-PRO-TOE)*

MILK TYPE: Goat

ORIGIN: Campania, Italy

The goats that roam the mountains in the Cilento region have access not only to some of the most beautiful land in Italy, but they also get to forage on all the fresh grass and herbs that grow in this terrain. The wheels are selected by the Madaio family to age in their cellars, a stone's throw away in the town of Castelcivita. These natural-rind, dense wheels wear the reliefs of the baskets they are formed in, are a pale straw color, and weigh between five and six pounds (2.3 and 2.8 kg) each. While the age profile varies based on the affineur's choice, you can expect to find them in the range of five months to one year old. For the more aged wheels, look to the rind for wear and slight mottling of gray and blue molds. Caprotto presents unmistakable notes of lemon peel, black pepper, and hazelnuts on the palate with aromas of wild herbs and minerals. It's a goat cheese for anyone who says they don't like goat cheese. And though it may be on the pricier side of the cheese spectrum, it is truly a showstopper on any cheeseboard.

Enjoy with a light Friulano and some sliced kiwi.

CHALLERHOCKER *(HOLLER-HOCK-ER)*

MILK TYPE: Cow

ORIGIN: Canton of St. Gallen, Switzerland

A true Swiss original, Walter Rass was once a famed Appenzeller (see page 86) maker who decided to take a chance on innovation. The production of Appenzeller is a highly regulated affair (see page 38), with much incentive for cheese makers, allowing them to feel secure and taken care of by the consortium. This is great on one level, affording the cheese makers a steady paycheck, but on another level, there is no room for creativity and very limited self-expression in the cheese being made. Using the same base recipe as Appenzeller, Walter blends together different starter cultures and adds secret ingredients to the brine used for washing these wheels. The end result is an exquisitely savory creation that has hints of vanilla yogurt, charred leeks, browned butter, and butterscotch. The rind smells slightly of honey roasted peanuts, and the fudgy paste is malty and sweet. This is a great cheese for anyone who loves the nutty tang of a Swiss cheese but is ready to take their taste buds to the next level of lactic love.

Enjoy with a bright Kölsch or a glass of Riesling.

COMTÉ *(CON-TAY)*

MILK TYPE: Cow

ORIGIN: Jura, France

Comté is one of the most widely loved cheeses throughout France. Due to its wide-ranging flavor profile, which varies depending on how long it is aged and the time of year it is made, Comté stands as an example of how a cheese can become the backbone of a community. The fruitières (cheese makers) in the valley work directly with the farmers to ensure the best quality milk possible. These fruitières make several wheels of cheese a day in the farmers' dairies, and a few days later, once the cheese has set enough to be moved up the mountain, the wheels are transferred to old military forts for aging. The younger cheeses—about nine to twelve months old—are mellow and silky, with a pliable texture that melts incredibly well and has slight notes of unripened bananas and cocoa powder. As they develop—about a year to eighteen months—they are infused with a sweet depth of burnt sugar and brown butter. After a few years of aging, they can develop a musky warmth that maintains the caramelly sweetness with a wide range of tropical-fruit notes, such as pineapple and guava. A fun cheese plate to present to friends is a "flight" of Comté at different ages, as each one really does taste unique.

Enjoy alone with a glass of slightly oxidized white wine from the Jura Mountains or as an addition to a fondue.

CONSIDER BARDWELL FARM RUPERT

MILK TYPE: Cow

ORIGIN: Vermont, United States

Inspired by alpine-style cheese production, the folks at Consider Bardwell Farm in West Pawlet, Vermont, make these large wheels of sweet raw Jersey cow's milk and leave them to age anywhere from six to upward of eighteen months. This whale of a cheese (by the way, there is a whale stamped into the rind of each wheel) is a richly flavored, densely textured example of what American farming and cheese-making are accomplishing. Starting out as a supple, approachable cheese with notes of rich cream and flowers, Rupert gains a refined complexity that develops into flavors of tropical fruit, dank stone, and rich soil. Taking its name from one of the oldest towns in Vermont, this cheese is a great example of old world traditions in new world production.

Enjoy with a crisp pilsner on a warm day.

EMMENTHALER *(EM-NN-TALL-ER)*

MILK TYPE: Cow

ORIGIN: Emmental, Switzerland

Probably the most visually recognizable Swiss cheese out there, this pure, almost plastically smooth cow's milk behemoth of a wheel is riddled with perfectly round eyes that range in size from acorns to golf balls. In "normal" cheese production, the presence of such large holes is considered a sign of bad cheese production, but in Emmenthaler, a special blend of three different types of bacteria is introduced to the milk before it is heated and turned to curd. As the wheels age, this combination of bacteria consumes the lactic acids present in the cheese and burps out carbon dioxide, which form the holes. Relatively mild in flavor, this is an incredible melter, and is most often found as an ingredient in fondues and mac 'n' cheese. The pleasantly buttery taste is heightened with a slightly sour milk tang that lends itself nicely as an addition to any starchy meal. Baked into a tray of penne or melted into mashed potatoes, Emmenthaler adds a mild "cheesy" quality without overpowering other flavors.

Enjoy with wheat beers and a cooked salami, such as mortadella.

FLIXER *(FLICK-SIR)*

MILK TYPE: Sheep

ORIGIN: Graubünden, Switzerland

A rarity in the Swiss world, this alpine-style sheep's milk cheese is a flinty joy ride of woolly bliss. Affineur Rolf Beeler works closely with the producer before selecting the perfect wheel to receive his stamp of approval, which is also known as his label. The producer has a small flock of twelve sheep that is only milked May through September. The small amount of milk produced accounts for the small size of these wheels. After being aged for about a month and a half, and receiving brief washings with a light salt brine, these wheels develop into robust little nuggets of explosive flavor. The roasted nutty flavor reveals hints of toasted hazelnuts and sautéed brown rice, while simultaneously having the distinctive floral notes of the fresh grass and wildflowers these sheep graze upon.

Enjoy with a light white wine, such as Chablis or Vinho Verde, as well as with a selection of marinated and pickled vegetables.

GRUYÈRE *(GREE-AIR)*

MILK TYPE: Cow

ORIGIN: Fribourg, Switzerland

One of the most famous Swiss cheeses around, Gruyère is similar to Comté (see page 125) in that its flavor profile ranges drastically depending on age and time of year that the wheels are produced. When on the younger side—about six to ten months old—the sweetness is balanced with an overt butteriness. As they age a bit—a year to eighteen months old—the cocoa notes become more prominent, and a slight tang develops from the frequent brine washing they receive in the aging rooms. After twenty months, the texture develops into a flinty firmness that sometimes has those pockets of amino acids that crunch and pop with every bite, and all the savory notes develop into a meatiness that can taste like a honey-glazed ham. There are several Gruyère producers but only eight aging facilities, which means that the art of the aging process is funneled through few hands. Gruyère is a highly regulated Swiss cheese that is not only name protected (see page 38) but each wheel is also graded on size, taste, smell, and appearance, with the most prestigious wheels receiving the top score in each category. Alpage productions are produced only in the summer months and have incredibly complex flavors that are wild and grassy, with no two wheels alike, depending on the patch of land the cows decide to graze upon that day. An incredible cheese to cook with, Gruyère elevates any quiche or frittata, but it is also excellent to munch on by itself.

Enjoy with a chilled glass of Riesling.

HOCH YBRIG *(HOCK-E-BRIG)*

MILK TYPE: Cow

ORIGIN: Canton of Schwyz, Switzerland

Produced from the raw cow's milk of a dairy near the famous ski area that is this cheese's namesake, Hoch Ybrig is a dense, musty, and nutty treat that feels like a smaller Gruyère (see facing page). The addition of white wine to the brining process provides a subtle sweetness that plays well with the controlled decay of the rind. Ah, yes, sweet rot! Selected by affineur Rolf Beeler and imported by Caroline Hostettler, the wheels weigh in at around fifteen pounds (7 kg) each, with a rust-colored rind that darkens with age. Use this fact as a guide when purchasing this cheese— you may want a younger wheel that has a more buttery flavor profile with notes of sweet, wet grass, or a wheel of more age that presents flavors of toasted nuts, dry hay, and a bright spiciness on the finish. Hoch Ybrig is a bold flavor to introduce into a pot of fondue, or simply munch on a wedge alongside some air-dried beef.

Enjoy with a tall glass of Scrimshaw Pilsner.

IDIAZABAL *(ID-E-OZ-EH-BALL)*

MILK TYPE: Sheep

ORIGIN: Navarre, Spain

A mildly smoked sheep's milk cheese from the heart of sheep country, traditionally these wheels were stacked next to the chimney of the cheese-maker's hut so that the smoke would gently permeate the paste, creating almost a whisper or afterthought, opposed to the heavy-handed smoked cheeses that taste a lot like an ashtray. The wood mix of cherry, birch, pine, and beech imparts a sweet, almost nutty quality to the cheese. Although Idiazabal has been name protected (see page 38) since the 1980s, there are two versions that can be found in the marketplace: The non-smoked version is floral and grassy when young, developing a brownish natural rind as it ages and becoming slightly bitter and flinty in flavor. The smoked version develops similarly, and is only smoked after the wheels have been aged to the desired texture and flavor profile. This cheese especially complements seafood and is lovely with a shellfish paella or grilled mussels

Enjoy with fruity rosés and luscious Vihno Verdes.

JASPER HILL FARM

Greensboro Bend, Vermont, United States

Brothers Andy and Mateo Kehler are Vermont boys through and through. Two carpenters who came to the realization that they would like to do meaningful work in the state that they love, they decided to hang up their hammers and focus on dairy farming and cheese-making. This meant understanding what their herd of cows would need to graze on, what would be the best cheeses to make, and where they were going to house it all. The Cellars at Jasper Hill were born from the age-old role of the affineur in the European cheese system (see page 32). The Cellars allow cheese makers to turn over their younger cheeses to the watchful and skilled eyes and hands of the cheese crew at Jasper Hill, helping the cheese makers to get a quicker return on their cheeses, because they don't need to wait months until the cheese is ready for market to get paid. The cheese makers can then focus on the care of their animals and the initial cheese-making process, both huge, time-consuming jobs. As Vermont continues to grow as a cheese mecca, the Kehler brothers continue to spearhead innovative community growth with everyone supporting each other and improving the cheese-making process.

KOOLPUTTER *(COOL-PUTT-ER)*

MILK TYPE: Sheep and cow

ORIGIN: Limburg, Belgium

Koolputter, or "coal miner," pays homage to the industry that once thrived in the Limburg province of Flanders near the Dutch border. This raw milk blend of sheep and cow's milk is made by Peter Boonen at Catharinadal (see page 182) in the town of Hamont-Achel, where he also produces Grevenbroecker (see page 182). Koolputter is a dense and spicy wheel that has strong elements of traditional Pecorino, yet holds a sweet, buttery character thanks to the addition of the cow's milk. Aged for roughly a year and coated in black wax to emphasize the importance of the coal miners to the history of the area, Koolputter has aromas of hay, butterscotch, and fresh grass, with a dense, somewhat flinty paste that melts brilliantly on the tongue. Rarely seen outside of eastern Belgium, if you can find this cheese, give it a try.

Enjoy with a tall glass of Achel Bruin.

LA JEUNE AUTIZE *(LA JUNE OH-TEES)*

MILK TYPE: Goat

ORIGIN: Bordeaux, France

Affineur Rodolphe Le Meunier (see page 68) gets these wheels, which are essentially a goat's milk version of Morbier (see page 134) at a young age—around two months old—from his chosen producer in Bordeaux and transfers them to his aging facility in Tours. There, he meticulously watches over them, washing the rinds when necessary with a brine measured specifically to achieve the flavor profile he desires. La Jeune Autize is an orange-colored-crusted wheel that weighs around nine pounds (4 kg) and has a pronounced sweet, earthy aroma on the rind. When cut open, the paste is ivory with a galaxy of vegetable ash strewn throughout, and gives off aromas of sour milk, lemon peel, and dried hay. The texture is fudgy yet semi-firm and breaks down incredibly well under the heat of the mouth.

Enjoy with a glass of Sancerre or Crémant de Loire, along with crisp apples.

YOU ARE WHAT YOU EAT

Mahón (right) has a slight but clearly pronounced saltiness to its flavor. This is due in part to the sea salt content of the grass that the cows eat on the windswept island of Minorca in the Mediterranean Sea. This feed-to-flavor corollary is also seen in other cheeses, such as Camembert avec Calvados (see page 90), which gets its apple overtones from both the Calvados that it is washed in and the fallen apples that are consumed by the cows who produce the milk to make this cheese.

L'ETIVAZ (LA-ET-EE-VA)

MILK TYPE: Cow

ORIGIN: Vaud, Switzerland

Created in the early 1900s by a collective of Gruyère producers who wanted to go back to the traditional cheese-making methods after the consortium started regulating how Gruyère (see page 128) was made, L'Etivaz is basically an old world Gruyère. Made exclusively from the milk of the summer months, when the cows are grazing freely along the mountainside, this milk is heated over open wood fires in large copper cauldrons. The process brings about a richer, creamier texture than the contemporary versions of Gruyère. Nutty and caramelly with a earthy tang and hints of smoke, these pure cow's milk giants—wheels weigh in around fifty pounds (23 kg)—are so layered and nuanced in flavor, that it's almost impossible to absorb the spectrum in just one bite. A great melter, L'Etivaz is just as impressive incorporated in cooking as it is as an addition to a cheese plate. Grate into a recipe for a gratin, or present on a cheeseboard with a salad of green apples with toasted sunflower seeds and bitter greens.

Enjoy with a funky, naturally fermented cider or a Jura white wine.

MAHÓN (MA-HONE)

MILK TYPE: Cow

ORIGIN: Minorca, Spain

The small island of Minorca is a dairy-producing dream. With more than six hundred cattle farms, Minorca is one of the leading cheese producers in Spain, with the milk yield being used for dairy production. Mahón has been a name-protected (see page 38) cheese since the 1980s and is one of the most famous cheeses to come from the island. With a unique squat shape, the form resembles a square paving stone, and has a golden rust-colored exterior. The rind is rubbed with either butter, oil, or a combination of both and pimenton (a Spanish paprika), giving it its reddish shade. When young, Mahón is pliable and mellow, with a buttery front and a slightly yogurty finish. As it ages, Mahón becomes slightly salty, with a mellow tang. All ages have a mild sweetness, resembling milk chocolate and honeycomb. Mahón melts incredibly well, lending itself nicely to the addition to many dishes. Try paired with smoked ham for a great snack or cubed up in a salad. It is also very nice thinly sliced and wrapped around scallions for a broiled dish of sweet and savory. Traditionally, Mahón is presented sliced, with a drizzle of good olive oil, a sprinkle of sea salt, and some coarsely chopped tarragon.

Enjoy with a bright red, such as a balanced Pinot Noir, or with a light pilsner.

MASTORAZIO *(MASTOR-AHT-ZEE-HO)*

MILK TYPE: Sheep

ORIGIN: Campania, Italy

The ode to the mastery of aging cheese, Mastorazio is a raw ewe's milk cheese that is selected at a young age by the Madaio family to age further in their caves in the southwest of Italy for anywhere between twelve to eighteen months. This timeline for maturation is considerable for a cheese of this size—five to six pounds (2.3 to 2.8 kg), on average—but does only good things to develop its flavor profile. Without becoming overly flaky and fragile, this Pecorino has a compact, pale-straw-colored paste that releases notes of minerals, herbs, and toasted hazelnuts. Mastorazio has a wonderful piquant and somewhat fatty finish on the palate, with the rich sheep's milk breaking down in the heat of the mouth.

Enjoy with a Nebbiolo or Dolcetto and a plate of smoked proscuitto and melon, or shaved atop a hot bowl of pasta.

MORBIER *(MORE-BEE-A)*

MILK TYPE: Cow

ORIGIN: Franche-Comté, France

Hailing from the mountainous region that Comté (see page 125) calls home comes this visually alluring masterpiece. It was originally created as the by-product from leftover curd from Comté production. When the cheese maker did not have enough curd to make another large wheel—Comté weighs in around eighty pounds (36 kg)—he would pile up the curd into a smaller cheese form—Morbier weighs in at around twelve pounds (5.5 kg)—and then dust the top with the ash from the fire used to heat the milk during the cheese-making process. The following day, the cheese maker would pile on the remaining leftover curd, and after a few weeks of aging in a cave and being flipped and washed every so often with a salt brine, a ripe wheel would be ready for market. Morbier proved to be so popular that it began to be the focal point of production, and no longer a means to use up too small amounts of curd. Morbier has a peach-toned rind with a pleasant, hay-like scent that can sometimes take on notes of wet soil and tree bark. The pliable, squeaky paste is a bit yolky in flavor, with gentle undertones of warm butter and overly ripe berries. Often confused for a blue cheese because of the vein of vegetable ash running down the center, Morbier is a beautiful addition to any cheeseboard, and is sublime thinly sliced over a pile of roasted potatoes.

Enjoy with a musky Sancerre or robust porter.

PAGLIERINO *(PAG-LEE-OH-RENO)*

MILK TYPE: Sheep

ORIGIN: Campania, Italy

These little sheep's milk balls weigh in at about five pounds (2.25 kg) each and are an incredible representation of high-quality milk being aged by experts to create an exceptional cheese. Literally translating to "straw," this cheese develops a deep yellow hue as it ages, along with an uncanny flavor reminiscent of its namesake. As the cheese is aged to about six months old, the paste develops a deep amber color, with a sweet, woolly flavor that is nutty and roasted at the same time, followed by an unmistakable Meyer lemon–like finish. The texture is dense yet creamy, and has the divine effect of melting in your mouth. The rich and lush sheep's milk gives off an animal-like butteriness to these wheels as they age. This is a great Pecorino for anyone who loves an Italian sheep's milk cheese, but wants something slightly more delicate and subtle.

Enjoy with a robust white, such as a Pinot Grigio, or a summer cocktail, such as a vodka gimlet, alongside a big tray of vegetable-filled lasagna.

PARMIGIANO-REGGIANO *(PARM-EE-JOHN-OH REG-EE-ON-OH)*

MILK TYPE: Cow

ORIGIN: Parma, Reggio Emilia, Bologna, Modena, and Mantua, Italy

The king of Italian cheese, Parmigiano-Reggiano has been a coveted craft since 1200 AD. The process to make these grand wheels is highly regulated by a consortium (see page 38). The cows are milked twice daily, and the evening milk is left out overnight in large shallow vats so that the cream rises to the top. That cream is then skimmed off in the morning and made into some of the sweetest butter known to man. After the cows are milked in the morning, the milk is combined with the now-skimmed batch from the previous night, which creates an incredibly balanced liquid that has hints of fresh grass and warm cream. The specialized copper-lined vats that the cheese is made in are big enough for only two wheels to be made at a time. Traditionally, any bits of leftover whey from the cheese-making process are used to feed pigs that are housed near the dairy. These pigs are later slaughtered and their meat is cured into Prosciutto di Parma. Throughout the specified regions of Italy that are granted permission to produce Parmigiano-Reggiano, farmers sell their wheels to Parmigiano "banks" that house and age the massive wheels—the average weight is about eighty pounds (36 kg)—so that the farmer receives payment faster, and the wheels can be tended to for a minimum of twelve months. The consortium then judges each wheel and classifies if it is good enough to receive the brand of Parmigiano-Reggiano. An incredible cheese to grate over any salad or pasta, it is perfect as a cheese plate focal point, drizzled with a reduced balsamic vinegar.

Enjoy with Prosecco.

PATA DE MULO *(PAT-AH DE MOUL-O)*

MILK TYPE: Sheep

ORIGIN: Castile and León, Spain

These flattened little logs of sheep's milk cheese are aged on wooden planks. The name, translating to the "foot of the mule," is derived from the unique appearance of these "wheels." Its relatively mild flavor leans away from the sometimes salty or pithy qualities familiar of Spanish sheep's milk cheeses. Much more minerally and sweet, Pata de Mulo is a great cheese for anyone who likes the richness of sheep's milk cheese, but prefers the robust nuttiness of an aged cow's milk cheese. Its firm-to-dry texture makes it a candidate to be shaved over roasted root vegetables, a frittata, or even a steaming bowl of gnocchi.

Enjoy with a sweeter white wine or fruit-forward red. It also pairs well with *membrillo*, also known as quince paste, and cured ham.

PECORINO DELLE BALZE VOLTERRANE DOP
(PECK-OH-RENO DELL BALL-ZAY VOL-TEAR-ANH-A)

MILK TYPE: Sheep

ORIGIN: Tuscany, Italy

Cheese maker Giovanni Cannas makes this raw milk Pecorino with vegetable rennet produced from a local wild artichoke. The rounds are then coated in organic extra virgin olive oil and delicately rolled in olive wood ash. Due to its unique flavor and appearance—*balze*, referring to geological outcroppings surrounding the nearby medieval hill city of Volterra—it now has official DOP (see page 38) status. Weighing in at about three-and-a-half pounds (1.5 kg) each and aged approximately three months, these rounds are made from some of the best sheep's milk in the world. It is a fantastic cheese to shred over roasted root vegetables or sautéed bitter greens.

Enjoy with a lighter-bodied red from the Tuscan region.

POINT REYES FARMSTEAD CHEESE CO. TOMA

MILK TYPE: Cow

ORIGIN: California, United States

The picturesque rolling hills leading to the Northern California coastline is where the Giacomini family has been making great cheese under the name Point Reyes Farmstead Cheese Co. since 2000. They first won our hearts with their Original Blue (see page 189), and then went on to score even more points with this quintessential table cheese simply named Toma. These buxom wheels weigh about ten pounds (4.5 kg) each, are made solely with the pasteurized milk from the Giacomini's herd, and are aged around three months before going to market. Toma is a semi-firm, extremely lactic cheese that has notes of sea-kissed grass and sweet butter. Every once and a while, we hold on to a few wheels and let them age, resulting in flavors of light caramel and almond. This is a fantastic cheese for cooking, as it melts extremely well and is quite flavorful without being overpowering.

Enjoy with fresh plums and a bottle of IPA.

RONCAL *(RON-CALL)*

MILK TYPE: Sheep

ORIGIN: Navarre, Spain

Hailing from the Spanish side of the Basque region, Roncal is a name-protected cheese (see page 38) that can only be produced from December until July. The sheep graze on the wild, open pastures of this valley, and the herbaceousness of the land comes out clearly in the milk as these wheels age. The marble-toned rind has a blue-green quality with a gray overtone. The floral paste develops a woolly bite and slight tang as it ages. Although the cheese develops little eyes throughout the paste, the texture is slightly grainy yet pliable. There are hints of green olive and caper berries, while at the same time, uncanny notes of almond and grass comes through on the tongue. A great sheep's milk cheese, and a must-have for anyone who knows and loves Manchego (see page 158), Roncal is a superb table cheese. It is especially indulgent crumbled over trout grilled with lemon and herbs.

Enjoy with a rustic red wine, such as a Tempranillo, as well as with hearty dark bread and fresh figs.

SCHARFE MAXX *(CHAR-FF MAXX)*

MILK TYPE: Cow

ORIGIN: Thurgau, Switzerland

Three cheese masterminds came together to create this raw cow's milk original that has extra cream added to the rich milk before being turned into curd. The milk that supplies these wheels comes from a collection of farms in the valley that surrounds the dairy. The young wheels receive a good washing with an herb-enriched brine as they age. The dairy has resided along the edge of Lake Constance since 1867 and used to only produce Emmenthaler (see page 126). The dairy now turns out a dozen original-recipe cheeses, and Sharfe Maxx stands out. The dense and fudgy paste holds a world of flavor: young garlic meets spring ramps, which meets roasted chicken skin and toasted cashews. These six-month-old wheels are packaged with a label of a charging bull. The name Scharfe Maxx loosely translates to "someone who is a bit aroused," and after one bite, you will understand why. Cubed up and baked with some boiled elbow pasta, this cheese will make any mac 'n' cheese a crowd favorite.

Enjoy with a robust lambic or even a honey wine.

SOVRANO *(SOH-VRAH-NO)*

MILK TYPE: Cow and water buffalo

ORIGIN: Lombardy, Italy

Aged for at least a year and a half, Sovrano is a unique cheese that blends the rich and lush milk from cows with the fatty and tangy milk of the water buffalo. Most people compare the sweet, fruit-forward tang with its cousin, Parmigiano-Reggiano (see page 135), but the difference really lies in the nuances. While Parmigiano-Reggiano develops a robust tropical tang, Sovrano stays in the balanced berry-fruit world. Hints of ripened raspberries and dark cherries hide within the crystalline paste, riddled with the crunchy pockets loved in aged cheeses. A great table cheese to accompany any steaming pile of pasta, try grating it into a meatloaf for an umami flare.

Enjoy with most beverages—from elderflower cocktails to sparkling reds, there is nothing this cheese can't stand up to.

SPRING BROOK FARM TARENTAISE *(TEAR-EN-TAY)*

MILK TYPE: Cow

ORIGIN: Vermont, United States

When their friends at the neighboring dairy, Thistle Hill, traveled throughout the Alps to learn about the best cheese to make that matched the climate and altitude of their home in North Pomfret, Vermont, they came up with an adaptation of the famed French Beaufort cheese that is truly an American innovation. In the spirit of true community, the cheese makers at Thistle Hill shared their discovery with the folks at Spring Brook Farm (see below), and now there are two very distinct flavor creations coming from one small corner of Vermont. Everything begins with the quality of the milk, and the Jersey herd grazes on the lush green of this region. The rather large wheels—on average about seventeen pounds (8 kg)—are aged in the on-site caves for about six months, being turned and tended to daily. As the rich milk ages, the sweetness of it is heightened, developing a burnt sugar, toasted almond quality. Tarentaise is an excellent table cheese and accompanies cured meats well. For a next level BLT, add a thick slab of this to that crispy bacon and ripe tomato, and be prepared to lose your mind.

SPRING BROOK FARM

MILK TYPE: Cow

Reading, Vermont, United States

The folks at Spring Brook Farm in Reading, Vermont, have a mission to educate children living in urban environments about agriculture and food systems. Their Farms for City Kids Foundation offers the hands-on engagement of cheese-making, as well as the awe-inspiring terrain of Vermont, and lets kids experience firsthand what it is like to not only know where food comes from, but to actually have a hand in producing it. Spring Brook currently makes three cheeses, all inspired by French cheese-making traditions. The longest-aged—about six months —Tarentaise, is a sweet and caramelly creation that has the grassy and floral hints found in aged alpine-inspired cow's milk cheeses. Their Reading Raclette is a great and buttery melter that has slight hints of wet soil and unripened banana. Their newest creation is the Morbier-inspired Ashbrook, a hearty cheese with the traditional line of ash separating the milkings that go into each wheel. Each of these cheeses is a great representation of an American cheese maker's creative interpretation of a European base, and the best part of eating Spring Brook Farm's cheese is that with every bite, you may be helping a future cheese maker.

TETILLA

MILK TYPE: Cow

ORIGIN: Galicia, Spain

Literally translating to "little breast," this squat Hershey Kiss–shaped cheese does resemble its namesake. A name-protected cheese (see page 38) since the early 1990s, these pure cow's milk dollops have a pleasantly squishy texture and rather mild flavor. After being aged in warm, humid cellars, they develop a rich, buttery, slightly tangy taste that has a balanced salt level. The yellowish paste develops little eyes throughout, giving a rather airy, pliable consistency. Ranging in weight from about two to four pounds (907 g to 1.8 kg), a whole wheel of Tetilla makes for an impressive presentation, surrounded by fresh figs and dates. Its tangy notes complement roasted chicken or braised meats, and it is incredible shredded over a piping hot bowl of turkey chili with lots of spices and cilantro.

Enjoy for a dessert course alongside a bottle of port.

TOMME D'ALSACE WELSHE *(TOHM D-AL-SAY-ACE)*

MILK TYPE: Cow

ORIGIN: Alsace, France

A superbly lactic cow's milk cheese from the Alsace region, these mellow wheels get a healthy bathing in local white wine as they age. The slightly earthy, truffly notes are balanced by a fruity sweetness that is elevated with the washing. A great melter, this buttery beauty is a worthy alternative for a Gruyère or Cheddar in an omelet or on a burger. It also has a meaty finish that pairs well with aged salamis, highlighting the cheese's earthy undertones.

Enjoy with a sweet Alsatian white wine and experience how it elevates the taste of the cheese on your palate.

BEER BUDDIES

Cooked/pressed cheeses tend to be grassy, nutty, funky, and fudgy. Their texture and flavor profiles make them a wonderful match for beers of many styles—whether it is a Saison with some fruity residual yeast and a light texture on the palate and a beautiful slice of Spring Brook Farm Tarentaise (see facing page) or a malty Doppelbock with a wedge of Challerhocker (see page 125), the world of beer and cheese pairings is a seemingly endless array of possibilities. Experimenting is part of the fun of serving cheese. Go to your local fine beer purveyor, pick up a mixed six pack (or two) and then head over to your favorite cheese counter and tell the monger what beer you have selected. Together you will be able to craft some exploratory tasting companions that may just unlock a whole new world of taste.

UPLANDS CHEESE PLEASANT RIDGE RESERVE

MILK TYPE: Cow

ORIGIN: Wisconsin, United States

An award-winning alpine-style creation that was mastered by the amazing cheese makers Mike Gingrich and Dan Patenaude has continued to evolve into greatness by the Hatch and Mericka families since they took over the Uplands farm in 2014 (see below) after apprenticing there for several years. Their herd of cows was one of the first in the country to be put on rotational grazing. This progressive yet extremely traditional feeding trend moves

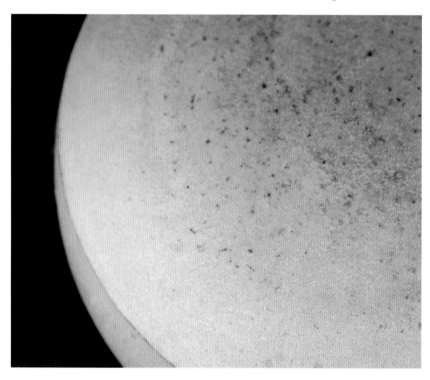

the herd throughout the rolling hills during the year, so they are munching on the freshest greens, while allowing the land they just left to regrow to its nutritious prime. The lush and rich milk that these cows yield from May to October is the base of perfection for the Pleasant Ridge Reserve. Aged from nine months to two years, the buttery paste develops into a sweet, caramelly, candy-like treat that will please even the most fickle of cheese lovers. Melted over a grilled beef patty with a spread of caramelized onions for an amazing burger, or grated over a steaming bowl of stew, this cheese adds layers of decadence.

Enjoy with a healthy pour of Bourbon and prepare for a good night.

UPLANDS CHEESE

Dodgeville, Wisconsin, United States

Situated in the Driftless Area of Wisconsin, Uplands Cheese has been producing handcrafted wheels made from the milk of their own herd since 1994. Neighboring farmers Mike Gingrich and Dan Patenaude invested in this three-hundred-acre plot of rolling hills with the mission to produce some of the best milk in the country. An innovative farmer, Dan had been practicing rotational grazing with his own herd since the 1980s. The two knew their herd was producing exceptional milk, and they wanted to find the best cheese to craft from this liquid gold. After years of researching traditional French and Swiss cheeses that were suited for the climate and quality of their own land, they came up with the recipe for Pleasant Ridge Reserve. Two young apprentices worked alongside Dan and Mike, learning the trade and craft of animal rearing and cheese-making. In 2014, these apprentices and their families— Andy and Caitlin Hatch and Scott and Liana Mericka—officially took over the farm and dairy, allowing the master cheese makers to relax and enjoy all that they have created, and thus giving the next generation of cheese makers the reins to evolve and grow.

WILDSPITZ *(VEAL-DUH-SPITS)*

MILK TYPE: Cow and goat

ORIGIN: Canton of Schwyz, Switzerland

Three generations of this cheese-making family have been producing alpine creations in this village dairy since 1926. An innovative twist on the classic pure cow's milk wheel, this cheese gets a tangy kick with the addition of goat's milk. The combination of the two milks creates a sweet and caramelly front that has a slight barnyard-like finish that ends with a wave of floral notes. The wheels are washed a few times a week with brine as they age for around four months in the caves of the dairy. The production and ingredients of the cheese are certified organic. The goat's milk is mellow and balanced, and infuses the cheese with a slight funk. Wildspitz is a great cheese to add to a classic mac 'n' cheese recipe, or to grate over thinly sliced boiled potatoes and place in the broiler for a bubbly, golden brown, gooey treat.

Enjoy with a Grüner Veltliner or a light rosé.

WOODCOCK FARM CHEESE COMPANY WESTON WHEEL

MILK TYPE: Sheep

ORIGIN: Vermont, United States

Using the raw ewe's milk from their flock of East Friesian sheep, Woodcock Farm has produced a round, nutty, and floral wheel that is reminiscent of a younger Pyrenees sheep's milk cheese. Aged from anywhere between four and ten months, the natural-rind Weston Wheel has a fudgy texture with a sweetness akin to burnt caramel and toasted hazelnuts. The aromas of wildflowers and lush grass are a testimony to the quality of the land these sheep graze upon. We like to bring these wheels in at a fairly young age and let them develop for a couple of months, when the more gamier, woolly notes begin to surface.

Enjoy with sliced figs and a glass of Dolcetto.

PULLED CURD

Pulled-curd cheeses are the family of cheeses also known as *pasta filata*, which literally translates from the Italian to "spun paste." After the initial process of coagulating the milk, the curds are cut into relatively large pieces—about the size of acorns and walnuts. The curds are then left to settle for several hours so that the whey drains naturally, meaning no pressing is done to extract more liquid. Once the whey drains, the curds are heated in hot water, making them supple and spongy. The curds are then gathered together and pulled to form long ribbons; these ribbons are twined and folded back onto themselves, and pulled again, in a similar manner to how taffy is made. The act of pulling the newly formed curds, as opposed to cutting and pressing them into a mold, creates a creamy, elastic texture that is pleasantly pliable and silky. The range of textures and flavors found in pulled-curd cheeses— from the young and supple Mozzarella (see page 145) to the brittler and beefy aged Provolone (see page 146)—comes from the aging process and, of course, the milk.

BURRATA

MILK TYPE: Cow or water buffalo

One of the most-loved and decadent cheeses from Italy, burrata is basically a satchel of freshly pulled Mozzarella (see facing page) cradling a center of cream and cut-up curd. To make this cheese, some of the curd is pulled into a smooth, silken sheet and cut curds and cream are placed in the center of the "sheet," and then it is cinched closed forming these yummy little sacks. This joyride of lactic wonder screams out summertime freshness, as this is the season when burrata is at its best, and the cows and water buffalo are yielding lots of rich milk. A great way to present one of these little balls—they average about three-quarters pound (340 g) each—is to split it over a bowl and watch the white wonder swirl about. Drizzle in some good olive oil and add some basil and cherry tomatoes for an incredible variation on a classic summer salad.

Enjoy with a white wine spritzer and a bowl of fresh berries.

CACIOCAVALLO *(CACHE-EH-O-KA-VALL-OH)*

MILK TYPE: Cow

ORIGIN: Southern Italy

Originating in southern Italy and bound together by rope during the aging process, these teardrop-shaped sacks of aged dairy were named Caciocavallo, which translates to "cheese on horseback," because the ropes often straddled a branch or hook as one would straddle a horse. During the make process, the curds are stretched and spun so the edible exterior forms a smooth and protective barrier for the developing strands of the slightly softer interior cheese. There are many kinds of Caciocavallo found throughout Italy, varying mainly in age and the cow's milk used, and the nuances these elements impart to the flavor make it a cheese that never gets old. It's the perfect accompaniment to a classic antipasti plate of mortadella, olives, and marinated artichokes.

Enjoy with a glass of spicy red wine.

MOZZARELLA

MILK TYPE: Cow or water buffalo

ORIGIN: Southern Italy

The most well-known cheese in the pulled-curd family, mozzarella is a beloved treat for anyone who loves dairy. Because of its pleasantly mellow and lactic flavor, mozzarella is a great accompaniment to many dishes. After the cow or water buffalo's milk has been coagulated, the curd is cut into large bits—about the size of a hazelnut—and are then heated through and pulled into velvety little balls. The shiny white exterior of the cheese opens up to a middle that is bursting with fresh flavor. Mozzarella melts like a dream and is great for traditional applications, such as on pizza or in a caprese salad, but it should also be experienced in other ways, including ribboned over a plate of sautéed zucchini that is then placed in the broiler to brown.

Enjoy with a big wet white, such as a Pinot Grigio.

PARISH HILL CREAMERY KASHAR

MILK TYPE: Cow

ORIGIN: Vermont, United States

One of only a few aged pulled-curd cheeses to be produced in the United States, Kashar is inspired by the famed Turkish cheese of the same name. The curd is pulled and then put into basket molds to drain, which imparts a textured pattern on the developing rind. The milk for these wheels comes from a herd of cows that graze upon the pristine pastures found in northern Vermont. This rich and nutritious milk ages to a flavor that is creamy and caramelly, with a slightly grassy finish. When young, the paste is satiny smooth and has a pleasant pliability. As the cheese matures, it becomes a bit brittler in texture but maintains its lovely mellowness. Kashar pairs perfectly with Mediterranean-inspired foods, such as grilled lamb kabobs or a lentil salad with lots of herbs and spices and topped with chunks of seared tuna.

PROVOLONE

MILK TYPE: Cow

ORIGIN: Campania, Italy

One of the most ubiquitous Italian cheeses, Provolone is a greatly misunderstood culinary treasure. These rather large pieces—weighing anywhere from fifteen to eighty pounds (9 to 36 kg) each—range in form from pear-shaped to giant loaves to oblong creations. As much as they differ in shape and size, provolone also varies widely in both flavor and texture. The young and silky Provolone Dolce, which is aged from two to four months, is sweet and creamy, with a slightly yeasty, sometimes tangy after note. The paste is lusciously smooth and melts incredibly well. The more aged (older than four months) Provolone Piccante can develop a brittle and grainy texture, with a bite and heat that borders on tannic and metallic in flavor. The aged versions are not  for the faint of heart and can sting your tongue, not unlike licking a battery. The Dolce is divine shaved over grilled sausages served on a soft roll for an incredible sandwich, while the Piccante is a great treat shredded over a bowl of vanilla gelato with a drizzle of a very aged balsamic vinegar.

Enjoy with most red wines, including a Nebbiolo for a younger provolone and a Barbera for a more aged version.

RAGUSANO *(RAG-EW-SAHN-OH)*

MILK TYPE: Cow

ORIGIN: Sicily, Italy

These massive loaves of cheese weigh in at about forty pounds (18 kg) each and are one of the oldest cheeses to come from Sicily. With production dating back to the 1500s, Ragusano is a DOP cheese (see page 38). The milk comes from the Modicana breed of cows that is required to graze on grass or be fed hay (depending on the time of year) in order to comply with the cheese production. When on the younger side, around four months old, the paste is creamy, buttery, and sweet with hints of soft caramel and clarified butter. When more aged, over six months, the pale yellow paste develops a lush golden hue and begins to intensify in tang and bite. The more aged variety starts off with a nutty bite, growing more peppery toward the back of the tongue. Ragusano is a great accompaniment to fresh green vegetables. Grate a generous dusting over a plate of sautéed broccoli di cicco and garnish with toasted almonds and marinated anchovies for an incredible summertime dish.

Enjoy with dark beers and stouts.

SCAMORZA *(SKA-MORE-ZAH)*

MILK TYPE: Cow

ORIGIN: Calabria and Apulia, Italy

Made in a similar fashion as Mozzarella (see page 145), Scamorza undergoes an aging process once it has been shaped. The cheeses are hung in suitably dry environments in small bunches, cultivating a rust-colored rind that protects the lactic, chewy paste. The hanging creates the pear shape of the cheese and also provides its name—in southern Italy, Scamorza translates to "beheaded." There are two versions of this cheese: Scamorza and Scamorza Affumicata, or Smoked Scamorza. The smoked version is more readily available and what one is most likely to encounter. While pleasant enough as a snack, scamorza is a good substitute for mozzarella in any cooking dish if you want to add a little more oomph to the taste. Try it in baked ziti or atop a pizza with mushrooms and speck.

PIZZA WITH STYLE

Most people wouldn't dare use an aged Provolone (see facing page) or Parish Hill Creamery Kashar (see facing page) for pizza, but isn't playing around with recipes in the kitchen a big part of the fun? When planning your next pizza party, offer some new cheeses instead of (or in addition to) that good old standby Mozzarella (see page 145). Having a variety of toppings, such as shaved asparagus, sautéed mushrooms, and sliced coppa, goes great with an assortment of cheese. We love these more robust, fuller flavor options to grate or ribbon over the top of the pie as it bubbles and browns in the oven.

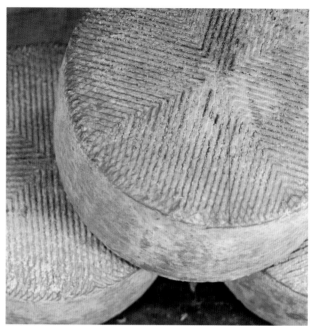

NATURAL RIND

Natural-rind cheeses have the most organic and feral exteriors, and also take on the most flavors of the places where they are aged. After the initial cheese-making process, a natural-rind cheese is placed into a cave or cellar, which allows it to attract the natural, positive bacteria and flora of the environment to create a colony on its rind. Some of the natural-rind cheeses receive an initial washing to encourage the development of the rind, attracting bacteria to other bacteria. Predominantly uncooked and pressed during the make process, this group has a wide variety of flavor profiles, textures, ages, and sizes. Each cheese forms a unique—as in one-of-a-kind—rind to protect and influence the developing paste. Natural-rind cheeses can vary tremendously depending on the seasons and regions in which they are produced.

ALPE LOCH *(ALP LOCK)*

MILK TYPE: Cow

ORIGIN: Allgäu, Austria

Only one wheel of this amazingly complex cheese is produced a day by the Fuchs family (see below). Crafted strictly during the summer months when the herd is high up the mountainside, eating the freshest, moistest green around, each wheel produced is fully unique, like a snowflake. Depending on what they chose to graze upon, the outside temperature, and their mood that day, the cows produce milk that is a fingerprint of the specific moment before they yield their liquid gold. These wheels are aged about one year before making their way to a counter, and the flavor is a rich illustration of just how complex and interesting cheese can be. A tropical wave of pineapple and guava paste is met with a metal tang and salty finish. The paste is riddled with the crunchy flavor pockets that occur when amino acids clump together with age. Normally pale brown, the rind can sometimes be more burnt ochre in color or a deep amber hue. The cheese holds so many complex flavor notes that it is hard to describe what you might find. Burnt chocolate, tobacco, cured ham, and tannic richness all lie inside. A real rarity and a true gem when found, this is a great cheese for anyone who loves bigger flavors and a little kick.

Enjoy with a crisp light ale to really elevate your palate to pick up on all of the cheese's subtleties.

FUCHS FAMILY

This husband-and-wife duo spend most of the year living in the lush valley of the Alpe Loch in Austria, where they raise, breed, and sell dairy cattle. Every summer, the two begin the journey with their herd up the mountain to their little milking chalet. While the low-lying grass begins to die out in the heat and dryness of the summer months, the grass and wildflowers in the higher elevation stay fertile and green longer into the season. The cows are left to roam freely along the mountainside, enjoying the lackadaisical lifestyle and consuming all the glorious green they desire. They are milked daily, yielding just enough milk to produce one wheel of Alpe Loch (see above), an amazing, truly handcrafted alpine cheese. The one wheel that is made daily is left to age in the cool stone cellar underneath the house. When fall comes, they pack up their herd, and their small lot of wheels, and begin the descent back to the reality of village life. But from June until September, the Fuchs get to live a pastoral life, enjoying the simple and solemn pleasures of being one with the land.

ARDI GASNA *(ARE-DEE GAW-SNAW)*

MILK TYPE: Sheep

ORIGIN: Midi-Pyrénées, France

The Basque region of France has a rich history of shepherding and cheese-making, and this cheese encapsulates the artistry of this area and its people. Ardi Gasna literally translates to "sheep cheese." The mountainous landscape of this territory is treacherous and isolating, the ideal spot for a shepherd and his flock to make a home. The milk for these wheels comes from a small cooperative of farmers whose sheep graze on the wildflowers and grass that blanket the rustic mountains. During the summer months, these sheep wander the land, satisfying their appetites on the rich green foliage. The cheese is at its best when made from the milk produced in the spring and summer because that is when the milk has the richest complexity as a result of the natural diet of the sheep. The wheels are aged anywhere from three months to a year in stone caves that are carved out in the mountainside, where they develop a tie-dye appearance of brown, gray, yellow, and orange molds on the rind. The paste is firm yet has a luscious melt-in-your-mouth quality. The flavors run the gamut from floral and lactic to woolly and rustic, with hints of almonds and oysters. This cheese is a great representation of the traditions and craftsmanship of cheese-making at its finest.

Enjoy with a chilled Chablis and a plate of grilled sardines drizzled with olive oil and a sprinkle of parsley.

BERKSWELL *(BERKS-WELL)*

MILK TYPE: Sheep

ORIGIN: West Midlands, England

Produced from the raw ewe's milk of their mixed-breed flock near the village of Berkswell, the folks at Ram Hall, a dairy and cheese producer, have perfected this cooked-curd, basket-drained cheese that is reminiscent of a fine Italian pecorino. Aged for approximately six months, on average, Berkswell is shaped like a flying saucer, displaying the marks from the draining basket on its light-brown rind that turns a darker shade of chocolate brown with age. Weighing about five pounds (2.3 kg) each and using only traditional animal rennet, the paste is pale straw in color, with a flinty yet dense texture. Aromas of bread and tropical fruit are complemented by a flavor of toasted hazelnuts and a bright acidity that resembles that of a pineapple.

BETHMALE *(BETH-MALL)*

MILK TYPE: Cow (traditionally) and goat (sometimes)

ORIGIN: Midi-Pyrénées, France

Dating back to the twelfth century and named after the town of its origin, Bethmale is an airy, fudgy flavor whirlwind for your mouth. Traditionally made with cow's milk, but sometimes a cow and goat's milk blend or only goat's milk, these wheels with peach-hued rinds are yolky, floral, earthy delights that encapsulate so many different flavors and nuances that no two wheels taste the same. The cow's milk and mixed-milk versions tend to be a bit earthier and slightly funky, with small pockets of white bloom on the rind. The pure goat's milk wheels are more floral and sweet, depending on the time of year the milk is yielded and how long the wheels are aged. Bethmale is great paired with fresh fruit, particularly apples. A fun plating is to serve it alongside a selection of different apples to see which notes of the cheese are highlighted with each apple. For example, a tart, tannic green apple brings out the minerality of the cheese, while a sweeter, juicier Fuji brings out the clover notes.

Enjoy with beer—a bottle of Affligem Blond is great alongside a wedge and a hearty helping of apple cobbler.

BRA TENERO (BRA TAH-NER-OH)

MILK TYPE: Cow

ORIGIN: Piedmont, Italy

The Tenero, or "tender" cheese of the town of Bra is a raw cow's milk wheel produced in Italy's northern region of Piedmont. There are three varieties of Bra—Tenero, Duro (aged), and Alpeggio (alpine)—made only with milk produced between the months of June and October when the cows are at pasture. While all three types of Bra are high quality, we find Tenero to be the most accessible and, thanks to a decent price point, versatile in the kitchen. Aged between three and six months, the rind is light amber in color, embracing a supple paste studded with small eyes and a semi-firm texture. The flavors range from fresh milk to grass to roasted nuts. Bra Tenero is a classic table cheese, amenable to a multitude of beverages and snacks, and will melt very nicely in the next calzone you make.

CANTAL (CON-TALL)

MILK TYPE: Cow

ORIGIN: Auvergne, France

A cheese whose name has been tarnished due to the industrialization of cheese-making, Cantal is one of the quintessential cheeses made in the mountainous Auvergne region of France. This cheese is named after the surrounding Monts du Cantal. The soil of this area is rich in minerals from ancient volcanic activity that affected the composition of the pastures on which the cows are raised. This cheese is made only between November and April, and during the winter months, the cows are fed hay that has been harvested throughout the warmer season. There are two types of Cantal available: Fermier (a farmhouse version made with raw milk) and Laitier (a commercial version made with pasteurized milk). We prefer the Fermier type. Each wheel weighs in at around eighty to ninety pounds (36 to 41 kg), and has a crumbly, cheddar-like consistency. Aromas of dank earth and soil are backed with a creamy, lactic assertiveness.

Enjoy with red wines of all types.

CLARA

MILK TYPE: Goat

ORIGIN: León, Spain

Made with pasteurized goat's milk, Clara is aged for about three months. It has a flaky texture and presents flavor notes of lemon peel and wet stone, with a subtle caramel sweetness on the finish. The small wheels—about one pound (454g) each—have a firm yet supple ivory paste. Resembling the stony crags the goats climb to get to the green that gives them nutrition, the exterior of Clara is naturally pock-ridden thanks to the microorganisms that feed off its rind's flora. Clara is a lovely treat for anyone who might enjoy a goat cheese but is a little timid of its barnyard factor. A nice way to present this cheese is alongside a rice salad with wedges of preserved lemon and topped with slivered toasted almonds.

Enjoy with citrusy whites and ales.

COBB HILL ASCUTNEY MOUNTAIN

MILK TYPE: Cow

ORIGIN: Vermont, United States

Cobb Hill Cheese was born out of a sustainable co-housing community in Hartland, Vermont, in 2000. Using only the raw Jersey cow's milk from the animals born and raised on the land, they produce two varieties of cheese: Four Corners, a Caerphilly-style cheese and Ascutney Mountain, the rugged-looking wheel that was originally based on a Swiss Appenzeller recipe. Named after a local mountain, Ascutney Mountain is aged between seven and eight months and has an evenly developed natural, brown-colored rind that shows light wear from aging, opening up to a buttery, straw-colored paste that can be flecked with small eyes and dashes of crystalline texture, depending on age. Notes of fresh grass, onion, and butter cream are topped off with a supple, easy-on-the-palate texture and finish.

Enjoy with hoppy pilsners, brown or red ales, or a glass of Viognier along with some fresh fruit.

CORNISH YARG

MILK TYPE: Cow

ORIGIN: Cornwall, England

Produced on England's southwest peninsula, this alluring wheel of rich, almost custardy pasteurized cow's milk is one of the more aesthetically pleasing cheeses you will come across. Taking its name from the inversion of the original cheese maker's last name (Gray) and wrapped in attractive deep green leaves from stinging nettle plants, Cornish Yarg begins its life similar to that of Caerphilly—the curd is produced, cut, and drained in the same manner. After an initial curing period, the wheels are wrapped with the nettle leaves that have had the sting removed from them, and then it is aged in humid conditions that cultivate slight blooms of white mold on the rind. The paste has a beautiful golden complexion with a semi-firm texture and yeasty notes.

Enjoy alongside some salty anchovies and a tall glass of cold Kölsch.

CORSU VECCHIU *(CORE-SURE VECK-EE-YOU)*

MILK TYPE: Sheep

ORIGIN: Corsica, France

The Mediterranean island of Corsica is home to nimble sheep that traverse the rugged terrain in search of wild herbs and foliage to munch on. The milk from the ewes is used to make wheels of Corsu Vecchiu, which are aged anywhere between six to nine months in humid cellars and average around five pounds (2.3 kg) each. The rind is a chalky-white to dusty-gray shade that gives way to a paste of pale gold with a smooth and rich texture. Notes of herbs, hazelnuts, and oysters combine with the fattiness of the milk to create a very seductive cheese that pairs well with seafood. Serve a wedge with a platter of garlic-dusted grilled shrimp and a chunk of crusty bread.

Enjoy with dry white wines and stone fruit.

GARROTXA (GAH-ROW-SHA)

MILK TYPE: Goat

ORIGIN: Catalonia, Spain

An incredible goat's milk cheese from the land of sheep, Garrotxa has been in existence for a long time, but its production was greatly decreased under the reign of Franco, who placed production limitations on the dairy industry. In the early 1980s, a cooperative of young cheese makers decided the traditions of this almost-forgotten cheese needed to be continued. These dense little pucks of cheese weigh about two pounds (907 g) each, on average, and are roughly the size and shape of a small loaf of boule bread—the small size shortens their aging time. The rather mellow and balanced milk from the Murciana goats develops into this pleasantly delicate and floral cheese. The soft, light-gray rind protects the slightly brittle yet velvety paste. The flavor gamut runs from raw hazelnuts and fresh wet soil to wild lilac and charred acorns, but with none of that bucky, goaty quality found in younger cheeses. Incredible when paired with fried potatoes, such as a patatas bravas, or diced and stuffed into a baked potato, Garrotxa is also lovely with a big bowl of toasted almonds.

Enjoy with a chilled glass of Chardonnay or Pinot Grigio.

GORWYDD CAERPHILLY (GORE-WID CARE-FULL-EE)

MILK TYPE: Cow

ORIGIN: Somerset, England

Sometime during the first half of the nineteenth century, the Welsh town of Caerphilly birthed this style of cheese, which is traditionally a crumbly cross section of flavors and textures. At Trethowan's Dairy, the tradition continues, as the wheels of Gorwydd Caerphilly are produced with the care and attention it takes to cultivate the complexity of this cheese. Using only raw cow's milk and traditional animal rennet, these wheels are aged in cellars of high humidity, creating an environment that encourages the gray and white molds that cover the rind. The interior is like two cheeses in one: near the rind, there is a dense line of chewy cheese; the center of the cheese is cakey and crumbly. Aromas of dank earth and mushrooms pop off the rind, and a pronounced citrusy lemon-peel flavor is balanced by the rich, lactic quality of the paste.

Enjoy with IPAs that have a citrusy hop profile or with white beers with residual yeast.

LA MAROTTE *(LA MARR-OH-TT)*

MILK TYPE: Sheep

ORIGIN: Massif Central, France

Produced by the Coopérative Fromagère des Bergers du Larzac, a group of eighteen families farming in the Larzac area in the south of France, La Marotte is a tommette made from thermised (a gradual pasteurization process) ewe's milk and aged in a multilevel cave construct nestled into the hillside. The aging environment for the cheese allows the natural rind to bloom colorful, positive bacteria across its exterior. Aged from anywhere between three and ten months, the paste of these little cylinders varies from being supple and chewy with notes of fresh herbs and flowers to a drier, more assertive texture that presents flavors of pineapple and roasted nuts.

LAVORT *(LA-VORE)*

MILK TYPE: Sheep

ORIGIN: Auvergne, France

A wholly unique creation, Lavort is a pure sheep's milk cheese that has a soft, gray, and furry rind, and a dense, caramel-hued paste with a floral aroma and flavor. This cheese was invented by the cheese makers at the Fromagerie de Terre Dieu, where the dairy specializes in raw-milk production, particularly focusing on the rich sheep's milk of the Lacaune breed that is also used in the famed Roquefort (see page 190). Lavort captures the rich, woolly characteristics of the milk, while highlighting the meaty, grassy undertones of the milk that develop with maturation. The sheep graze on pasture from April to September, which is the only time of year this cheese is crafted. Made in two sizes—the larger version weighing in at about five pounds (2.3 kg) and the smaller version around two pounds (907 g)—the cheese has a round form with indentations on the top and bottom. Once the wheels have been formed, they are aged on fir planks that impart a roasted, woodsy quality to the cheese. The natural environments where they mature impart a rainbow of bacteria on the rind, ranging from pockets of soft yellow and white to streaks of orange and brown. There is a musky aroma on the rind and a sweet fermentation to the paste. Serve a wedge alongside fresh figs and blueberries as the beginning to a meal of roasted leg of lamb and springtime asparagus.

Enjoy with medium-bodied reds, such as a Merlot with melon overtones, or a hoppy ale, such as Maine Beer Company's Mo, a vibrant pale ale.

MANCHEGO *(MAN-CHAY-GO)*

MILK TYPE: Sheep

ORIGIN: La Mancha, Spain

Probably the most well-known Spanish cheese, manchego is an incredible example of what a truly great sheep's milk tradition can become. Historically and exclusively made from the milk of Manchega sheep and crafted by the women of the villages throughout La Mancha, manchego has grown to be almost a name brand. When the region began to industrialize the cheese, you could only find versions that were cranked out of factories. In the last few decades, there has been a rebirth of farmstead productions, and now the "true" version can be found again. A quality manchego should have a grassy, flinty, woolly explosion of flavor. Think of a slightly wet wool sweater—that smell is this taste. Riddled with hints of green almonds, fried garbanzo beans, and grilled sardines, there is so much going on in terms of flavor depth that the rubbery, bland industrial imposters should not be called "manchego." You can go the classic Spanish route and pair it with some dried chorizo, Marcona almonds, quince paste, and a glass of Estrella Damm beer, or try something new and have a wedge alongside a pile of toasted pumpkin seeds dusted with a bit of cayenne, some dense, dark seedy bread, and a Dunkel beer.

MONTGOMERY'S CHEDDAR

MILK TYPE: Cow

ORIGIN: Somerset, England

Often called the king of cheddars (and we can't really argue with that moniker), Montgomery's Cheddar is a clothbound, farmhouse work of art and a surefire hit for anyone in the market for this particular style of cheese. By wrapping the wheels in layers of linen adhered with lard, Mr. Montgomery's Cheddars (see page 160) are able to ferment and embrace the positive molds that are present in the aging facility through the porous nature of the cloth, giving them a well-rounded depth of flavor. Selected by Neal's Yard Dairy for export to the United States, the wheels vary in age from twelve months to upward of eighteen months. The buttery, grassy, crumbly paste gains a pleasant peppery complexity with age, and it is not uncommon to find wheels with slight bluing in the paste. Each wheel weighs in at around forty-five pounds (20 kg), and it is always a pleasure to break them down, inhaling the deep aromas of dank basement and fresh pasture and nibbling on the finest crumbles from the heart of the cheese.

Enjoy with ales of various hop profiles along with the sweetness of crisp apples.

MONTGOMERY CHEESE

In southwest England, in the village of North Cadbury in Somerset, Jamie Montgomery and his crew produce cheese every day of the week, including one of the best clothbound cheddars on the market. A third generation cheese maker, Mr. Montgomery is hands on with every aspect of the cheese-making process, working to ensure the flavor profiles of the wheels going to market are representative of the land he cares for. Montgomery Cheese produces their signature cheddar (see page 159), a smoked cheddar, and an alpine-influenced wheel, named Ogleshield, from the milk of Jersey cows that also graze the pastures of the farm. Ogleshield is a robust, nutty creation that is a rare treat that should be sought out from your cheesemonger.

MRS. KIRKHAM'S LANCASHIRE (LANE-CASH-EAR)

MILK TYPE: Cow

ORIGIN: Lancashire, England

A true family affair, Mrs. Kirkham's Lancashire is a plump, buttery, and crumbly wheel of raw cow's milk produced in northwest England. Selected by Neal's Yard Dairy for maturation and export, the wheels are made by Graham Kirkham following his mother's recipe and using the milk his father pulls from the cows. The complexity of this curdy, sour treat derives from the combining of curds from three days of cheese-making, a tradition that dates back to when farmers did not have enough cows to yield milk for an entire wheel of cheese on a given day. By using very little starter culture, this allows the cheese to naturally ferment over the make process, producing flavor profiles that are expressive of the natural spirit of the milk. The exterior of the cheese is layered with butter to not only protect the development of the interior, but to also boost the creamy, lactic explosion this cheese has on the palate. This is a great cheese for Welsh rarebit or served alongside green apples.

Enjoy with a pint of Fuller's London Pride.

OLD FORD

MILK TYPE: Goat

ORIGIN: Somerset, England

Few cheese makers have the patience and care it takes to craft a wheel of this nature. Using the raw milk from her goat herd, Mary Holbrook creates each wheel of Old Ford herself, striking a balance of sweet, salty, and bitter. This is a rare cheese that exhibits a true mastery of craftsmanship and control over the cultivation of decay. Aged at ambient temperatures during the warmer months in an old stone shed on her farm, Old Ford has a rugged exterior, exhibiting impressions of the cheesecloth used to wrap the wheels in their formative stages, as well as deep-earth-tone colors, such as topsoil brown and mossy green. The paste of the cheese is dense and somewhat brittle and flinty, with a sharp, tannic bite that evens out the sweetness of the goat's milk. This piquant cheese is excellent when delicately shaved over a summer vegetable and grain salad.

Enjoy with a bottle of off-dry cider.

OSSAU IRATY *(OH-SAW EE-RAW-TEE)*

MILK TYPE: Sheep

ORIGIN: Midi-Pyrénées, France

There are only two sheep's milk cheeses in all of France that are granted the AOC label (see page 38), and this is one of them. A wheel that has come to represent the rich history of the Basque cheese makers, Ossau Iraty is an incredibly complex creation that has all the nuances of the wide-ranging diet that the sheep in this region feast upon. Although this cheese has been name protected since 1980, the recipe is hundreds of years older. Once upon a time, the remote and isolated Basque region was a cocoon, as not many people traveled up to this mountainous area. When these wheels eventually made their way down to the marketplace, people fell in love with this flinty, floral, tangy, and nutty creation. The paste has a seductive firmness that can develop a slightly grainy texture when on the older side, after being aged for around a year. The rind is light gray in color, with slight tones of browns and olives from the cacophony of bacteria that are in the air of the caves where the wheels are aged. Try a plate of cured olives and pickled cauliflower with a wedge to bring out its subtle brininess.

Enjoy with light-bodied reds and whites, or a funky hard cider.

PECORINO MASCHIO *(PECK-OR-ENOT MA-CHI-OH)*

MILK TYPE: Sheep

ORIGIN: Tuscany, Italy

Known for its beautiful sheep's milk cheese, Tuscany has provided us with this treasure: Percorino Maschio, a raw, organic wheel aged a minimum of twelve months in its homeland. Each wheel weighs in around five pounds (2.3 kg) and looks like a cylinder of stone. Rust- and gray-colored spots cover the rind—which is embossed with small notches from the basket the cheese was formed in—that protects a paste that is dirty gold in color and spotted with small eyes. The aging process brings out the intense mineral flavor of the sheep's milk, with notes of pepper and dried herbs. There is a marked animalistic quality to this cheese, as flavors of mutton and barnyard bounce off each other, accompanied by the silky fat that announces its presence when brought to a proper temperature (i.e., not cold). For those who are looking for a full-flavored pecorino for snacking or as an addition to a recipe, Pecorino Maschio is the one for you.

PUITS D'ASTIER *(PAH-WEE DUH-STEE-AA)*

MILK TYPE: Sheep

ORIGIN: Auvergne, France

A powdery, donut-shaped wheel, Puits d'Astier is made from the mineral-laden sheep's milk from the Auvergne and can be found in various states of age. Translating to "well of Astier," this cheese with a pillowy rind has an affinity for blossoms of yellow flowers across its brilliant white exterior. Aged on straw mats to create a truly balanced and developed rind, Puits d'Astier has a slight cream line when very young that develops into a fudgy and dense cheese with a more intense layer of yellow mold between the rind and paste with age. This cheese is truly a work of art and should be paired with whatever fruit is in season.

Enjoy with a glass of Orvieto.

RASCHERA *(RAW-CHER-AH)*

MILK TYPE: Cow, sheep, and goat

ORIGIN: Piedmont, Italy

One of our favorite cheeses for the table and cooking, Raschera takes its name from the alpine huts found in the Cuneo province in northern Italy. The cheese is shaped in large squares, a form that was traditionally made for easier transport when the wheels came down from the mountains, where the Alpeggio version of the cheese is still made. Each slab weighs in at around twenty pounds (9 kg) and presents a dark gray, almost stone-like exterior appearance. The chalky-white interior is a semi-firm  explosion of sweet-and-sour milk, studded with very small eyes produced during the fermentation process. The three types of milk incorporated into the mix create an appealing flavor that is at once buttery and earthy yet also acidic and tart. Raschera is mellow enough to appeal to the timid cheese consumer, but rich and flavorful enough to keep the connoisseur going back for more. Its application in the kitchen is what endears this cheese the most: it melts like a dream and should become a staple when making pizza.

Enjoy with about any red wine.

ROCCOLO *(ROW-KO-LOW)*

MILK TYPE: Cow

ORIGIN: Lombardy, Italy

One of the most far-out and interesting cheeses available, Roccolo comes via the alpine valley of Val Taleggio in northern Italy. These richly colored brown cylinders are named after the traditional hunting lodges of the province that are similar in shape. Translating to "bird snare," Roccolo is an exquisite cheese. When it is right, the rind smells of dank earth and charred nuts. The paste is a beautiful cross section of cakey and crumbly sweet-and-sour cow's milk in the center and a silky, somewhat elastic texture near the rind, which is given gentle washing during maturation to feed the bacteria and bring out a smoky, aquatic flavor profile.

Enjoy with a glass of Verdicchio and some fresh berries.

WHEN MOLD IS A GOOD THING

Mold and bacteria may not sound very appetizing, but they are a key component in creating cheese. Bacteria are purposely introduced into cheeses at either the milk stage or after they have been shaped. Cheeses have to be carefully monitored, however, to make sure that the bacteria are helpful and not harmful.

Natural-rind cheeses are a sturdy lot and love a good mix of bacteria in the air to develop the proper rinds. A controlled aging area that has harbored many natural-rind cheeses to maturation has developed a force field, in a sense, of positive molds to protect the cheeses from harmful intruders, such as insects or negative bacteria that could harm the final product. The molds that grow contribute to the flavor and help protect the cheeses while they age.

ROS *(ROWZ)*

MILK TYPE: Sheep

ORIGIN: Catalonia, Spain

One of the lesser-known sheep's milk cheeses to come from Spain, Ros is made from pasteurized ewe's milk by Can Pujol, a cheese producer in Catalonia. The milk is sourced a stone's throw away from the dairy, where the sheep graze on the hillsides that are kissed with a Mediterranean seabreeze and possess a mineral-rich soil that encourages the growth of the wild foliage. This cheese has a quite firm exterior, dusted with gray molds, which protects a dense interior that is crumbly and sweet when young and a harder texture when aged for about a year. Ros is a sweet and earthy cheese, holding notes of roasted almonds, brown butter, and pears and is a great accompaniment to smoky chorizo.

Enjoy with dry Spanish ciders.

SAINT NECTAIRE *(SAINT NECT-TEAR)*

MILK TYPE: Cow

ORIGIN: Auvergne, France

The milk from the hearty Salers, Holstein, and Montbéliarde breeds of cows are used exclusively in the production of Saint Nectaire. These cows graze on the volcanic soil of the Auvergne, creating a base that has a strong mineral flavor for this classic French cheese. The recipe dates back to the seventeenth century, and although there are two distinct types of Saint Nectaire, it is an AOC-protected product (see page 38) and must be aged a minimum of sixty days. After the initial steps of transforming this rich and slate-flavored milk into curd, draining the whey, and forming it into a tomme shape, Saint Nectaire receives a washing of salt brine. This helps stimulate the growth of the rind as well as attract the positive bacteria. Once the cheeses have set for a day, they are transferred to straw mats made from rye where they develop their natural rinds as they age. Aging on rye mats imparts a roasted, grassy flavor to the earthy milk. Saint Nectaire is a rich and earthy cheese with notes of blanched cashews and damp grass. A great addition to any meal, try serving a wedge alongside a beef stew.

Enjoy with similarly earthy wines, such as a Burgundy or Bordeaux.

ST. SULPICE (SAINT SAUL-PIECE)

MILK TYPE: Sheep

ORIGIN: Midi-Pyrénées, France

Aged by a cooperative of affineurs in the Auvergne, this fudgy, dense, sheep's milk cheese is a bit more chocolaty and candy-like than its sheep's milk brethren. The wheels are produced by a small community of shepherds, and they begin their aging lives in the caves of the dairy; a few days after the wheels are made, they are transferred to the facilities in the Auvergne, where they are flipped, brushed to remove mites, and tended to for about six to nine months before being ready for market. St. Sulpice is a great divergence from the normally floral and flinty flavor profiles of the milk produced by Pyrenees sheep. The compact paste can develop slight eyes, or holes, as it is aged, but for the most part, the smooth and continuous paste is great for melting as a whole slab over a slice of toasted dark, seedy bread with a smear of grainy mustard. Although this cheese is excellent as a centerpiece on any cheeseboard, it also would make an amazing topping for a tuna melt.

Enjoy with an Anchor Steam or a nutty ale.

TOMME BREBIS FEDOU (TOHM BRAY-BEE FAY-DO)

MILK TYPE: Sheep

ORIGIN: Languedoc-Roussillon, France

This cheese arrives to us with a bow on it. Birthed from the high-quality sheep's milk produced in the plateaus of southern France, Tomme Brebis Fedou is aged between three and six months and is a well-balanced representation of the rich, fatty dairy that these sheep produce. The cheese is wrapped in a raffia bow, and the rind has an even distribution of gray "cat hair" (Mucor) over the exterior. Wheels of Tomme Brebis Fedou have vegetal notes of string beans and mushrooms, leading to a sweet, candy-like yet musty flavor profile on the palate. This cheese can be quite gamy, suitable for people who like a sheep's milk tomme that is a little wilder than the usual round and nutty varieties.

Enjoy with a glass of Mourvèdre and some roasted chestnuts.

TOMME BREBIS TUNNEL *(TOHM BRAY-BEES TOO-NELL)*

MILK TYPE: Sheep

ORIGIN: Midi-Pyrénées, France

A raw sheep's milk cheese that is selected and cared for by a collective of affineurs in the Auvergne, Tomme Brebis Tunnel is a dream of a cheese to sell and to eat. By choosing the young wheels from a cooperative of Basque shepherds, these magicians of maturation cultivate a cheese of such character and nuance, it is unlike any other cheese that we import. The stone-like relief of the rinds shows the wear and pockmarks left behind from the microorganisms present in the aging caves that feed on the rind and varies in shades of brown—darker when younger and paler and more worn with age. The dense paste has a fudgy give when young and a flinty, more crystalline texture with significant maturing time. Pronounced tropical-fruit notes of pineapple, along with roasted hazelnuts, accompany the rich, fatty, lanolin-driven sensations on the palate. Tomme Brebis Tunnel is an all-out crowd pleaser and a surefire way to make your cheese plate shine.

Enjoy with a glass of Côtes du Rhône or a bone-dry farmhouse cider.

TOMME CHÈVRE TUNNEL *(TOHM SHEV TOO-NELL)*

MILK TYPE: Goat

ORIGIN: Midi-Pyrénées, France

One of the more obscure cheeses to grace the pages of this book, Tomme Chèvre Tunnel is the masterpiece of a group of affineurs located in the Auvergne. They take a young goat's milk Bethmale (see page 152), made from the raw milk of Pyrenees goats, and place it in their caves (or tunnels, if you will) until the microorganisms present on the cheese and in the aging environment develop the cheese into a well-rounded wheel with notes of sweet graham cracker, lemon peel, and rich soil. Encrusted with a porous, rust-colored rind, the paste is ivory white, studded with small eyes, and has a plush, toothsome texture. Due to its funky, sometimes earthy notes, this cheese is a great companion to big roasts, such as an herb-encrusted leg of lamb with bulbs of roasted garlic.

Enjoy with demi-sec white wines and pilsners.

TOMME CRAYEUSE *(TOHM CRAY-USE)*

MILK TYPE: Cow

ORIGIN: Rhône-Alpes, France

This cheese is often referred to as "two cheeses in one" due to the duplicity of the paste: the center of this cow's milk tomme is chalky and velvety, while toward the rind, it develops a gooey, custardy texture. This dual-ripening process stems from the ultra-moist caves where Tomme Crayeuse is aged. The deep auburn-colored rind develops spots of yellow and white molds, giving a moth wing–like coloring to the furry exterior. The aroma of the rind is riddled with wet mud and rotting mushrooms, and although the flavor holds an earthy quality, there is a pleasant milkiness that veers toward brown butter and charred hazelnuts with hints of egg yolk. Due to the high moisture that is retained in the cheese during the aging process, Tomme Crayeuse is supple and creamy on the palette. This relatively young cheese, dating back only to the late 1990s, came to be from acclaimed cheese maker Max Schmidhauser who was looking to develop a better Tomme de Savoie (see facing page). Crayeuse translates to "chalky," referencing the center paste's texture. Tomme Crayeuse is excellent with dried salami or a frittata.

Enjoy with a big red wine, such as a Pinot Noir or Nebbiolo.

TOMME D'ESTAING *(TOHM DEE-STANG)*

MILK TYPE: Sheep

ORIGIN: Massif Central, France

Hailing from the plateaus of Larzac in the south of France, this fuzzy-rind sheep's milk tomme resembles a slab of granite in its color and texture. Its light-gray natural rind is speckled with oranges, yellows, and browns—a beautiful mottling derived from the different bacteria in the caves where the wheels are aged. The aroma on the rind is earthy, with a wet grass note, while the paste holds a rich brown-butter aroma, with hints of caramelized lamb fat. As the wheels age from three months to six to nine months, the relatively mellow and floral paste develops a rich earthiness that begins to sweeten as it ages. A fun plating is to serve a slab of this with a wedge of Roquefort (see page 190) from the nearby village, and taste how the caramelly base of milk, from the same breed of sheep, has developed into such different yet complementary creations.

Enjoy with a light sparkling wine or Champagne and notice how the effervescence lightens your palette and plays with all the nuances of this sheep's milk cheese.

TOMME DE SAVOIE *(TOHM DUH SAV-WAH)*

MILK TYPE: Cow

ORIGIN: Rhône-Alpes, France

Traditionally a cheese reserved for the farmer, Tomme de Savoie is made using the leftover skimmed milk from a day of butter production. Historically, dairy farmers would fetch a good amount of money from butter, as there was no wait in the return from milking to market. The cheese was made from the by-product and usually reserved for the farmer and his family to feast upon. The buttery, earthy, supple cheese that became known as Tomme de Savoie was so popular in the marketplace that it carved out a reputation as a fantastic table cheese to be enjoyed with everything from fresh fruit to green salads to a roasted leg of lamb. There are several producers of Tomme de Savoie and at least a dozen affineurs who create their own flavor profiles by aging the cheeses to their liking. Wheels are available in a range of flavors from those that are mellow and balanced, taking on the subtle lactic notes of freshly soured milk, to those that are funky, dank, and slightly manure-esque.

Enjoy with a Beaujolais.

TOMME HAUT BARRY *(TOHM HOT BERRY)*

MILK TYPE: Sheep

ORIGIN: Massif Central, France

On the plateaus of Larzac in the south of France, sheep graze on a variety of wild flora sprouting from the mineral-rich soil. Incorporating the thermised (gradually pasteurized) milk from these ewes, Tomme Haut Barry is a stout, dome-shaped cheese with a firm gray rind that is often flecked with yellow- and rust-colored blooms, or flowers. Continuous dry brushing of the rind during aging allows these flowers to spread positive bacteria across the exterior of the cheese, providing an environment that enhances the mineral qualities of the cheese. Aged for about five months, the interior of the cheese is a mellow golden hue with a dense and pliable texture. Notes of butter, fresh grass, hazelnuts, and wet stone make this a cheese with a great depth of character.

Enjoy with a glass of Chenin Blanc alongside some fresh peaches.

TOMMETTE DE YENNE

(TOHM-ETT DUH YEN)

MILK TYPE: Cow

ORIGIN: Rhône-Alpes, France

A fairly unknown cheese, these raw, organic, semi-firm tommettes come to us from the mountains of eastern France, where they are made by a dairy cooperative in the town of their namesake, Yenne. Surrounded by lakes and rivers, the land has fertile soil, which provides the cows some seriously good green to graze on, giving their milk a wonderful boost of flavor and quality. The natural rind of Tommette de Yenne that envelops the paste is a hodgepodge of colors: steely-gray, rusty-brown, and yellow blooms are all common on its exterior. Uncooked and pressed during the make process, the texture of the cheese is smooth and pliable, with some studding of eyes throughout the golden-hued paste. The custard-colored interior leans toward flavors of asparagus, fresh grass, and touches of pine sap.

Enjoy with red wines from the region or a Bière de Garde.

TOURMALET *(TOUR-MA-LAY)*

MILK TYPE: Sheep

ORIGIN: Midi-Pyrénées, France

These farmstead-produced, little sheep's milk top hats are a great representation of what quality can be when crafted by hand. Super luscious and floral, this dense-paste wonder has all the spring-like freshness that makes the Pyrenees renowned for their sheep's milk cheeses. The rind is golden with a pink hue and smells of hay and daffodils. The sheep graze on the open fields of the mountainside, eating all of the fresh foliage they desire. The mild yolky overtones break through to a caramelly crispness that has a tangy undercurrent of yogurt. This is an example of an extraordinary cheese from a mecca of great cheeses. Pair alongside a meal of grilled trout and boiled potatoes doused with lots of fresh spring herbs.

Enjoy with a lightly sparkling rosé.

TWIG FARM GOAT TOMME (TOHM)

MILK TYPE: Goat

ORIGIN: Vermont, United States

This miniature top hat of a cheese of pure goat's milk has a soft, velvety, and gray exterior, and a dense, ivory paste. The herd of goats that produces the milk for this cheese graze freely in the thick forest that surrounds the creamery. Each day, Twig Farm's proprietor, Michael Lee, takes his ladies for a stroll, where they dine upon fallen pine bark, fresh shrubs, and anything else they can get their teeth into. The wheels are aged in cool stone cellars, where they attract a cacophony of naturally occurring bacteria that develop into beautiful rinds. The flavors are floral and sweet, with a slightly flinty note. There are hints of charred asparagus and roasted cauliflower with an after note of toasted peanuts and roasted mutton. This is an incredible cheese for anyone who thinks he doesn't like goat cheese; the flavors are so layered and nuanced that it is hard not to fall in love with these wheels, as well as Twig Farm. An incredible addition grated over a steaming bowl of penne with a fresh primavera sauce, or sliced thin with watermelon and a drizzle of olive oil, this is a great cheese for cooking with.

Enjoy with a wheat beer, such as Allagash White, or a crisp apple cider.

VERMONT SHEPHERD "VERANO"

MILK TYPE: Sheep

ORIGIN: Vermont, United States

The Major and Ielpi families tend to their flock of two-hundred-and-fifty sheep on their acreage of rolling green hills in the Vermont countryside. Having learned their craft from working with Basque shepherds in the Pyrenees, they translated and adapted these practices to their farm near the New Hampshire border, and over the past decades have crafted one of the best American cheeses available. They produce two types of raw milk cheese: Verano and Invierno. Verano, which is Spanish for "summer," is made during the summer months from 100 percent sheep's milk, produced when the flock is out frolicking in the pastures. Invierno, which is Spanish for "winter," is made with a blend of sheep and cow's milk during the colder months when the animals are tended to indoors. The cheeses are aged in the cave on wooden planks, which, due to their porous and stout nature, provide a proper base for the development of the cheeses, allowing the rinds to breathe and absorb any positive bacteria that may reside in the cave. Aged anywhere between five and eight months, Verano is a brilliant expression of the luscious nature of sheep's milk. The rind is a sandy-beige color that shows signs of age by its pockmarks. The paste is a beautiful shade of gold that releases flavors of toasted nuts and sweet herbs; the texture is firm but pliable, with the cheese melting away on the palate in an extremely pleasant manner.

Enjoy with a traditional Basque cider and watch the sparks fly.

VULTO CREAMERY HAMDEN

MILK TYPE: Cow

ORIGIN: New York, United States

After various experiments to cultivate a wild natural-rind cheese, cheese maker Jos Vulto of the Vulto Creamery has struck gold with his creation called Hamden. Collecting and using only raw milk from a neighboring farm in upstate New York, he crafts each wheel in a similar fashion as his cheese Ouleout (see page 112), but instead of ripening them with a brine solution, he allows the wheels to age in his humid cellars and take on the aerobic molds present in the environment, cultivating a woolly rind that is a combination of gray and white blooms, with the occasional sprouting of blue and green molds. The paste is a rich butter yellow with a pliable, semi-soft texture that releases notes of wet earth, touches of mushroom, grass, and clover. This cheese reminds us of tommes from eastern France, such as Crayeuse (see page 168) and Savoie (169). Hamden is a wonderful domestic cheese from a man who continues to set the bar high with his artistry.

BLUE

Blue cheeses are an enigma in the cheese world due to their variances in appearance, texture, and taste. But what unites them is that they all have the presence of blue molds in them. These bacteria, the desired Penicillium glaucum and Penicillium roqueforti, can be introduced in a few ways. A common method is to inoculate the milk, meaning adding the bacteria to the liquid before the curd is formed. Another process involves dipping metal needles into a slurry that has the bacteria present, and then piercing the formed wheels with the needles so that the molds grow along those channels. The formed wheels can also be placed in an environment that already has the blue bacteria present, and over time, it is attracted to the cheese and attaches itself, creating its own little colony. Blue cheeses can have a natural rind, a washed rind, or even be wrapped in foil. They run the flavor-profile gamut from stereotypically sharp and piquant to delicately citrusy with a light sweetness that is gentle and alluring. Texturally, this group is as varied as it is in flavor and form—from the gloopy Gorgonzola (see page 181) to the brittle and crumbly Cabrales (see page 179). All in all, blue cheese is an often-feared group that really should be explored to be understood and appreciated.

ARETHUSA FARM BLUE

MILK TYPE: Cow

ORIGIN: Connecticut, United States

In the town of Litchfield, Connecticut, Arethusa Farm and Dairy produces some of the finest milk around. The farm's herd of Holstein, Jersey, and Brown Swiss cows is milked twice daily, and then the liquid is transported to the creamery across town where it is pasteurized, but never homogenized. Inspired by Stilton (see page 193), these natural-rind wheels weigh in at around eight and a half pounds (3.8 kg) each, on average, and have a mottled brownish-gray exterior. The interior of the cheese is ivory white with a healthy dose of blue veining that creates an explosion of flavors. The smooth and supple texture bequeaths notes of fresh butter, toasted bread, and subtle pine. If you like Stilton, try a piece of Arethusa Blue on your next cheese plate or crumble on top of pears and then broil them.

BEENLEIGH BLUE *(BEEN-LEE BLUE)*

MILK TYPE: Sheep

ORIGIN: Devon, England

Cheese maker Robin Congdon and his crew create these wheels in the southwest of England from the pasteurized milk of ewes, which he sources from a farm in Cornwall. Based on a Roquefort (see page 190) recipe, Beenleigh has a dense, moist, slightly chewy texture and a rich, full-bodied mouthfeel—the fat from the sheep's milk creates a pronounced and seductive layer of smoothness. Notes of wet stone, hazelnuts, and burnt caramel mingle with spicy molds of green and blue. Seasonally made from milk produced in the spring and summer, Beenleigh is aged for a minimum of five months before going to market.

Enjoy with sweeter ciders, stouts, and smoky meats.

BLAUSCHIMMEL/CHIRIBOGA BLUE *(BLAU-SHIM-MEL/CHEER-E-BOW-GA)*

MILK TYPE: Cow

ORIGIN: Bavaria, Germany

One of the most unique blue cheeses to be found, this dual-named cow's milk creation is a textural wonder. Reminiscent of softened butter, Blauschimmel, also known as Chiriboga Blue, has a seductively creamy texture with a melt-in-your-mouth quality. The milk for these wheels that weigh, on average, five pounds (2.3 kg) comes from a collection of thirty family-run organic farms all within an hour of the dairy. The freshness of the milk is evident in the creamy and lactic flavor profile. Slightly sweet, in the vein of vanilla ice cream, this blue cheese is an exception to the rule of production. During the cheese-making process, the milk is not inoculated with any blue cultures. After the curd has been cut and the wheels have been formed, the extremely supple and moist drums are turned about a half-dozen times during the first twenty-four hours of their lives. This act ensures that the wetness is consistent throughout the cheese. After a few days, metal needles are dipped in the blue cheese cultures and the cheese is pierced with these needles. The effect is a very controlled bluing throughout the cheese, with none of the peppery tang that takes place when the cultures intermix with the milk proteins. Blauschimmel is wrapped in plastic to help maintain the creamy texture and moisture levels; there is no rind developed. This blue is a decadent treat for anyone who loves cheese, and a great gateway for anyone who thinks they don't like blue cheese.

Enjoy with dark stout beers and sweet sherries.

OBERE MÜHLE

Cheese maker Arturo Chiriboga left his war-torn home in Ecuador over fifteen years ago and found a new home in his wife's country of Germany. As a cheese maker in his native land, it was a natural fit for him to land a job at the Obere Mühle dairy where the delicious Blauschimmel/Chiriboga Blue (see page 177) is made. This small facility operates as a self-sustaining venture, generating most of their own energy in the form of hydropower from the creek that runs down the mountainside and under the dairy. Obere Mühle works with a collection of organic dairy farmers, who all ensure the freshness of their product by delivering it only a few hours after the cows have been milked. This small cooperative of farmers has relatively small herds—some as little as three cows ranging up to around eight. This intimacy allows for each farmer to prioritize the care of their animals and the quality of the milk. The dairy also operates as a small inn, providing an education to their guests on their practices and cheese-making methods.

BLEU D'AUVERGNE *(BLUE DOW-VERNE)*

MILK TYPE: Cow

ORIGIN: Auvergne, France

In the 1850s, an inspired cheese maker came up with the recipe and process that began the production of Bleu d'Auvergne. Antoine Roussel realized that the same blue molds that grew on his rye bread would create a wonderfully rich blue inside his cheese. After cutting the curd, he left a good amount of whey remaining and did not press the cheese, in order to leave pockets of air to help the growth of the bacteria. Today, this creamy, sweet, slightly fungal blue has little pockets of fuzzy mold throughout its luscious paste. The rich cow's milk lends a buttery taste that has an earthy appeal due to the bacteria. Blue d'Auvergne is great crumbled into a bowl of red wine vinegar and emulsified to make an incredible blue cheese dressing to drizzle over endives with candied walnuts.

Enjoy with big floral whites and wheat beers.

BLEU DE CHÈVRE *(BLEW DUH SHEV)*

MILK TYPE: Goat

ORIGIN: Loire Valley, France

Produced in the style of Roquefort (see page 190) but without the molds being harvested from rye bread, this goat's milk blue from France is sweet, supple, and barnyard-like, all at the same time. These wheels are produced during the summer months, when the goats graze on the green and lush hilly pastures. The flavor is both floral and candy-like, and is an incredible representation of what a great blue can be. The paste is supple and creamy while being a little grainy on the tongue. There is a slightly musty or goaty aroma that breaks away to the smell of fresh flowers. For a decadent treat with a real flavor explosion, smear a thin amount of this cheese over a hot, fudgy brownie.

Enjoy with a crisp ale or a bright Chenin Blanc.

BLU DEL MONCENISIO *(BLUE DEL MON-CHEN-E-SEE-O)*

MILK TYPE: Cow

ORIGIN: Piedmont, Italy

Produced in small quantities in the area surrounding the Moncenisio Pass between the borders of France and Italy, the Blu del Moncenisio we receive is selected by the master affineurs at Luigi Guffanti for development in their cellars in Arona, Italy. These drums are produced year-round, with the cows on pasture at higher elevations during the summer months, where wildflowers grow among the hearty grass. The curds are ladled into forms, but are not pressed, allowing some moisture to be retained in the body and creating a damp and creamy cheese. Aged for about twelve weeks, they arrive wrapped in foil, weighing about six pounds (2.7 kg) each, on average, and have a soft texture that is densely studded with blue mold. Balanced flavors of pepper, tree bark, and topsoil announce their presence while being subtly whisked away by the lush creaminess of the cheese. Blu del Moncenisio is great for crumbling on salads or stuffing into bacon-wrapped dates and will tempt a person who swears she doesn't like blue cheese into testing her boundaries on a cheeseboard.

Enjoy with a glass of Sauternes.

CABRALES *(KAH-BRA-LESS)*

MILK TYPE: Cow, sheep, and goat

ORIGIN: Asturias, Spain

Aged anywhere from two to four months in humid limestone caves, Cabrales is a peppery joy with a rind of animal funk. Raw cow, sheep, and goat's milk comprise the barnyard-like base for this exceptionally spicy blue. All the animals must be raised and graze in this small mountainous region per the PDO regulations (see page 38). The wheels are aged on wooden planks to help retain moisture and to impart a subtly sappy note. Cabrales is known for its acidic bite and salty start. The deep flavors range from coarsely ground black pepper to the face-numbing, floral hit of a Szechuan peppercorn. Dry and a bit brittle yet with a moist quality, this cheese lends itself to crumbling easily, and is particularly good alongside fresh fruit, such as red grapes. Try this cheese cubed up and tossed in a salad of toasted sunflower seeds, halved grapes, and parsley.

Enjoy with a fruity Vinho Verde or a sharp cider.

CASHEL BLUE
(CASH-EL BLUE)

MILK TYPE: Cow

ORIGIN: County Tipperary, Ireland

Cashel, a beautiful Irish blue, is named after the Rock of Cashel that overlooks the fertile pastures grazed upon by the cows that produce the milk for this cheese. Made by the Grubb family in County Tipperary since the 1980s, Cashel Blue uses milk sourced from surrounding farms and delivered to the dairy at Beechmont Farm, where it is treated with blue molds so that the cheese blossoms with dense blue veins. Each wheel weighs in around three to three and a half pounds (1.4 to 1.6 kg) and has a very white paste when young, evolving to a rich butter yellow at around five months of age. Cashel has a very smooth and creamy mouthfeel—the fat

provides a seductive coating on the tongue, with a sharp, peppery tang from the Penicillium roqueforti. This is a blue cheese for people who love blue cheese.

Enjoy with a pint of Murphy's Irish Stout.

CROZIER BLUE *(CROW-ZUR)*

MILK TYPE: Sheep

ORIGIN: County Tipperary, Ireland

There are a lot of sheep in Ireland—the country boasts some high-quality wool products and some fine shepherd's pie. But as far as dairy sheep go, there aren't a whole lot of them on the Emerald Isle, which makes a cheese like Crozier somewhat of a rarity. In fact, it is the only blue in Ireland made with sheep's milk. Translating to "crook," in reference to the hook on a shepherd's staff, and weighing about three pounds (1.4 kg) a wheel, Crozier has a smooth consistency and a rich, creamy mouth feel, with hints of toasted hazelnuts and earth.

Enjoy with a dry cider.

FOURME D'AMBERT
(FOUR-MA DAM-BEAR)

MILK TYPE: Cow

ORIGIN: Auvergne, France

This cylindrical-shaped blue cheese hails from the lush lands of Auvergne, a region in France known for its cattle-rearing traditions. As one of France's oldest cheeses, Fourme d'Ambert dates back to the Roman Empire. Today, cooperatives throughout this region work together to produce these wheels. Farmers tend to the cows, milking their herd twice daily. The milk is then transported daily to the dairies for cheese production. During the make process the milk is inoculated with Penicillium roqueforti, which develops a mellow sugariness in the cow's milk, as opposed to the peppery heat it becomes in Roquefort (see page 190). Creamy in texture, with a floral earthiness on the nose, this blue is a spreadable wonder that pairs well with any form of rare meat. Melted atop ribbons of rare roast beef for an incredible sandwich, or smeared on top of a seared steak, this cheese loves the iron bite of blood.

Enjoy with a light-bodied Pinot Noir or a tawny port.

GORGONZOLA *(GORE-GONE-ZO-LA)*

MILK TYPE: Cow

ORIGIN: Lombardy, Italy

A classic blue from the mountainous territory in northern Italy, Gorgonzola comes in several different styles. The firmer, more aged Piccante, also known as Mountain, has a beautiful white interior with streaks of blue and green molds, resembling a slab of precious marble. The younger, creamier Dolce is pleasantly supple with a gooey interior and pockets of the same blue and green molds. Gorgonzola Cremificato is a Dolce mixed with heavy cream, creating an indulgent puddle of creamy blue bliss. All of these types are known as Gorgonzola, and they all are made of pure cow's milk from the same region. The history of this cheese tells us that the farmers used to walk their herds up the mountain during the beginning of summer to let the cows feast on the fresh green grasses and wildflowers. At the end of summer, during the procession back to their farms, they would stop in the bustling town of Gorgonzola, which was hub of commerce due to its location. The cheese would be sold there, and legend has it, that's how it got its name. Because there are so many varieties of this blue cheese, it is an excellent addition to any meal. A bowl full of the Cremificato with a drizzle of extra-aged Balsamic vinegar is a seductive dessert. The Piccante is great cubed up and tossed with some steaming hot penne pasta and a dollop of sour cream.

Enjoy all of them with a balanced Barolo.

GREAT HILL BLUE

MILK TYPE: Cow

ORIGIN: Massachusetts, United States

Fifty miles (80 km) south of Boston on Buzzards Bay, the town of Marion is home to Great Hill Dairy, where the milk from a local herd of Guernsey cows is used to create Great Hill Blue, a well-balanced wheel made with raw, non-homogenized milk. Each wheel clocks in at about six pounds (2.7 kg), is wrapped in foil, and has a bone-white appearance with streaks of blue in the interior paste, from where the piercing prior to its maturation allowed the mold to develop. Aged for a minimum of four months, Great Hill Blue has a creamy and slightly granular mouthfeel, with touches of smoke and pepper on the finish. While a pleasant addition to a cheese plate, we find this blue to be excellent crumbled over a salad of mixed greens, apples, and walnuts, or melted atop a perfectly cooked rare steak.

GREVENBROECKER/ACHELSE BLAUWE *(GREV-N-BROKER/ACK-ELSE BLA-OW)*

MILK TYPE: Cow

ORIGIN: Limburg, Belgium

Faced with the task of producing a blue cheese his wife would actually like, cheese maker Peter Boonen of Catharinadal (see below) worked tirelessly to create a recipe that expressed the full-flavored sweet cream of the raw cow's milk he was using and brought out the earthy, fruity flavors of the Penicillium roqueforti he was incorporating. Sometime later (and after patenting the process to make the cheese), Mr. Boonen shaped wheels of Grevenbroecker, which is also known as Achelse Blauwe, by layering the curds into molds and spraying the blue in between each layer to create a beautiful marble effect when the cheese is cut open. The cheese has a supple, very creamy mouthfeel, with notes of fresh butter, dank earth, and pepper. Since the blue is dispersed in an irregular fashion, it is common to have a great variance in the flavors of each bite—some may be more lactic, others more spicy. This cheese feels like a work of art in appearance, quality, and flavor.

Enjoy with an Achel Trappist Dubbel.

CATHARINADAL

Hamont-Achel, Limburg, Belgium

In what was once a Franciscan nunnery in the Limburg province of Belgium, Catharinadal, a cheese-making and retail facility, is run by Peter and Bert Boonen, along with their families. Using the milk from their herd of cows pastured in the province, they produce a litany of cheeses and fresh dairy products (their ice cream is some of the best we have tasted), always experimenting with washes on their cheeses and incorporating traditional herbs and ingredients into their products. Having recently erected a larger cheese-making and aging facility, the Boonens may be able to increase their production, but they will never compromise their standards of quality. Using only raw milk with no preservatives other than salt in their process, Catharinadal is keeping centuries-old traditions alive in Flanders. Look for their Grevenbroecker (see above) or Koolputter (see page 130) and take a taste of history.

HARBOURNE BLUE

MILK TYPE: Goat

ORIGIN: Devon, England

Sourcing the goat's milk from a nearby farm, Robin Congdon follows the same recipe as his Beenleigh Blue (see page 177) to make Harbourne. The wheels resemble giant marshmallows flecked with blue mold—the brilliant whiteness of the goat's milk is somewhat hypnotic once the outer gold foil wrapper is removed. The sweetness of the goat's milk is heightened during the ten weeks or so of maturation time, while the development of the spicy and assertive blue mold takes hold throughout the body of the cheese. Harbourne's texture can vary from dense and creamy toward the exterior to crumbly near the center, and has aromas of candied alfalfa and powerful barnyard. This is a big blue cheese, and not one for the timid.

Enjoy with full-bodied reds or dessert wines.

JASPER HILL FARM BAYLEY HAZEN BLUE

MILK TYPE: Cow

ORIGIN: Vermont, United States

A handmade original from the great dairy dream team in Vermont (see page 130), Bayley Hazen is a Jasper Hill Creamery creation that is aged in their cellars. Made from the raw milk of their own herd of cows, this Stilton-inspired blue is dense and fudgy, with a sensually creamy quality. The flavors run the gamut of a candy shop, with hints of peanut brittle, red licorice, dark chocolate, and burnt caramel. The slightly earthy undertone heightens the butteriness of the rich cow's milk. The natural, delicate rind helps retain just the right amount of moisture so that the paste develops an even quality. Tended to daily, these wheels are matured for at least sixty days, and come out in perfect condition. Crumble into a cauliflower gratin and then brown in the broiler for a great fall treat.

Enjoy with Saison-style beers.

JERSEY BLUE

MILK TYPE: Cow

ORIGIN: Canton of St. Gallen, Switzerland

Willi Schmid samples the raw milk he collects each morning in order to determine which of his cheeses it will be best suited for. When he deems that the rich Jersey cow's milk tastes just right, he creates these dome-shaped, earthy, creamy bombs. By cutting the curd into various sizes and shapes and hand-ladling them into the molds, Schmid creates a brilliant scene of blue veining throughout the paste. The cheese starts its aging process in the cheese-maker's cellar, giving it a dank, moldy aroma amid the nutty notes from the coagulated milk. When ripe, the exterior of Jersey Blue is enrobed completely with bluish-gray mold, and the paste is a rich ivory with shocks of mold running through it. This is a full-flavored, lactic, fruity, and peppery work of art from one of the most forward-thinking cheese makers in the world.

Enjoy with fresh pears and a glass of Gewürztraminer.

LADY'S BLUE

MILK TYPE: Goat

ORIGIN: Drenthe, Netherlands

One of the rarest treats to grace our presence, this exceptional goat's milk blue from the Netherlands is unlike any other cheese we have tried. The couple that makes this cheese lives an almost-utopian existence on their little plot of land. He tends to the herd of mixed-breed goats that live in a barn without doors, free to roam the land and graze whenever they wish. She milks them daily, turning their super floral and herbaceous yield into two cheeses: this blue and an aged tomme. Lady's Blue is dense yet creamy, decadent yet nuanced—a duality unto itself. With hints of clover and spring onions, there are also layers of bright citrus and wet goat. The moist paste is similar in texture to a perfectly toasted marshmallow—slightly gooey, but still holding shape. Lady's Blue is like the Haley's Comet of the cheese world, so if you're lucky enough to come across it, it's a must buy. Eat it on its own, perhaps with some raisin fennel bread and a bowl of fresh raspberries.

Enjoy with a Sancerre or Saison.

MONJE (MOAN-HAY)

MILK TYPE: Cow

ORIGIN: Asturias, Spain

Enrobed in maple leaves, this raw cow's milk blue from Spain's north coast has a really big flavor and a texture that will engage a serious cheese enthusiast. Monje, translating to "monk," has been made for over a century in the town of Panes located on the Rio Deva that leads to the Bay of Biscay. The cows enjoy the fertile pastures of this Asturian town, producing a milk of such richness that it is able to stand up to the powerful, spicy blue and green molds that densely populate this cheese. Its texture is quite creamy, with a slightly granular component throughout its mottled complexion due to the mingling of mold and paste. Monje is a blue cheese that will challenge you.

Enjoy with a glass of Fino sherry and some cured Iberian ham.

PARISH HILL CREAMERY WEST WEST BLUE

MILK TYPE: Cow

ORIGIN: Vermont, United States

Done in the style of Gorgonzola (see page 181), West West Blue is a creation from the domestic cheese-making guru Peter Dixon. At his small creamery in Westminster, Vermont, Peter plays around with classic DOP Italian cheese recipes and adds his own innovative twist. As in the production of Gorgonzola (see page 181), West West Blue combines the curd produced from the evening milking with the following morning's yield. The curd that is left out overnight has the opportunity to begin a slow and natural fermentation process. The milk from a neighboring farm is inoculated with blue cheese cultures before the curd is formed. Aged anywhere between 90 to 180 days, West West Blue develops a delicate, pale earth-toned rind that encases a supple and slightly fudgy paste. The earthy depth of flavor is elevated with a peppery kick and pockets of soil-like funk. This is a great blue cheese to serve alongside a hearty meal, such as a beef Bourguignon, or to incorporate into a tray of sausage lasagna.

PENACORADA (PEN-YA-CORE-AH-DA)

MILK TYPE: Cow

ORIGIN: León, Spain

This relatively mild and fudgy blue cheese is a gentle creation from a creamery that usually specializes in the famed Valdeon. The wet landscape of this Spanish region offers a bounty of fresh grasses and wildflowers for the cows to feast upon. Unlike Valdeon, Penacorada is sweet and earthy with round notes of chestnuts and brown sugar. The paste is dense yet creamy, with even, deep blue-gray veining throughout. This is a great addition to any cheeseboard for someone who wants to dabble in the world of blue cheese but wants to avoid the peppery heat of other blues. It goes very well with dried cherries and pecans, or crumbled over slices of smoked ham and then broiled for an incredible open-faced sandwich.

PERSILLÉ DU BEAUJOLAIS *(PEAR-SEE DUH BOW-JUH-LAY)*

MILK TYPE: Cow or goat

ORIGIN: Rhône-Alpes, France

A unique cheese created by the Lapierre family in the south of France, this delicately veined wheel is a true testament to a family tradition. Now made by two sons of the couple who conceptualized this cheese, Persillé du Beaujolais can be found as either a pure cow's milk or pure goat's milk version. Although the shapes of the cheeses are different, the production process is the same. After the wheels have aged for a few months in their own caves, they are moved into the hands of renowned affineur Hervé Mons to develop their round, fudgy perfection. The taste is both floral and slightly fungal, with a sweetness similar to butterscotch and berries. Accompany a wedge with a plate of fresh melon slices during the summer for a real treat that truly celebrates the season.

Enjoy both versions with sparkling whites.

PERSILLÉ DE CHÈVRE *(PEAR-SEE DUH SH-EV-RAH)*

MILK TYPE: Goat

ORIGIN: Île-de-France, France

This is a relatively new goat's milk blue to the United States and is produced by Ferme de la Tremblaye in La Boissière-École. The thermized milk is inoculated with blue mold prior to the curds being cut and hand-ladled into forms. After the cheese has lost enough moisture, the wheels—weighing around two to two and a half pounds (907 g to 1.1 kg) each—are dusted with vegetable ash and aged for about ten weeks. Persillé de Chèvre is very supple, with a rich and gooey cream line surrounding a buttery brick of dense goat's milk studded with greenish-blue molds. The flavors range from dirty, minerally earth to sweet, creamy barnyard and white pepper. The folks at Ferme de la Tremblaye really hit the nail on the head with this goat's milk bomb.

Enjoy with a glass of Sancerre and crisp green apples.

PICÓN BEJES-TRESVISO *(PEE-CON BAY-HESS TRAY-VEE-SO)*

MILK TYPE: Cow, sheep, and goat

ORIGIN: Cantabria, Spain

This piquant Spanish creation has been a name-protected cheese (see page 38) since the mid-1990s. Sheep, cow, and goat's milk are mixed together, rennet is added, the slurry is heated, and then the curd that forms is cut into hazelnut-size bits. These curds are then placed loosely into molds, but are not pressed, allowing for a good amount of moisture to be retained and enough air between the curds, so there is room for the bacteria to grow. Salt is rubbed on the exterior once these wheels are formed, to begin a bit of a washing process. The wheels are then moved into damp limestone caves, where they age for a minimum of two months. A natural rind develops in these caves, introducing a musky, earthy quality to the already complex flavor from the mixing of the milks. Peppery and bright, there is a bite to this cheese. The texture is milky and creamy but can develop into a more granular and gritty feel as the cheese ages. The bluing manifests in teal and aquamarine patches that are pretty evenly dispersed throughout the cheese. A great big blue, pair Picón Bejes-Tresviso with tart green apples and a big bowl of frisée salad, with bits of crisped serrano ham.

POINT REYES BAY BLUE

MILK TYPE: Cow

ORIGIN: California, United States

Inspired by the world-renowned Roquefort (see page 190), Bay Blue is an all-American interpretation of a classic and loved blue cheese. Sweet and candy-like, this Penicillium roqeuforti–studded cow's milk cheese resembles the fertile landscape these cows graze upon: lush, green, and fresh. The crumbly paste has a melt-in-your-mouth quality while maintaining a texture that lends itself to be shredded over a bowl of crisp endive. The rich and hearty milk is inoculated with the blue cheese cultures before the curdling process begins. After the curd has been cut and the wheels formed, the pure white rounds are pierced through with metal needles to help aerate the rind, allowing a channel for the bacteria to breath and grow. The overt sweetness is a testimony to the quality of the milk and the way the milk proteins break down during the aging process. The flavors are reminiscent of sour cherry with hints of mandarin-orange rind.

Enjoy with a big, dark stout beer, or incorporate into a blue cheese salad with tart Fuji apples and crisp Little Gem lettuce.

POINT REYES ORIGINAL BLUE

MILK TYPE: Cow

ORIGIN: California, United States

Point Reyes Farmstead Cheese Co. operates on some of the most picturesque and tranquil landscapes in all of California. A stone's throw from the Point Reyes National Seashore, the rolling green hills are blessed with ample sunshine and crisp, sea-kissed air, cultivating high-quality grass for the dairy's cows to graze upon. The milk from these blessed animals is used to create Original Blue, the first cheese that was made by Point Reyes. Aged for about six months, these raw-milk wheels are coagulated with microbial rennet, weigh about six pounds (2.7 kg) each, and have a sweet-cream flavor profile that mellows out the blue mold staggered throughout the paste. Superb on a cheese plate or broiled on top of honey-glazed pears or melted on a burger, this is a gateway blue for people who claim to not like this type of cheese.

ROGUE CREAMERY CAVEMAN BLUE

MILK TYPE: Cow

ORIGIN: Oregon, United States

If you're in the mood for a cheese that balances very dirty earth with very sweet cream, look no further than this cheese from these cheese makers in Central Point, Oregon. Rogue Creamery's Caveman Blue is a raw cow's milk dream of a blue cheese, showcasing the time and attention the creamery dedicated to this cheese during its years of development. Adding to its depth of flavor is the natural mold that develops on the rind during aging that protects the paste while allowing some moisture to escape, cultivating a dense, buttery paste. Once the cheese makers are satisfied with the progress of the cheese, it is then wrapped in foil to help retain moisture as it goes to market. The result is a wonderfully lactic mouthfeel that gets an earthy kick from the Penicillium roqueforti dispersed throughout the cheese. This is one of the best blue cheeses to come out of the United States.

Enjoy with a glass of AleSmith Speedway Stout.

ROGUE CREAMERY ECHO MOUNTAIN BLUE

MILK TYPE: Goat and cow

ORIGIN: Oregon, United States

Specialists in the blue cheese game, Rogue Creamery concocts these raw mixed-milk wheels from the milk of the goats and cows that graze upon the green grass and clover that sprouts on the banks of the Rogue River in southern Oregon. Aged anywhere between six months and a year—the cheese is only released when the Rogue cheese makers feel it is ready—Echo Mountain is a full-flavored, slightly crumbly blue cheese with balanced acidity; the tang from the goat's milk is ever-present but never overwhelms the rich fat from the cow. The foil wrapping unveils a pale ivory wheel that has a dense consistency with slight bluing on the exterior. The interior is a balance of blue veins and creamy paste, with hints of lemon peel, churned butter, and fresh dirt.

Enjoy with a glass of Tokaji and sliced pears after a meal.

ROGUE CREAMERY ROGUE RIVER BLUE

MILK TYPE: Cow

ORIGIN: Oregon, United States

This is like the holy grail of blue cheese. Rogue River Blue is made solely with the raw milk from a neighboring herd of Holsteins and Brown Swiss, and only when they are out to pasture in the late summer and early fall. Rogue Creamery develops wheels of their signature Oregon Blue (the base for Rogue River Blue) by aging them in their caves between eight months and one year. When the wheels are to the liking of the cheese makers, they are then wrapped in Syrah leaves that are sourced from a vineyard in nearby Medford and macerated in pear brandy from a distillery in Portland. The soaked leaves add a level of moisture and protection to this cheese, while imparting a sweet, boozy, mellow earthiness to the already buttery and spicy paste. The end result is a wheel of cheese with various textures—from smooth and creamy to granular and crumbly—and flavors—think candied hay to an earthy fruitiness—that truly represents the southern Oregon landscape.

Enjoy with three fingers of Eagle Rare bourbon.

ROGUE CREAMERY SMOKEY BLUE

MILK TYPE: Cow

ORIGIN: Oregon, United States

Let's face it: we all have a soft spot for smoked cheese every now and then. Maybe it's triggered from the smoked Gouda that you had in school lunch sacks or the smoked mozzarella your grandma used to put out on the antipasti plates at the holidays. Regardless, it's always a treat to come across a smoked cheese that is of upstanding character and quality, such as Smokey Blue from Rogue Creamery. Made from the raw milk of Brown Swiss and Holstein cows, the wheels are cold-smoked over hazelnut shells and aged for a minimum of six months. The flavor of the smoke combines with the sweetness of the milk to create a porky, caramelly, toasty treat that has a dense, sometimes crumbly consistency and makes you feel like you're eating campfire butter. Smokey Blue is a versatile ingredient—melt it on a burger, make into a killer wing sauce, or crumble over a salad of endive and pears. Or heck, just eat a slice of it by itself.

Enjoy with a glass of Reisling.

THE PERFECT DIP

You already know what's great with blue cheese. Chicken wings. Nothing beats dipping spicy, crispy chicken wings into a ramekin of creamy, cool blue cheese dip. Here's a not-so-secret recipe from our kitchen to yours—now get marinating and fire up the grill.

In addition to chicken wings, this is a great dip for crudité.

1 clove garlic, minced

Salt and pepper, to taste

2 teaspoons red wine vinegar

½ pound (225 g) Cashel Blue (see page 180) or, for a smokier alternative, use Rogue Creamery Smokey Blue (see left)

1 cup (240 ml) crème fraîche

½ cup (120 ml) mayonnaise (we like Duke's)

1. Mince garlic, sprinkle with salt, and mash into a paste.

2. Combine garlic and vinegar in a bowl and mix together.

3. Add cheese and mash until it is crumbled and combined with the vinegar/garlic slurry

4. Mix in crème fraîche and mayonnaise and combine until desired consistency is achieved.

5. Add salt and pepper to taste.

ROQUEFORT *(ROW-K-FOUR)*

MILK TYPE: Sheep

ORIGIN: Aveyron, France

Probably the most famous blue cheese in the world, Roquefort has been name protected since 1925 (see page 38). The distinct aqua-green molds, known as Penicillium roqueforti, are naturally occurring in the floors of the Combalou caves where these cheeses are aged. The pure sheep's milk wheels are pleasantly creamy, with a sweet, granular texture. The peppery heat is balanced well with the rich, fruity undertones of the milk. This is a great cheese to crumble over a pile of fresh Little Gem lettuce and sliced apples, or incorporate into a ground beef patty before searing for an incredible, blue cheese–studded burger.

SHROPSHIRE BLUE

MILK TYPE: Cow

ORIGIN: Nottinghamshire, England

Originally produced in the 1970s in Scotland, the Shropshire we receive today comes by way of Neal's Yard Dairy through their selection of wheels produced by Colston Bassett Dairy in Nottinghamshire using traditional animal rennet. This highly recognizable, natural-rind blue has a distinctive orange paste littered with little blossoms of blue veining. The annatto added to the milk gives Shropshire its color, imparting very slight touches of spice, but subtle enough to not overpower the peppery aspect of the blue, nor the rich, grassy complexion of the cheese itself. Aged between six to twelve weeks, Shropshire is quite smooth, with a plush mouthfeel, and is prone to crumbling.

Enjoy with a pint of robust porter.

STICHELTON *(STICH-EL-TON)*

MILK TYPE: Cow

ORIGIN: Nottinghamshire, England

This raw-milk, Stilton-inspired cheese is a relatively new product, only being produced since about 2004. A creation of the fine folks at Neal's Yard Dairy with cheese maker Joe Schneider, Stichelton is a throwback to how Stilton (see facing page) was traditionally made, with the use of raw milk and animal rennet to start the coagulation process. After a case of food poisoning was inaccurately linked back to a dairy that made Stilton, producers decided to only make wheels using pasteurized milk. Although the outbreak was proved to have no correlation to the cheese, Stilton has remained in its new form. Stichelton has a moist and velvety paste that is light and crumbly on the tongue, with a seductive, melty quality. The straw-yellow paste holds notes of tart raspberry jam and toasted shortbread cookies. There is an undeniable earthy quality where the little pockets of

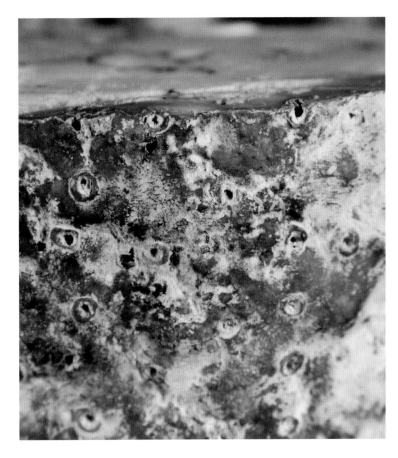

fuzzy gray-blue molds have blossomed in the paste. The slightly tacky, peach-toned rind has a grainy, salty quality. Serve alongside a plate of dried cherries and toasted walnuts for a decadent snack.

Enjoy with herbaceous whites, such as a Chablis or even a slightly oaked Chardonnay.

STICHELTON DAIRY

When the last of the raw-milk Stilton (see facing page) producers switched to pasteurization in the 1990s, Neal's Yard Dairy's Randolph Hodgson set out on a mission to create a cheese that would incorporate the depth of flavor that he found lacking in the pasteurized versions. After meeting cheese maker Joe Schneider, the two hatched a plan to begin producing the cheese again in its original form, on their terms; however, Stilton is a name-protected cheese (see page 38), meaning it may only be called such if it is produced in the determined manner—that is, with pasteurized milk. With a little help, the two decided on the name Stichelton (see above), from the Old English *stichl*, meaning "style," and *tun*, meaning "village." Neal's Yard Dairy prides itself as an entity that works closely with cheese makers to not only nurture innovative and new dairy traditions, but to also retain the time-honored and cherished versions of true English artisanal cheeses.

Stilton

STILTON

MILK TYPE: Cow

ORIGIN: Nottinghamshire, England

The history of this world-renowned English trademark blue dates back to the eighteenth century. Although the recipe has changed a bit over time, this is a name-protected cheese (see page 38), and as such, it must be produced with local, pasteurized milk, have a natural rind, and be formed in a tall, cylindrical shape. After the initial cheese-making process, where the milk is inoculated with the blue bacteria, long, thin needles are used to pierce the exterior, creating the air channels that the bacteria will thrive in. The wheels are then left to age for about nine to twelve weeks before the bluing process sufficiently permeates the paste. The rather buttery and crumbly interior has notes of fresh hay and wild buttercups, indicative of what the cows graze upon in the countryside. The beige rind has spots of pink and browns, signs of the natural environments where they are aged. A bit more tangy and salty toward the rind, and earthy and robust at the core, Stilton is a classic blue. A great way to serve a wedge is at the end of a classic British meal of rib roast and Yorkshire pudding.

WOODCOCK FARM KINDA BLUE

MILK TYPE: Cow

ORIGIN: Vermont, United States

American cheese makers have a way with names, and this fudgy, dense, pudding-like cheese shows you why. The subtly dispersed veins of blue break down the paste of this rich and gooey cow's milk cheese to help impart an earthy, slightly soil-like taste to this otherwise lactic and creamy cheese. Not as aggressive, peppery, or downright "blue" as most in the marketplace, this cheese borders on a Brie or Camembert in both texture and flavor. A robust barnyard quality finishes off a wave of rich milkiness that is only "blue" in the color and flavor of its earthy veins, and not in the overt or aggressive ways other blues are known for. A great cheese, alongside red grapes and fresh cherries, to round out a cheeseboard, Kinda Blue is just as good smeared on grilled corn on the cob or a piece of toasted walnut raisin bread.

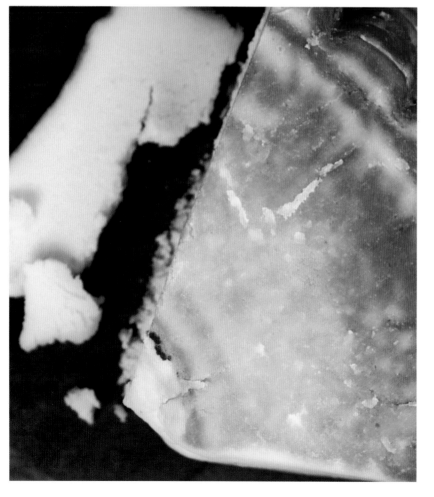

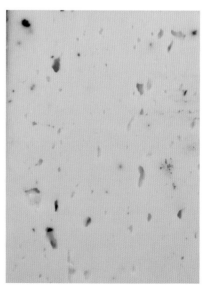

FLAVORED

We accept the fact that people like "things" in their cheese, and who can deny a brick of pepper jack over nachos or a scoop of a garlic and herb cream cheese? However, the majority of commercially produced flavored cheeses are really nothing more than subpar dairy being masked with more subpar ingredients to make a perfectly marketable but subpar product. Not all flavored cheeses are bad, and we do appreciate the ones that strive to use quality milk and combine it with quality ingredients such as the ones here, to create a quality cheese.

Many cultures look to flavor cheeses in the same manner as they flavor breads and beers—as staples of sustenance turned into art forms in their culinary landscape. Just like adding raisins and walnuts to a loaf of bread or adding fresh fruit to a light wheat beer brewed during the summer months, the addition of spices, grains, and fresh and dried fruits that are readily available, allow the producers to be innovative with classic creations.

There are two primary ways to introduce flavoring into cheeses. The ingredient can either be incorporated into the milk or curd during the make process, or the flavors can be added to the exterior once the wheels have been formed. In either case, the end result is the addition of another flavor element that hopefully enhances the experience and cohesiveness of the milk and cheese.

BREBIS AU PIMENT D'ESPELETTE *(BRAY-BEE OH PEE-MONT DUH ESS-PELL-ETTE)*

MILK TYPE: Sheep

ORIGIN: Midi-Pyrénées

The famed shepherds of the mountainous Pyrenees region of France are known for their love of their flocks. These sheep are watched over by a caring eye that has a strong lineage in animal care. The mellow, floral, dense, and buttery sheep's milk cheese gets elevated to a smoky sweet, slightly spicy level of intensity with the addition of the regionally loved pepper, piment d'Espelette. The local chile is dried and smoked over wood fires, and used in everything from breakfast eggs to the potato-based Spanish-style tortilla. A pure sheep's milk tomme, the cheese on its own is slightly caramelly, with decadent notes of wildflowers and green grass. The residual heat from the pepper is more of a nuanced afterthought, rather than having the overt smack of most peppers. Incredible grated into a quiche of roasted red peppers and sautéed mushrooms, or served on its own as a bulk wedge for a picnic in the park, Brebis au Piment d'Espelette is a great addition to any cheese lover's repertoire.

Enjoy with a malty ale or a bright, sparkling red.

COTSWOLD

MILK TYPE: Cow

ORIGIN: Gloucestershire, England

The legendary English cow's milk cheese Double Gloucester gets elevated to new heights of culinary wonder with the addition of green onions and fresh chives. The full-fat cheese is similar to a cheddar in its tangy seduction, yet has a slightly suppler paste and creamier finish. Nutty and tangy, the cheese is overwhelmed with a spring-like bounty of oniony heat. A great snacking cheese to pair with a midday ale, Cotswold is a meal unto itself, with a meaty, savory quality that matches the creamy richness of the milk. The perfect cheese to pair with a smorgasbord of tasty victuals, this cheese is a stand-alone classic for anyone who likes the floral heat of raw onions mellowed out with the fattiness of good cream. Pair with a meal of grilled lamb kebabs and a rice pilaf salad, and you won't be disappointed.

Enjoy with different types of cocktails, especially ones made with a herbaceous gin.

CREMEAUX DES CITEAUX AUX TRUFFES *(CRÈME DAYS SI-TOE OH TRUE-FAYES)*

MILK TYPE: Cow

ORIGIN: Normandy, France

What's more decadent than a triple crème with a pillowy rind? How about a triple crème stuffed with a plump layer of black truffles? Selected by affineur Rodolphe Le Meunier (see page 68), this cheese begins its life just like Brillat Savarin (see page 61), but during the aging process, the cheese gets a healthy dose of black truffles spread right through the center of its rich, buttery paste. The cheese is then aged longer, as the Penicillium candidum encases and protects the cheese. Cremeaux des Citeaux aux Truffes can come in individual pieces—about five ounces (142 g) each—or as a larger wheel—roughly one and a quarter pounds (567 g). The truffles give a deep, earthy, fungal kick to the fatty, buttery nature of the cheese itself. It's definitely a crowd-pleaser, and makes a great addition to a New Year's Eve snack assortment.

Enjoy with Champagne.

CYPRESS GROVE TRUFFLE TREMOR

MILK TYPE: Goat

ORIGIN: California, United States

Cypress Grove has made quite a reputation for themselves as one of the best goat cheese producers in the United States. By adding earthy black truffles to their full-flavored goat's milk, they have created one of the most addictive flavored wheels to come across cheese counters. A surefire hit for the truffle lover in you, Truffle Tremor has a bright, bloomy rind that gives way to a gooey, oozy cream line, surrounding a crumbly, rich, white core that is studded with flecks of truffle throughout. The sweet-and-tart nature of the goat's milk is well balanced by the earthiness of those little truffles. The cheese comes in wheels weighing around three pounds (1.4 kg) each, and is a nice addition to an omelet served with leafy greens or as part of a cheese plate.

Enjoy with a nice glass of port.

FLEUR DU MAQUIS (FL-AIR DO MAH-KEYS)

MILK TYPE: Sheep

ORIGIN: Corsica, France

A decadent, herbaceous treat from the small island off the coast of France, Fleur de Maquis is at its root a superb sheep's milk tomme. The exterior is coated with a mix of local herbs and peppers before the natural rind develops in the caves. The floral mixture permeates the cheese from the outside in, imparting subtle notes of a spice cabinet. The springtime herbs lighten the rich sheep's milk, creating a wondrous flavor joyride that is a gooey, rich mess of a wheel at its peak and is a bit more velvety and melty in texture when younger. Corisca is known for its rough terrain and its shepherding history, and this cheese perfectly integrates both of those criteria in a lactic dream that rivals all others. Not as assertive as if the seasonings were added to the milk during the make process, the herbs and spices lend a complementary warmth rather than taking away from the quality base of the wheels. A showstopper on a cheese plate, Fleur du Maquis is as visually appetizing as it is tasty.

Enjoy with a mineral-forward or a slightly effervescent white.

HUNTSMAN

MILK TYPE: Cow

ORIGIN: Leicestershire, England

One could argue that Huntsman isn't a flavored cheese but that it is just two cheeses in one. But into which category should this combination of Double Gloucester and Stilton (see page 193) be placed? Blue? Natural rind? Huntsman is a cheese that defies such categorical malarkey, and that's what makes it so special. Sure, it's commercially made, but when you gaze into its eyes, its hypnotic layers of rich orange and deep, foamy, ocean blue create a romantic feeling of watching a warm Pacific sunset with a loved one. We're not quite sure how you want to eat this, but we reckon it will be enjoyed at your next PTA meeting with slices of apples and soda water, but could be just as lovely paired with an IPA and some fresh fruit after mowing the lawn on a spring day.

KEIEMNAAR MET KRUIDEN *(KAI-EM-NAR MET CREW-DEN)*

MILK TYPE: Cow

ORIGIN: Flanders, Belgium

Made by a father-and-son team in the Belgian countryside, these wheels are comprised of whole, raw, EU certified–organic cow's milk and a whole mess of herbs harvested from the pastures the cows graze upon. With an incredibly fun name to say and a rich, plump texture, Keiemnaar met Kruiden is an example of a cheese that does a good job of minimally masking the high-quality milk used with the addition of the herbs (i.e., the cheese still tastes like cheese). This cheese really shines melted on a roast beef sandwich.

Enjoy with a crisp, cold pilsner.

LEMON BAKED RICOTTA

MILK TYPE: Cow and water buffalo

ORIGIN: Lombardy, Italy

This sweet, snacktastic northern Italian cheesecake is made from the milk of cows and the docile water buffalos of Lombardy. By using very few ingredients (rice flour, sugar, and lemon), the richness of the milk is still expressed even with the highlights of tart lemon and the balanced sugar content. Try a piece with your next brunch spread of smoked fish, or crush pistachios over a piece, drizzle some honey on top, and serve as a sweet treat after a hearty meal.

LEYDEN *(LAY-DEN)*

MILK TYPE: Cow

ORIGIN: Southern Holland, Netherlands

Do you like the smell of grilled tacos? Or, how about roasted cumin and steak drippings? Well, then, have we got a cheese for you! Leyden is named after the town it originates from in the Dutch province of Southern Holland and is made on a number of large farms in the area. Using pasteurized cow's milk and additional cream, this cheese has toasted cumin seeds kneaded into the curd prior to ladling into draining baskets. After aging for about three months, the cumin seeds form a flavor archipelago, ranging from dry hay to sweet butter cream. What was once a way to cover up the off flavors of the milk when the cow's yield was watery and bland has become a tasty tradition that has global appeal. Nutty and savory, with a meaty robustness, Leyden is a Christmas-time treat and melted between two slabs of a pullman loaf makes an incredible grilled cheese sandwich, or try it ribboned over crisp pieces of bacon for a beast of a breakfast.

Enjoy with dark, rich stouts and big, robust reds.

LI BLANC COUCOU TRUFFEE *(LE BLONK KOO KOO TRUE-FAYE)*

MILK TYPE: Cow

ORIGIN: Liege, Belgium

In the Belgian town of Stoumont, Fromagerie Counasse produces EU certified–organic farmstead cheeses in a variety of styles and ages. Li Blanc Coucou Truffee (aka, the "White Cuckoo with Truffles") is a natural-rind, raw-milk wheel that weighs about four pounds (1.8 kg) and possesses a supple texture and a pleasant, milky flavor profile. The beige-colored rind has flecks of black spots, a sign of the earthy black truffles that adorn the soft, chewy paste, which shows very small eyes produced during the fermentation process. The brightness of the milk is a soft landing for the earthy truffles, as their combination produces a very likeable cheese.

Enjoy with a glass of light-bodied red wine and some smoked meats.

MANCHEGO PIMENTÓN
(MAN-CHAY-GO PIMM-EN-TONE)

MILK TYPE: Sheep

ORIGIN: La Mancha, Spain

The Spaniards love their sheep's milk, and they also love their pimentón. Manchego Pimentón is made from the smoke-dried, ground red chiles native to the land. The spice is incorporated into the curd before ladling it into basket molds, and the process from then on is pretty much the same as the production of good ol' plain Manchego (see page 158). The gentle smoky heat complements the complex sheep's milk flavors, leaving a residual heat as opposed to an aggressive punch. An excellent cheese to incorporate into a Spanish-style tortilla or frittata, Manchego Pimentón is just as lovely in a meal as it is accompanying one. Arrange a plate of this cheese with sliced, cured chorizo, a handful of Marcona almonds, and a dollop of *membrillo* (quince paste), alongside a crusty peasant loaf of bread and you will be transported to the rustic Spanish countryside of La Mancha.

MARIEKE FOENEGREEK GOUDA
(PHEN-UH-GREEK GOW-DA)

MILK TYPE: Cow

ORIGIN: Wisconsin, United States

Continuing the long history of the Dutch adding flavoring to their cheeses, Marieke Penterman takes her award-winning Gouda and adds fenugreek seeds to the paste to create a sweet-and-savory raw cow's milk treat. Aged around four months, these wheels weigh in around eighteen pounds (8.2 kg) each and have a traditional Gouda-style waxed exterior. The paste is the shade of light butter, with the seeds adorning it in a very dense manner. The sweet and nutty nature of the spice combines with the full flavor of the cheese, producing a flavor profile reminiscent of pecan praline ice cream, with a definitive taste of true maple syrup. Marieke Foenegreek Gouda will take your grilled cheese to new heights, but it can also be savored on its own.

PETIT THEODORE

MILK TYPE: Cow

ORIGIN: Loire Valley, France

These super creamy, little balls of fresh cow's milk are rolled in a blanket of dried fruit and nuts. The rich and decadent cheese is a great blank canvas for the addition of all sorts of flavors. Sometimes the raisins are soaked in a liqueur, sometimes not, but they're always tasty. The nuts range from toasted hazelnuts to crushed almonds to whole pine nuts, adding a great texture to the otherwise slightly gooey cheese. Chewy and crunchy, each bite holds a new sensation. The companionship of fruit and cheese is a long-standing one, as the sweet-and-savory seduction plays pleasantly on the palate. The addition of nuts also adds a great salty bite and roasty quality. The variations of ingredients found with this cheese come from the affineur's desires. Rodolphe Le Meunier (see page 68) is known for his cutting-edge flavor collaborations. Although rooted in tradition, this man loves to push the boundaries of food.

RICOTTA AL PEPPERONCINO

MILK TYPE: Sheep

ORIGIN: Abruzzi, Italy

The classically subtle and creamy Ricotta (see page 54) is pressed down into a little basket mold to drain out more whey making these wheels are a bit firmer than their fresher cousins. After receiving a light dusting of salt to help with the drying process, they are then encased in a rub of crushed red pepperoncini. The heat from the peppers gently permeates the paste, creating a salty, flinty flavor cacophony that will make your mouth sweat in the best possible way. A great treat for anyone who loves a little heat. Perfectly paired with a big red wine that can compete with the bold flavors— try with a Barolo.

RIVER'S EDGE CHÈVRE UP IN SMOKE

MILK TYPE: Goat

ORIGIN: Oregon, United States

Cheech and Chong have nothing on these dumplings of pure Oregon goat's milk that are gently wrapped in maple leaves collected from the woods surrounding the farm. These leaves are then washed and smoked over hickory and alder chips, and just prior to wrapping the cheese, they receive a healthy spritz of bourbon. The cheese itself is incredibly smooth and creamy, with the sweetness of the goat's milk mingling perfectly with the smoky earthiness of the leaves. Up in Smoke is a stunning addition to a cheese plate and a real crowd-pleaser. It's not too often you find such quality in a smoked cheese, but River's Edge Chèvre really hits the nail on the head with this one.

SAGE DERBY *(SAGE DARBY)*

MILK TYPE: Cow

ORIGIN: Derbyshire, England

Derby, a style of cheese from East Midlands, is made with pasteurized cow's milk and has a semi-firm texture and a mild, milky flavor. With such a pleasantly creamy base, some genius had the idea to incorporate flavors into this blank canvas—one of them being the herb sage. Traditionally, fresh sage leaves were chopped and mixed in with the curd, but as production techniques have changed over the years, spinach and other green herbs, such as parsley, have been added to give the cheese its signature yellow-and-green appearance. Originally made only during the harvest season and for Christmas, the popularity of this cheese has led it to become available year-round. While it may look like a phantasm, this is actually a very real, very accessible cheese. The buttery, herby flavors of Sage Derby are a good match for melting atop a root-vegetable casserole

Enjoy with a Chardonnay.

SOTTOCENERE
(SO-TOE-CHEN-AIR-AY)

MILK TYPE: Cow

ORIGIN: Veneto, Italy

A complex, almost gothic-looking wheel of pasteurized cow's milk, Sottocenere translates to "under ash," referencing the crusty, ash-laden rind that coats the cheese. Hailing from the northern Italian province of Veneto, the cheese is aged between three and four months and has a semi-firm texture. Flecks of black truffle are woven throughout the yellow-white paste, and during its formative days, Sottocenere is rubbed down with olive oil infused with truffle to give the cheese another dimension of earthy flavor. Once shaped, the cheese is enrobed with a combination of ash, nutmeg, cinnamon, coriander, and other baking spices, and left to age until the cheese makers deem it fit for consumption. Notes of scalded cream, whipped butter, soil, and sweet spice undulate over the palate while memories of mother's kitchen come to mind. Try melting Sottocenere over a bowl of polenta or serve alongside some fresh grapes.

Enjoy with a bottle of Prosecco.

TOMME DE FONTENAY (TOHM DUH FAWN-TEN-AY)

MILK TYPE: Goat

ORIGIN: Bordeaux, France

Weighing in at about ten pounds (4.5 kg), Tomme de Fontenay also goes by the name Tomme Bordeaux, depending on its affineur. Rodolphe Le Meunier's (see page 68) version is known as Tomme de Fontenay, named after the area of the Loire Valley where he calls home. After carefully selecting his preferred wheels, Le Meunier brings these prizes back to his caves to receive his care and attention. These dense and fudgy wheels of pure goat's milk are encrusted with a mixture of herbs and peppers that are native to the lands these goats graze upon. The ivory white paste develops a rustically gray-colored natural rind that resembles the forest floor in autumn. The sweetness of the goat's milk balances nicely with the herbaceous crust, eliminating any potential barnyard qualities from developing. Tomme de Fontenay pairs extremely well with berries and fruits. Plate a wedge alongside green grapes, fresh figs, and a drizzle of some wildflower honey and watch as it quickly disappears accompanied by euphoric oohs and aahs.

Enjoy with floral whites and dry rosés.

TRIFULIN *(TREE-FUL-EEN)*

MILK TYPE: Cow and goat

ORIGIN: Piedmont, Italy

The truffle craze continues with this mixed-milk drum that calls northern Italy its home. Hailing from the rolling hills known as the Langhe in Piedmont, Trifulin is a pasteurized blend of cow and goat's milk that is traditionally made between the months of July and November. Each wheel comes in weighing between two to three pounds (907 g to 1.4 kg) and carries a rustic ivory rind that may occasionally have some mottled brown spots. Aged for a minimum of thirty days, but usually closer to two or three months, the paste is dense with a flaky texture that has a delicate crumbly character. The truffles adorn the paste in a fluid manner—their aroma and dank flavor combine with the rich cow and tangy goat's milk to create a varied and esoteric deluge of flavors that will challenge any concept of flavored cheese you may have. Try shaving it over a bowl of gnocchi and asparagus.

Enjoy with a minerally red wine.

WESTFIELD FARM HERB GARLIC CAPRI

MILK TYPE: Goat

ORIGIN: Massachusetts, United States

This is an incredibly fresh goat's milk cheese from a small family-run farm in Hubbardston, Massachusetts. The citrusy, bright, slightly floral base gets a savory kick with the addition of fresh garlic and herbs. Crumbly yet creamy, this super spreadable cheese is a great base for grilled flatbreads and fish tacos, or simply smeared on a toasted piece of fruit-flavored bread. There are all sorts of fresh Chèvre (see page 53) infused with a myriad of flavors available, and how can you blame producers for it? When you have a base of great milk, the addition of herbs and spices complement the flavors and nuances of the cheese. Westfield Farm's chèvre (or "capri," as they call it) stands out from the industrially produced versions, with the pureness and quality of the products used. Not the least bit goaty or barnyard-like, this is a great gateway cheese for anyone who thinks they don't like goat's cheese. The salt level of the milk elevates the freshness of the herbs and garlic. An excellent dip for crudité or an enjoyable addition to any picnic or barbecue, this cheese will not last long, as it is always the first to be eaten!

Enjoy with wheat beers.

PART FIVE
ENJOYING CHEESE

BEVERAGE PAIRINGS

Cheese and booze go together like hand in glove. The process of fermentation binds these two art forms in a flavor explosion that not only represents the lands from which they originate but also the tradition of their craftsmanship. With effervescent beverages, such as beer or sparkling wine, there is a marriage of flavor and texture—bubbles create a sensation on your tongue that, when comingled with cheese, elevates and alters the appreciation of the individual ingredients. Beverages such as wine and spirits find harmony with cheese through the nuances of their flavor profiles. But it's not just about alcohol and the dairy; teas and coffees are often unexplored partners to cheese, and their floral and roasty qualities bring out certain flavors that may go unobserved otherwise. Drinking and eating are a time-honored tradition, and we implore you to have fun with the process of pairing to find what works best for your palate. You might enjoy a classic marriage, such as Champagne paired with a triple crème cheese, but we believe that there are many unexpected yet perfect combinations out there, and the only way to know is to taste, drink, and savor. In this section, we share some of our thoughts and recommendations on exploring the vast world of pairing cheeses and beverages. Cheers!

BEER

One of the greatest joys of working in the world of food is witnessing and participating in the evolution of the field as a whole and enjoying the various elements available within it. Over the last twenty-some odd years, beer has undergone a watershed transformation from a beverage your grandparents used to crush out of a can while fishing in reservoirs to a beverage of such stature that it has begun to challenge the revered and time-tested wine as the people's choice to pair with cheese.

The ability of the craft beer industry to develop and expand on styles has created a spectrum of beverages that, when coupled with its effervescence, makes it perhaps the most versatile of libations for cheese pairing. From kriek lambics to coffee-infused imperial stouts, here are some of our favorites to quaff with that other fermented beauty: cheese.

BLOOMY

Farmhouse ales are our go-to for this category. Originally brewed by Belgian farmers in the late winter to be enjoyed by the field hands in the warmth of summer, farmhouse ales are bright and crisp, with a light, refreshing body and notes that can range from hay to stone fruit. The residual yeast in the bottles of these beauties allows the maturation of the beverage to continue until the bottle is popped, and it creates a slight element of funk. Depending on the yeast used, notes of banana, fresh bread, or tropical fruit can be found. This fermentation process also tends to create sourness in farmhouse ales. We enjoy this style of ale with young and supple cheeses—one of our favorites to pair with farmhouse ales is a Belgian Sainte-Maure (see page 76) that we receive unaged and allow to develop a Geotrichum rind over a couple of weeks, or a cakey and funky Robiola Tre Latte (see page 75). The acidity and tang of the cheeses matched with the bright and clean flavors of the beer are a summer match made in heaven. The Commons Brewery out of Portland, Oregon, pays homage to the clean and simple vision of the original Belgian farmhouse ales and is worth seeking out.

WASHED RIND

We're talking funky, ooey, and gooey—you know, touches of manure, barnyard hay, peanuts, and bitter greens. For a beverage to hang with these cheeses, there needs to be a touch of sweetness, but not too much—too sweet and you've destroyed your ability to find harmony. Trappist (or trappist-style) dubbel ales are a great fit for these little stinkers. Malt forward and round with just a touch of bitterness, these brown bombers beckon for a slab of Vulto Creamery Ouleout (see page 112) smeared over a piece of dark rye bread. Westmalle Trappist Dubbel is a wonderful expression of this style and is still brewed by the monks at the Westmalle Abbey. Creamy in texture with hints of dates and brown sugar, this beer can stand up to the funkiest of the funky. Russian River Supplication, with its woody and sour profile, is a wonderful beer to pair with one of our shop's favorites, Charmoix (see page 93).

WASHED CURD

Sweet and crystalline with floral notes, the cheeses in this category pair very nicely with beers of high-hop character. Some of our preferred super-hoppy IPAs are Maharaja from Avery Brewing Company, Pliny the Elder from Russian River, and Sticky Hands from Block 15 out of Oregon. Additionally, hearty Trappist ales with bitter finishes and malty profiles, such as Orval Trappist Ale, also work wonderfully with this class of cheese.

COOKED/PRESSED

These cheeses tend to be grassy, funky, dense, and fudgy. The variety of flavor profiles makes them versatile for beer pairing; they could work with a crisp kölsch, a farmhouse ale, or a malty brown depending on the age and the treatment of the cheese during maturation. The best advice we can give is to grab a few different beers and try out combos that work for you. Yeah, we know it's tough drinking good beer and eating good cheese.

NATURAL RIND

Dank, moldy, and buttery, these cheeses match up well with medium-bodied beers that have touches of residual yeast, such as Old Speckled Hen, French bière de garde, or even rich, malty German bock, which has a sweetness that can cut through the bitterness that these molds can sometimes impart on the cheeses they envelop.

BLUE

Whether it's a creamy pile of gooey goodness with soil and root-vegetable overtones, or a flinty, fruity masterpiece, blue cheese is a make or break for most people. Paired with the right brew, it can be a gateway for both the novice and the experienced cheese lover. We find that most blue cheeses pair well with beers that can stand up to the challenge of the mold. Think porters, stouts, and malt-forward Trappist ales. The balance is of utmost importance. Some of our favorite pairings include Rogue Creamery Caveman Blue (see page 188) with AleSmith Speedway Stout; Blu del Moncenisio (see page 179) with Rodenbach Grand Cru; and Achelse Blauwe (see page 182) with Achel Trappist Brune.

WINE

Wine and cheese—it's the quintessential match and there's good reason why wine has long been the beverage of choice to pair with cheese. From light and acidic to full and peppery, the fruit of the vine has so many varietals and styles that it's hard not to find something that pairs well with every cheese in this book. Here are some general guidelines to keep in mind for pairing cheeses with the various categories of wines.

Bubbly wines, such as Champagne, Blanc de Blanc, and Cava pair well with buttery triple crèmes, including Pierre Robert (see page 74) or Nettle Meadow Farm Kunik (see page 73), but yeasty young goat cheeses such as the Belgian Sainte-Maure (see page 76) or Painted Goat Farm Cinderella (see page 73) are also fun to eat alongside a sparkler. Goat's milk cheeses are a great match for a spectrum of white wines, and we can never balk at a glass of Sancerre with a Couronne de Touraine (see page 67). A big, buttery Chardonnay is a good fit with the lavish Cowgirl Creamery Mt. Tam (see page 68), or try it with Arethusa Blue (see page 176). Sweeter whites tend to partner well with more pungent cheeses, so give a bottle of Gewürztraminer a brick of Limburger (see page 101), or try a floral and tropical fruit–laden Tokaji with some Stracchino di Vedeseta (see page 108). Rosés and yellow wines, such as the ones from Jura, are fun to pair with alpine-style cheeses, such as Comté (see page 125) and Uplands Cheese Pleasant Ridge Reserve (see page 140). The light tannins and sometimes flower-forward notes in these wines also complement a sheep's milk cheese such as La Marotte (see page 157) and Vermont Shepherd "Verono" (see page 172). The world of red wine has so many variations and complexities that the most fun way to dive into it is by buying a few bottles and performing your own private taste tests. Here are a few of our favorite combinations: try a light Nebbiolo with a Robiola Tre Latte (page 75); a full-bodied Pinot Noir with Bergfichte (see page 88); and a Rioja with some Torta La Serena (see page 109). The best part about pairing cheeses and wines is that you can discover your own favorite partners through experimentation.

SPIRITS

WHISKEY

These brown liquors are quite an exquisite pairing with cheese when done correctly. One of the most popular classes we hold at our shop is Whiskey and Cheese 101, where we go through a few different styles of whiskey and play around with types of cheeses that complement the spirit. But if you can't make it to one of our tastings, we can bring the tasting to you. While there are hundreds of whiskeys out there for you to imbibe in, here's a rundown of some of our favorite pairings we've discovered over the years.

SCOTCH

Scotch flavors can range from smoky and mossy to astringent and malty. The scotch you choose to drink will obviously dictate what cheese you should serve alongside it. If you are leaning toward a really smoky scotch—one that has medicinal notes that often remind you of a freshly unveiled Band-Aid, such as Bowmore or Laphroaig—cheeses such as Wilde Weide (see page 119) and Consider Bardwell Rupert (see page 126) are good matches. If a mellower lowland scotch is more your speed, try a piece of Alpe Loch (see page 150) alongside a dram of Auchentoshan 12 Years Old.

BOURBON AND RYE

These American originals create a spectrum of spice, sweetness, and downright "hotness"—that is, they are astringent and very alcohol forward. If you find yourself inclined to enjoy bourbons that are less sweet, such as Woodford Reserve or Buffalo Trace, may we suggest pairing them with Uplands Cheese Pleasant Ridge Reserve (see page 140) or Spring Brook Farm Tarentaise (see page 138). If you prefer a sweeter bourbon, such as Eagle Rare, give Consider Bardwell Dorset (see page 94) or Montgomery's Cheddar (see page 159) a chance to balance out the sweet woodiness. Now if rye whiskey is your game, enjoy a glass of High West Double Rye with a ripe piece of Vulto Creamery Ouleout (see page 112) or a nice snifter of Willett Family Reserve alongside Capriole Farms Mont St. Francis (see page 91).

IRISH WHISKEY

Irish Whiskey is so much more than shots of Jameson you may have knocked back in your early drinking days. The spectrum of Irish whiskey ranges from briny and sharp to sweet and buttery. And what better way to celebrate the Emerald Isle's gift to the spirit than to pair it with the fine dairy of the land. Try a glass of Knappogue Castle with an oozy piece of Ardrahan (see page 87) or three fingers of Redbreast 12 Year with a slab of hearty Coolea (see page 117), and celebrate with friends and family.

TEQUILA

Cultivated from the hearty agave plant by the skilled laborers known as *jimadores*, tequila is an earthy treat that undergoes certain aging processes, developing ranges of flavors from creamy and citrusy to woodsy and spicy. The style of the spirit you choose will play an integral part in what cheeses you pick to enjoy with it. Here are some of our favorite pairings with different aged tequilas.

BLANCO: Usually creamy, with occasional hints of vanilla, blanco or silver tequila is amenable to a number of cheeses, but we really like this style with a piece of Stompetoren Grand Cru (see page 119) because the slight sweetness of the blanco complements the sweetness of the cheese, almost like a cream frosting on a caramel cake.

REPOSADO: Aged in oak barrels from anywhere between two and eleven months, reposado extracts a more robust and fruitier flavor profile from the wood it rests on, making slightly funkier cheeses, such as Stracchino di Vedeseta (see page 108), a nice fit with this spirit.

AÑEJO: The elder statesman of tequila undergoes a maturation process in oak barrels between one and three years. The aging process mellows the astringent nature of the alcohol and tends to impart notes of caramel and some tannins. This is a perfect style of tequila to pair with blue cheeses, such as Fourme d'Ambert (see page 181) or Gorgonzola (see page 181).

GIN

The herbaceous world of gin is vast and varying. There are the more overt juniper-based versions, such as Junipero, or the more balanced, almost luscious Barr Hill from Vermont. Due to the liquor's diverse flavoring, gin lends itself to a wide variety of cheeses. From the more blueberry-noted craft gins that pair well with young goat's milk and mixed-milk cheeses, such as Andante Dairy Duet (see page 59), to the more piney variations that go great with English cheddars, such as Montgomery's Cheddar (see page 159), there is a lot of room for creativity when crafting gin cocktails for a cheese party.

VODKA

A great "blank canvas" for all sorts of cocktails, this rather light, slightly astringent liquor lends itself wonderfully to the overwhelming flavor world of cheese. Although it might be difficult to discern all of the notes and aftertastes of a chilled glass of Stoli, the warmth and tongue-lightning qualities of vodka leave your palate ready to receive all the flavor compounds of a great piece of Manchego (see page 158). Acting as almost a cleanser in ways, the pithy and sometimes bitter qualities of a good vodka go great with leaf-wrapped robiola-type cheeses, such as Capriole Farms O'Banon, or the more seductive, gentle goat's milk cheeses, such as Sainte-Maure (see page 76).

TEA/COFFEE

Often overlooked as beverages to pair with cheese, coffees and teas hold a vast world of flavors that lend themselves well to accompanying the wide variety of lactic loves. Black teas, running the gamut from the citrusy, bergamot-infused Earl Grey to the malty, floral notes of English breakfast lend themselves nicely to an evenly balanced sheep's milk tomme, such as La Marotte (see page 157), or a goat's milk cheese, such as Twig Farm Goat Tomme (see page 172). The floral notes of the milk are balanced with the rich flavors of the teas. The mouth-coating black teas are lightened with the wash of warm caffeine. Try a wedge of La Marrote (see page 157) with your morning tea to see them both open up into different flavor experiences. For herbal teas, like chamomile and citrus blends, a rich and creamy triple crème such as Pierre Robert (see page 74) or Nettle Meadow Farm Kunik (see page 73) acts almost like a dollop of cream or custard atop a fruit pie. Green teas, with their vast array of smoky and nutty notes, pair well with the decadent nuances in alpine-style cheeses, such as Gruyère (see page 128) and Comté (see page 125).

Coffee, with its ever-expanding flavor compounds depending on bean origin and roasting techniques, has a lot of room to play in pairings. A more chocolaty blend, such as a dark roast, is well suited to an alpine-style cheese, such as the domestic Challerhocker (see page 125) or the Wildspitz (see page 141), plus a number of blue cheeses, including Stilton (see page 193) or Jasper Hill Bayley Hazen (see page 183). The fatty cow's milk balances nicely with the rich roasts. Lighter roasts, such as Ethiopian Yirgacheffe, pair well with sharply flavored, woolly pecorinos, such as Calcagno (see page 123), or nuttier and sweeter Goudas, such as Coolea (see page 117).

Espresso drinks, including the "straight" varieties and those combined with milk, go well with lemon-forward fresh chèvres from the Loire Valley like Crottin de Chavignol (see page 68) and Valençay (see page 80). The natural acidity levels in the espresso beans bring out the more rounded, custardy nuances of the barnyard-like cheeses.

ACCOUTREMENTS

We love how certain foods go so well together and enjoy discovering accompaniments that complement cheese. A wedge of farmhouse cheddar is great on its own but excellent when eaten with a dollop of homemade chutney. Cheese shouldn't be treated as an isolated culinary adventure because it goes well with so many other foods. Cheese is magical on its own, but when paired with friendly flavors, there is a transformation—certain nuances stand out, becoming bolder and more pronounced, while other notes become more subdued.

Cured meats are a natural accompaniment for cheeses. The curing and fermentation these meats undergo is in lockstep with the way our beloved cheeses are aged. Similarly, pickles and bread, both lovely arms of the fermented family, combine wonderfully with cheese.

Sweet treats can also pair just as well as savory accompaniments. A wedge of dark chocolate can be sublime when paired with an aged alpine-style cheese. An aged balsamic will transform a wedge of Parmigiano-Reggiano (see page 135). Shredding Comté (see page 125) into the dough of an apple pie is divine. Here are some of our favorite food items to pair with cheese and why.

PICKLED PRODUCTS

Whether you are pickling a classic Kirby cucumber or watermelon rinds or dilly beans, this form of preservation is the closest to the aging of cheese in the culinary world. The root concept of combining a basic brine and time to transform a fresh vegetable into a completely different product is similar. The acidic tang of vinegar-based pickles brightens up flavors, and as most pickles have a combination of spices in their juices, the addition of pickled products to a cheese plate can create a fabulous spectrum of flavors. Try pickled onions with Limburger (see page 101) or dainty cornichons with a slab of Comté (see page 125). Pairing should be fun and exploratory, so let your tastes lead the way to find what combinations work for you and your friends.

MUSTARD

One of our own personal weaknesses is mustard. The wide variety of flavors that are coaxed from these little pearls is mind boggling. From the classic English version with a heat similar to wasabi to the more vinegary bite of a French Dijon, mustards are a great companion to many cheeses. Firmer goat's milk cheeses, such as Garrotxa (see page 156) or Old Ford (see page 160), complement the astringent, peppery notes of the mustard seed while lending a more grassy background. Comté (see page 125) and Gruyère (see page 128), as well as many alpine-style cheeses, go great with a dollop of a mustard smoothed out with the addition of beer. There are literally hundreds of different combinations to try.

JAM, HONEY, AND COMPOTE

The classic sweet-and-savory flavor combos have a certain pull on the heartstrings of our taste buds. A much-loved pairing is a fig jam, well, with anything, but specifically with a Pyrenees sheep's milk cheese, such as Ossau Iraty (see page 161). A beloved traditional pairing is a wedge of Parmigiano-Reggiano (see page 135) and a drizzle of chestnut honey. The overt woodsy nature of the honey brings out the sweet and nutty notes of the cheese. Another fun pairing is floral lime flower honey with some fresh Chèvre (see page 53). A fruit mustard, such as an Italian *mostardo* goes splendidly with a slab of pecorino, such as Calcagno (see page 123), and a dollop of strawberry rhubarb jam is lovely with a triple crème, including Nettle Meadow Farm Kunik (see page 73) or Pierre Robert (see page 74).

OLIVES

Just like cheese, olives come in a variety of shapes, colors, textures, and flavors, and are an essential part of a cheese plate built for snacking. Whether it's a buttery Castelvetrano or a grassy and bitter Lucques, these fruits are a great match for most cheeses produced throughout the Mediterranean region. Try a wedge of Idiazabal (see page 129) with the sweet and buttery Arbequina olive, or a chunk of Tourmalet (see page 171) with the wine-like Gaeta olive.

CURED FISH

Cured fish is often overlooked in cheese-plate pairings. The oily, sometimes smoky quality of the fish lends itself to the rich tang of a Manchego (see page 158) or Idiazabal (see page 129). Sardines and anchovies are divine with any Spanish cheese. Yellowtail tuna is a great companion to Feta (see page 113) and Marieke Gouda (see page 118).

OILS AND VINEGARS

It's amazing what a little drizzle of olive oil can do to transform a soft, buttery cheese such as Scimudin (see page 77), or the way a vinegary reduction of Montepulciano adds an earthy sweetness to a sharp and salty cheese such as Parmigiano-Reggiano (see page 135). The key is to not completely saturate the cheese with these complementary liquids, but allow both the cheese and the oil or vinegar to express themselves harmoniously.

FRESH FRUIT

In our opinion, there is no better match for cheese than fresh, seasonal fruit. The fleeting nature of seasonal produce creates a greater appreciation for the foods you are enjoying, and experimenting with fruit and cheese pairings is always an eye-opening experience. The natural sweetness of fruit is a good balance to the salty, barnyard-like aspects of cheese. From a snappy Macoun apple with a slab of Montgomery's Cheddar (see page 159) in the autumn months to fresh berries picked off the vine and eaten with creamy mascarpone or sweet, ripe peaches enjoyed with Many Fold Farm Condor's Ruin (see page 71) during the summer months, nothing brightens up a cheese plate like fresh fruit.

DRIED FRUIT AND NUTS

Can't get to the farmer's market? Is the season so dire that there's nothing in the produce aisle catching your eye? Have no fear, dried fruits and their good friends nuts (all kinds of nuts) are a perfect adornment to a cheeseboard. While maintaining their natural sweetness in a preserved state, dried fruit provides enough texture and flavor variations to match with a grand spectrum of cheese, while nuts, such as Marcona almonds, pecans, and walnuts, have dense textures and rich, earthy flavors that are complementary to many styles of cheese. Pair dried apples with a farmhouse cheddar, dried figs with Roquefort (see page 190), or cranberries and cherries with Consider Bardwell Farm Rupert (see page 126). Weaving a galaxy of dried fruit and nuts across a cheese plate can really tie the whole thing together visually, too.

CURED MEATS

Though the world of charcuterie-making is rooted in certain formulas, the variety of techniques and culinary inventiveness of these producers fuels an integral component of a hearty cheeseboard. Salami; cured whole muscle meats such as prosciutto and coppa; pâté; and tender-cooked meats create another dimension in the flavor spectrum of a cheese spread. Some of our favorite combos are proscuitto with Scimudin (see page 77), coppa with Puits d'Astier (see page 162), pate with Comté (see page 125), and salami with Taleggio (see page 108). Whether it is a pâté of pheasant and fig, a dried sausage chock-full of hot peppers, or a sweet and nutty slice of prosciutto, cheese and charcuterie are two foods that belong together.

CHOCOLATE

Consider chocolate a complement to a cheeseboard (especially one served after a meal for dessert). Whether it is a dark, bitter square paired with a rich, gooey, and lactic cheese, such as Nettle Meadow Farm Kunik (see page 73), or a higher-percentage milk chocolate (45 percent and above) with a firm and nutty sheep's milk cheese, such as Ros (see page 164), experimenting with chocolate and cheese pairings brings an element of creativity and playfullness to a cheese plate.

BREAD

One of the most commonly asked questions at the cheese shop is, "What is your favorite cracker?" The answer: fresh bread. Hey, crackers are great; they have all sorts of shapes, thicknesses, and flavors. But nothing beats fresh, crusty bread as a vehicle for putting cheese in your mouth. And, just like crackers, bread comes in all sorts of shapes, thicknesses, and flavors. Beware of subpar bread—find a good bakery, one that is using interesting fermentation techniques, old-world baking methods, and creating alluring crusts and crumbs in their loaves. Behold the power of true bread and its harmonious relationship with cheese.

CREATING A CHEESEBOARD

There is a lot of anxiety and stress that can revolve around the concept of crafting a cheeseboard. People often ask us what the "rules" are and what is the "right way" to create a proper cheese plate. Honestly, there is no right or wrong answer here. There are a number of ways to proceed. There are the more traditional options, a classic being to serve four different cheeses, ranging in texture and flavor intensity, representing all milk types and a blue cheese. Although we believe that this is a good option for novices and a safe bet, we do not think you should feel locked into any one way of creating a tasty presentation. The root of what you are trying to do is present a selection of cheeses that you like. As the customer, you will find yourself in front of a dizzying array of cheeses. You are the one who is going to taste through the case, selecting wedges of wonders that you enjoy. You are going to be sharing these finds with your friends and loved ones—you are feeding them and they will be happy. Here are a few things to take into account when assembling a selection: What will everyone be drinking? Is this for a cocktail hour event or will it be presented before a meal or after a meal as a dessert course? What else will you be serving? All of these questions should be asked by the monger who is offering you service, and this communication will help you arrive at the best options for your event. For more information on communicating with a cheesemonger, see Visiting a Cheese Counter on page 36. Here are a few fun and creative cheese plates to experiment with.

THE THREE-CHEESE PLATE FOR DESSERT AFTER A HEARTY MEAL

After a decadent meal, it's nice to have a few bold flavors to compete with your tired palate. An all French selection includes:

Comté (see page 125)

Pierre Robert (see page 74)

Fourme D'Ambert (see page 181)

THE GREAT ALL-GOAT SELECTION FOR BEFORE A LIGHT MEAL

To the people who think they don't like goat's milk cheese, I tell them that they haven't tried the right goat cheeses. For people who know how vast and diverse goat's milk cheeses are, this is a fun board to play with. From the light and much-loved Capriole Farms Sofia (see page 63) to the lemony and firm Caprotto (see page 124), goat's milk cheeses go well with a handful of dried cherries and a drizzle of wildflower honey. Serve with a variety of white wines or gin martinis.

Capriole Farms Sofia (see page 63)

Caprotto (see page 124)

Sainte-Maure (see page 76)

Tomme Chèvre Tunnel (see page 167)

Lady's Blue (see page 184)

AN ALL-AMERICAN CELEBRATION OF CHEESE

Everybody loves a theme—whether it's a children's circus birthday party or a backyard summer luau, adding a motif to an event adds a certain *je ne sais quoi* for you and your friends. Take for example the innovative and high-quality American dairy currently being produced. Celebrate these cheese makers' craftsmanship and go for the gusto with a bountiful spread of the following, perhaps to celebrate the Fourth of July.

Jasper Hill Farm Harbison (see page 70)

Many Fold Farm Garretts Ferry (see page 72)

Alemar Cheese Company Good Thunder (see page 85)

Twig Farm Goat Tomme (see page 172)

Vermont Shepherd "Verano" (see page 172)

Rogue Creamery Caveman Blue (see page 188)

THE CENTERPIECE CHEESE PLATE

Sometimes simplicity is nice. And all you need is one great cheese to stand alone and dazzle. We appreciate selections and options, but with cheeses, as with a great piece of chocolate or that phenomenal bottle of wine, superior ones should stand alone. Two great cheeses that fall into this category include:

Vacherin Mont-d'Or (see page 110)

Gruyère (see page 128)

GLOSSARY

AFFINEUR: a person who selects, cares for, and matures cheese

ARTISAN: one who makes a product by hand

BATCH: a yield of cheese from one vat of milk

BIODYNAMIC: an organic production

BREVIBACTERIUM: the bacteria found on washed-rind cheeses that lends an orange hue and footy aroma; also known as B. linen

BRINE: a salt bath that cheese is often set in, anywhere from a few hours to overnight, right after being formed, as well as a solution that is used in washing cheeses as they age

BUCK: a male goat

BUCKY: the flavor characteristic that resembles a petting zoo: very animalistic and beasty, and most often associated with goat's milk cheeses

BULL: a male cow

CASEIN: a protein that is found in milk

CAVE: an aging environment for cheese, which can be a cave, a cellar, or a refrigerated unit

CHYMOSIN: the enzyme found in rennet that occurs naturally in the fourth stomach of ruminant animals that curdles the mother's milk making it digestible for the offspring

CREAM LINE: the thin layer of supple, sometimes almost liquidy cheese that develops just underneath the rind

CURD: the solid matter that is made by coagulating milk

DOE: a female goat

EYES: the small holes that develop in cheeses, such as the Swiss cheese Emmenthaler, as a result of fermentation during the aging process

FARMSTEAD: a product that is made using the raw materials from the place of origin, meaning a cheese that is made on a farm that uses the milk from their own herd exclusively

FERMIER: the French term for farmstead, meaning the milk that is used to make the cheese comes from the herd of the cheese-maker's farm

FRUITIÈRE: a group of Comté cheese makers who work with neighboring farmers to gather their milk and craft the wheels

GREEN CHEESE: a very young cheese that is intended to be aged but has yet to begin the process

INOCULATION: the act of introducing a certain bacteria to the milk prior to coagulation

MICROBIAL: rennet made using vegetarian-friendly means, usually in a laboratory

MUCOR: bacteria that grows in long wisps that resemble cat fur; also known as Rhizomucor

NAME PROTECTED: a cheese that is regulated by a government supported agency; the cheese is held to standards that control taste, milk type, area of production, aesthetics, etc., depending on the type of cheese

NEEDLING: the act of piercing a blue cheese with long, hollow needles to introduce bacteria to the cheese

PASTE: the edible center of the cheese, excluding the rind

PENICILLIUM CANDIDUM: the bloomy white mold that grows on the exterior of cheeses such as Camemberts and Bries

PENICILLIUM ROQUEFORTI: the bacteria that creates streaks of blues, grays, and greens in blue cheeses

RENNET: an enzyme usually derived from the stomach lining of a ruminant animal that helps in the coagulation process of cheese-making

RUMINANT: a mammal who has multiple stomachs and whose digestion system ferments the ingested feed before the feed is actually digested

SEASONING: the environment of a cave that is suited to a particular rind of cheese

SILAGE: a fermented mash of farm residuals (hay, corn husks, etc.) that is given to animals as feed during the winter

THERMISED: a process of treating milk, which is gentler than flash pasteurization, taking the milk to a lower temperature for a longer period of time, so as not to shock the bacteria and composition of the milk

TRIPLE CRÈME: a cheese that has a butterfat content that is 75 percent or higher

TYROSINES: small, crunchy white crystals in the paste of certain cheeses that are a crystallization of the amino acid tyrosine, a result of the breakdown of casein (the main protein in milk) as the cheese ripens; certain aged cheeses, such as Gouda and Gruyère, often have a large number of them

WHEY: the liquid that is released from coagulated curd

INDEX

ACKNOWLEDGMENTS

We would like to thank all of the hardworking cheese folk out there who have their feet rooted in both tradition and the soil, and who continue to grow and support the cheese world that has welcomed us into their family. We honor this craft and all those who work tirelessly to preserve it. A special thank you to Daphne Zepos for being an incredible person who changed the landscape of cheese in America. And a huge thank you to Ellen Cronin for having a visionary lens that made this book look so pretty.

CREDITS

All photos by E.M. Cronin unless otherwise noted. iStock: Cover, linen texture throughout, and on back cover, 1, 6–7, 8, 9, 10 (top), 11, 12 (top, bottom), 13, 15, 18–19, 21, 22, 25, 32, 204–205; Deposit: 10 (bottom); Getty: 12 (middle); courtesy of Essex St. Cheese: 33; Courtesy of Rodolphe Le Meunier: 68; Courtesy of Columbia Cheeses: 39, 150; Courtesy of Jasper Hill Farm: 130; Sophie Kamin: animal drawings, throughout.